ASEAN AS AN ACTOR IN INTERNATIONAL FORA

ASEAN as an Actor in International Fora addresses a blind spot in ASEAN research and in comparative regionalism studies by assessing why, how, when and to what extent ASEAN member governments achieve a collective presence in global fora. Written for academic researchers and practitioners working in areas such as international relations, political science and international law, it examines ASEAN's negotiating behavior with a novel four-point cohesion typology. The authors argue that ASEAN's "cognitive prior" and its repository of cooperation norms have affected ASEAN's negotiation capacities, formats, strategies and cohesion in international fora. Using two case studies – one on ASEAN's cohesion in the WTO agricultural negotiations and one on UN negotiations on forced labor in Myanmar – they examine ASEAN's collective actions at different stages of negotiation, in different issue areas and in different negotiating fora. The book concludes by providing recommendations for strengthening ASEAN's international negotiation capacities.

PARUEDEE NGUITRAGOOL is a lecturer at the School of International Affairs, Faculty of Political Science and Public Administration, Chiang Mai University (CMU), Thailand. Before joining CMU, she was a research associate at the Department of Political Science, University of Freiburg, Germany, and a guest researcher at many institutions in Southeast Asia, including

Institute of Southeast Asian Studies (ISEAS) in Singapore, Center for Strategic and International Studies (CSIS) and University of Indonesia (UI) in Jakarta, Indonesia. Her main research interests include the images of the West in Indonesia, and environmental politics and international relations in Southeast Asia.

JÜRGEN RÜLAND is Professor of Political Science in the Department of Political Science at the University of Freiburg, Germany. He is also the Chairman of the university's Southeast Asia Program and Chairman of the Academic Advisory Board of the GIGA German Institute for Global and Area Studies, Hamburg (2006–2014). Professor Rüland has published extensively on Southeast Asia and, in 2007, *Pacific Affairs* awarded him and Christl Kessler the William L. Holland Prize for the best article in 2006. He was the Stanford University/National University of Singapore Distinguished Fellow for Contemporary Southeast Asia 2010 and fellow at the Freiburg Institute of Advanced Studies (FRIAS History) 2010/2011 and 2014/2015.

INTEGRATION THROUGH LAW

The Role of Law and the Rule of Law in ASEAN Integration

General Editors

J. H. H. Weiler, European University Institute
Tan Hsien-Li, National University of Singapore
Michael Ewing-Chow, National University of Singapore

The Association of Southeast Asian Nations (ASEAN), comprising the ten member states of Brunei Darussalam, Cambodia, Indonesia, Lao PDR, Malaysia, Myanmar, Philippines, Singapore, Thailand and Vietnam, has undertaken intensified integration into the ASEAN Community through the Rule of Law and Institutions in its 2007 Charter. This innovative book series evaluates the community-building processes of ASEAN to date and offers a conceptual and policy toolkit for broader Asian thinking and planning of different legal and institutional models of economic and political regional integration in the region. Participating scholars have been divided up into six separate thematic strands. The books combine a mix of Asian and Western scholars.

Centre for International Law, National University of Singapore (CIL-NUS)

The Centre for International Law (CIL) was established in 2009 at the National University of Singapore's Bukit Timah Campus in response to the growing need for international law expertise and capacity building in the Asia-Pacific region. CIL is a university-wide research centre that focuses on multidisciplinary research and works with other NUS or external centres of research and academic excellence. In particular, CIL collaborates very closely with the NUS Faculty of Law.

INTEGRATION THROUGH LAW
The Role of Law and the Rule of Law in ASEAN Integration
General Editors: J. H. H. Weiler, Tan Hsien-Li and Michael Ewing-Chow

ASEAN AS AN ACTOR IN INTERNATIONAL FORA

Reality, Potential and Constraints

PARUEDEE NGUITRAGOOL AND JÜRGEN RÜLAND

CAMBRIDGE
UNIVERSITY PRESS

CAMBRIDGE
UNIVERSITY PRESS

University Printing House, Cambridge CB2 8BS, United Kingdom

Cambridge University Press is part of the University of Cambridge.

It furthers the University's mission by disseminating knowledge in the pursuit of education, learning and research at the highest international levels of excellence.

www.cambridge.org
Information on this title: www.cambridge.org/9781107503885

First published 2015

A catalogue record for this publication is available from the British Library

ISBN 978-1-107-50388-5 Paperback

CONTENTS

TABLES

GENERAL EDITORS' PREFACE

This monograph is published within the context of a wide-ranging research project entitled, Integration Through Law: The Role of Law and the Rule of Law in ASEAN Integration (ITL), undertaken by the Centre for International Law at the National University of Singapore and directed by J. H. H. Weiler, Michael Ewing-Chow and Tan Hsien-Li.

The Preamble to the ASEAN Charter concludes with a single decision: "We, the Peoples of the Member States of the Association of Southeast Asian Nations ... [h]ereby decide to establish, through this Charter, the legal and institutional framework for ASEAN." For the first time in its history of over four decades, the Legal and the Institutional were brought to the forefront of ASEAN discourse.

The gravitas of the medium, a Charter: the substantive ambition of its content, the creation of three interlocking Communities, and the turn to law and institutions as instruments for realization provide ample justification for this wide-ranging project, to which this monograph is one contribution, examining ASEAN in a comparative context.

That same substantive and, indeed, political ambition means that any single study, illuminating as it may be, will cover but a fraction of the phenomena. Our modus operandi in this project was to create teams of researchers from Asia and elsewhere who would contribute individual monographs within an overall framework which we had designed. The project framework, involving several thematic clusters within each monograph, is thus determined by the framework and the place of each monograph within it.

As regards the specific content, however, the authors were free, indeed encouraged, to define their own understanding of the problem and their own methodology and reach their own conclusions. The thematic structure of the entire project may be found at the end of this Preface.

The project as a whole, and each monograph within it, display several methodological sensibilities.

First, law, in our view, can only be understood and evaluated when situated in its political and economic context. Thus, the first studies in the overall project design are intended to provide the political, economic, cultural and historical context against which one must understand ASEAN and are written by specialists in these respective disciplines. This context, to a greater or lesser degree, also informs the sensibility of each monograph. There are no "black letter law" studies to be found in this project and, indeed, even in the most technical of areas we encouraged our authors to make their writing accessible to readers of diverse disciplines.

Comparative experience suggests that the success of achieving some of the more ambitious objectives outlined in Article 1 of the Charter will depend in no small measure on the effectiveness of legal principles, legal rules and legal institutions. This is particularly true as regards the success of establishing "an ASEAN Community comprising the ASEAN Security Community, the ASEAN Economic Community and the ASEAN Socio-Cultural Community as provided for in the Bali Declaration of ASEAN Concord II". Article 2(2)(n) stipulates the commitment of ASEAN Member States to act in accordance with the principle of "adherence to multilateral trade rules and ASEAN's rules-based regimes for effective implementation of economic commitments and progressive reduction towards elimination of all barriers to regional economic integration." The ASEAN Member States therefore envisage that rules of law and the Rule of Law will become a major feature in the future of ASEAN.

Although, as seen, the Charter understands itself as providing an institutional and legal framework for ASEAN, the question of the "role of law and the rule of law" is not advocacy but a genuine enquiry in the various substantive areas of the project as to:

- the substantive legal principles and substantive rules of the various ASEAN communities;
- the procedural legal principles and rules governing institutional structures and decision-making processes;
- implementation, enforcement and dispute settlement.

One should not expect a mechanical application of this scheme in each study; rather, a sensibility that refuses to content itself with legal enactments as such and looks to a "living" notion of law and institutions is ubiquitous in all the studies. Likewise, the project is sensitive to "non Law." It variously attempts to locate the appropriate province of the law in this experience. That is, not only the role of law, but also the areas that are and should remain outside the reach of legal institutionalization with due sensitivity to ASEAN and Asian particularism and political and cultural identities.

The project, and the monographs of which it is made, are not normatively thick. They do not advocate. They are designed, for the most part, to offer reflection, discuss the pros and cons, and in this way enrich public awareness, deepen understanding of different options and in that respect contribute indirectly to policymaking.

This decisive development of ASEAN has been accompanied by a growing Asian interest in various legal and institutional forms of transnational economic and political cooperation, notably the various voices discussing and showing an interest in an East Asia Integration project. The number of Free Trade Agreements (FTAs) and Regional Trade Agreements (RTAs) has increased from six in 1991 to 166 in 2013, with a further 62 in various stages of negotiations.

Methodologically, the project and many of the monographs are comparative in their orientation. Comparative law is one of the few real-life laboratories that we have in which to assess and understand the operation of different legal and institutional models designed to tackle similar objectives and problems. One should not need to put one's own hand in the fire to learn that it scorches. With that in mind a couple of monographs offer both conceptual reflection and pragmatic "tool boxing" on some of the key elements featuring in all regional integration systems.

Comparative law is in part about divergence: it is a potent tool and means to understand one's own uniqueness. One understands better the uniqueness of Apples by comparing them to Oranges. You understand better the specialness of a Toyota by comparing it to a Ford.

Comparative law is also about convergence: it is a potent tool and means to understand how what are seemingly different phenomena are part of a broader trend, an insight which may enhance both self-understanding and policy potentialities.

Although many studies in the project could have almost immediate policy implications, as would the project as a whole, this is not its only or even principal purpose. There is a rich theory of federalism which covers many countries around the world. There is an equally rich theory of European integration, which has been associated with the advent Union. There is also considerable learning on Free Trade Areas and the like.

To date, the study of the legal aspects of ASEAN specifically and other forms of Asian legal integration has been derivative of, and dependent on, theoretical and conceptual insight which were developed in different contexts.

One principal objective of ITL and these monographs will be to put in place the building blocks for an authentic body of ASEAN and Asian integration theory developed in, and with sensitivity to, the particularities and peculiarities of the region and continent. A theory and conceptual framework of Asian legal integration will signal the coming of age of research of and in the region itself.

Although the monographs form part of an overarching project, we asked our authors to write each as a "standalone" – not assuming that their readers would have consulted any of the other titles. Indeed, the project is rich and few will read all monographs. We encourage readers to pick and choose from the various monographs and design their own menu. There is, on occasion, some overlap in providing, for example, background information on ASEAN in different studies. That is not only inevitable but desirable in a project of this amplitude.

The world is increasingly witnessing a phenomenon of interlocking regional organization where the experience of one feeds on the others. In some way, the intellectual, disciplinary and comparative sensibility of this project is a microcosm of the world it describes.

The range of topics covered in this series comprises:

The General Architecture and Aspirations of ASEAN
The Governance and Management of ASEAN: Instruments, Institutions, Monitoring, Compliance and Dispute Resolution
Legal Regimes in ASEAN
The ASEAN Economic Community
ASEAN and the World
The Substantive Law of ASEAN

ACKNOWLEDGEMENTS

This book, which explores thus far largely uncharted waters of the meanwhile voluminous research on the Association of Southeast Asian Nations (ASEAN), could not have been completed without the great support of many institutions and individuals. Foremost of those to whom we owe great gratitude is the Centre for International Law (CIL) of the National University of Singapore. The study is part of a large and pioneering research project entitled "Integration through Law" (ITL) conducted by the Centre, in which about seventy scholars have been involved. At the center of the project is the comprehensive study of all principal legal issues associated with the process of regional integration in Southeast Asia, including the pertinent institutional context to which our study contributes. The project leaders, Professor J. H. H. Weiler (European University Institute, Florence), Professor Michael Ewing-Chow and Dr. Tan Hsien-Li, have not only provided us with the highly valued opportunity to participate in this challenging endeavor; we also greatly benefited from their excellent guidance and the inspiring research atmosphere they created. All this is greatly appreciated as well as the Centre's financial and institutional support, which enabled us to carry out fieldwork in Europe and Southeast Asia.

We received excellent feedback in two workshops in Singapore and Jakarta at different stages of the project.

The workshops brought together an impressive array of leading scholars of regionalism and numerous high-caliber government practitioners from all over the ASEAN region. In particular, we would like to thank Professor Pascal Vennesson, Mr. Peter Govindasamy, Mr. Termsak Chalermpalanupap and many other – unnamed – participants of the Integration through Law project for their thoughtful comments and suggestions on the first, then still incomplete, draft version of this book. We would likewise thank two anonymous reviewers of the completed manuscript for their meticulous reading of the text, their encouragement, but also their candid critique of some of our conceptual choices. We took their advice very seriously and we sincerely hope that the revised manuscript comes as close as possible to their high-quality standards. The University of Freiburg's Southeast Asia program, sponsored by the German Federal University of Education and Research (BMBF), was an invaluable pool of expertise from which we greatly benefited through innumerable informal conversations and discussions.

Without the help of our interviewees in Singapore, Jakarta, Bangkok, Manila, New York, Geneva, Brussels and Berlin it would have been impossible for us to understand how ASEAN members interact inside and outside the negotiation rooms of global forums. We greatly appreciate that they shared with us their precious time, information, knowledge and experience. In addition, we would like warmly to express our sincere thanks to our able research assistants at the Department of Political Science and the Southeast Asian Studies program of the University of Freiburg, namely Jan-Simon Dörflinger, Felix Idelberger, Vanessa Guinan-Bank,

Verena Lais, Anna Leiber, Mareike Well and Lukas Müller for their dedicated support. Jan-Simon Dörflinger, Felix Idelberger and Lukas Müller have compiled and pre-reviewed numerous resolutions of the United Nations General Assembly and have traced ASEAN's voting behavior in this UN body. Berenike Feldhoff has helped us in searching for ASEAN's joint statements in the WTO. Without their competent assistance, we would have spent much more time on data collection and some mistakes would most likely have gone undetected.

In Singapore Renee Chan Lai Sang has eased our administrative and logistical burdens with great competence, reliability and efficiency. Last but not least we thank Alec Crutchley for his careful proofreading of the final versions of this manuscript. Yet, while we are very grateful for all the great support we have received, any errors that remain are the sole responsibility of the authors.

ABBREVIATIONS

3G	Global Governance Group
ABAC	ASEAN Business Advisory Council
ABC	ASEAN Business Club
ACD	Asian Cooperation Dialogue
ACFTA	ASEAN–China Free Trade Area
ACSC	ASEAN Civil Society Conference
ACT	Accountability, Coherence and Transparence
ADM	Asian Developing Member
AECF	Asia–Europe Cooperation Framework
AFL–CIO	American Federation of Labor and Congress of Industrial Organizations
AFTA	ASEAN Free Trade Area
AFTINET	Australian Fair Trade and Investment Network
AIPMC	ASEAN Inter-Parliamentary Myanmar Caucus
ALMM	ASEAN Labor Ministers Meeting
AMAF	ASEAN Ministers on Agriculture and Forestry
AMF	Asian Monetary Fund
AMM	ASEAN Ministerial Meeting
AMRO	ASEAN+3 Monetary Research Office
APA	ASEAN People's Assembly
APEC	Asia-Pacific Economic Cooperation
APF	ASEAN People's Forum

APN	Asia-Pacific Network
APRIS	ASEAN Project for Regional Integration Support
APT	ASEAN Plus Three
ARF	ASEAN Regional Forum
ASA	Association of Southeast Asia
ASEAN	Association of Southeast Asian Nations
ASEAN-5	ASEAN founding members (Indonesia, Malaysia, the Philippines, Singapore and Thailand)
ASEAN-CCI	ASEAN Chamber of Commerce and Industries
ASEM	Asia–Europe Meeting
AUN	ASEAN University Network
BDF	Bali Democracy Forum
BIMSTEC	Bay of Bengal Initiative for Multi-Sectoral Technical and Economic Cooperation
BRICS	Brazil, Russia, India, China, South Africa
CAP	Common Agricultural Policy
CAS	Comparative Area Studies
CIL	Centre for International Law
CINAPS	Centre for Indonesian National Policy Studies
CLMV	Cambodia, Laos, Myanmar and Vietnam
CMI	Chiang Mai Initiative
CMIM	Chiang Mai Initiative (Multilateralized)
CPR	Committee of Permanent Representatives
CSIS	Center for Strategic and International Studies
D8	Developing 8

DNPI	Dewan Nasional Perubahan Iklim (National Council on Climate Change)
EAEG	East Asian Economic Group
EAS	East Asian Summit
EC	European Community
ECOSOC	Economic and Social Council
ECOWAS	Economic Community of West African States
EEC	European Economic Community
EEZ	Exclusive Economic Zone
EPG	Eminent Persons Group
ERIA	Economic Research Institute for ASEAN and East Asia
EU	European Union
FAO	Food and Agriculture Organization
FLACSO	Facultad Latinoamericana de Ciencias Sociales (Latin American Faculty of Social Sciences)
FLC	Forced Labor Convention
FOSS	Forum of Small States
FSB	Financial Stability Board
FTA	Free Trade Agreement
G7/8	Group of 7/8
G15	Group of 15
G20	Group of 20
G33	Group of 33
G77	Group of 77
GATT	General Agreement on Tariffs and Trade
GDP	gross domestic product
GMM	Global Movement of Moderates
GSP	Generalized System of Preferences

HIV/AIDS	Human Immunodeficiency Virus/ Acquired Immune Deficiency Syndrome
HLT	[International Labor Organization]High-Level Team
HLTF	High-Level Task Force
ICTSD	International Centre for Trade and Sustainable Development
ICWA	Indonesian Council of World Affairs
IFI	international financial institution
IFPRI	International Food Policy Research Institute
ILC	International Labor Conference
ILO	International Labor Organization
IMF	International Monetary Fund
IPU	Inter-Parliamentary Union
ISEAS	Institute of Southeast Asian Studies
ISIS	Institutes of International and Strategic Studies
ITD	Italian–Thai Development Public Company Limited
ITL	Integration through Law
JIM	Jakarta Informal Meeting
KFG	Kolleg-Forschergruppe
KNLA	Karen National Liberation Army
LDC	least-developed country
LFS	labor force survey
LIPI	Lembaga Ilmu Pengetahuan Indonesia (Indonesian Institute of Sciences)
MAI	Multilateral Agreement on Investment
Maphilindo	Malaya, the Philippines and Indonesia
MDG	Millennium Development Goal

Mercosur	Mercado Común del Sur (Common Market of the South)
MTID	Markets, Trade and Institutions Division
NAFTA	North American Free Trade Agreement
NAM	Non-Alignment Movement
NePAD	New Partnership for Africa's Development
NGO	non-governmental organization
NIEO	New International Economic Order
NLD	National League for Democracy
NPR	nominal protection rate
NTU	Nanyang Technological University
OECD	Organisation for Economic Co-operation and Development
OIC	Organization of Islamic Cooperation
P5	Five Permanent Members of the UN Security Council (USA, Russia, China, France and United Kingdom)
PECC	Pacific Economic Cooperation Council
R2P	Responsibility to Protect
RAM	recently acceded member
RM	Malaysian ringgit
RSIS	Rajaratnam School of International Studies
S5	Small Five Group
SAARC	South Asian Association for Regional Cooperation
SADC	Southern African Development Community
SAPA	Solidarity for Asian People's Advocacy
SARS	severe acute respiratory syndrome
SCO	Shanghai Cooperation Organization

SDT	special and differential treatment (for Developing Countries)
SEANWFZ	Southeast Asian Nuclear-Weapon-Free Zone
SIIA	Singapore Institute of International Affairs
SOM	Senior Officials' Meeting
SP	special product
SPDC	State Peace and Development Council
SSM	special safeguard mechanism
SVE	small, vulnerable economy
TAC	Treaty of Amity and Cooperation [in Southeast Asia]
TF-WAR	Task Force on Agreement on Agriculture (Re)negotiations
UN	United Nations
UNBISNET	United Nations Bibliographic Information System
UNCTAD	United Nations Conference on Trade and Development
UNDP	United Nations Development Program
UNGA	United Nations General Assembly
UNPA	United Nations Parliamentary Assembly
UNSC	United Nations Security Council
USDP	Union Solidarity and Development Party
WHO	World Health Organization
WTO	World Trade Organization
ZOPFAN	Zone of Peace, Freedom and Neutrality

Chapter 1

Introduction

This book is part of a larger project entitled "Integration through Law."[1] As the project title suggests, the organizers believe that accelerated legalization, contractualization and, perhaps, even constitutionalization are among the key drivers of regional integration. Greater legalization creates a more rules-based type of regional cooperation with binding obligations for the members and is associated with the expectation that it makes cooperation more enduring, predictable and effective. With precisely these objectives in mind, the leaders of the Association of Southeast Asian Nations (ASEAN) passed the ASEAN Charter, a quasi-constitutional landmark document, in late 2008. In their view, legalization is a requisite not only for a deeper-integrated regional grouping, but, in particular, also a more cohesive one as well. In a globalized world, in which the lives of Southeast Asians are increasingly affected by decisions made far beyond their region in arcane bodies of international organizations, regional cohesion is not only direly needed to settle complex regional cross-border problems but also to develop the "voice opportunity" (Grieco 1996) essential for negotiating successfully in global forums.

[1] For details, see Centre for International Law, National University of Singapore, available at: http://cil.nus.edu.sg/research-projects/cil-research-projects/asean/ (accessed 2 January 2014).

In other words, cohesion has not only an intra-regional dimension but also an extra-regional one.

This extra-regional dimension of cohesion is the main theme of this book. Regional organizations have proliferated since the early 1990s, mainly in the Global South. With this new wave of regionalism, there are no longer "regions without regionalism" (Palmer 1991). Since then, in an increasingly vertically and horizontally differentiated emerging system of global governance, regional organizations have more and more been becoming actors in their own right (Rüland 2010). On first sight, this may appear surprising given the fact that all newly formed regional organizations are intergovernmentalist in nature. Yet the increasing actorness of regional organizations has been well documented in the field of interregionalism studies (Hänggi, Roloff and Rüland 2006; Doidge 2011; Wunderlich 2012). And with increasing actorness regional organizations also adopt collective actor roles in global forums, mainly to strengthen the bargaining power of smaller countries in particular.

Interestingly, though, very little is known about regional organizations and their cohesion as collective actors in global forums. The scant literature that exists is strongly influenced by studies on the European Union and particularly on its role in the United Nations (see, inter alia, Schmitter 1969; Schmitter 1971; Nye 1967; Nye 1971; Meunier 2005; Rhinard and Kaeding 2006; Laatikainen and Smith 2006). Non-Western regional organizations have hardly ever been studied in this respect,[2] perhaps because, unlike in the case of the EU with

[2] For exceptions, see de Lombaerde, Baert and Felício (2012) and Panke (2013b).

its partial supranationalist institutional architecture, very little joint activity is expected of intergovernmentalist regional groupings. While much is known about ASEAN's practices in intra-regional cooperation and some information exists about ASEAN's agency in international forums of the East Asian and Asia-Pacific region, hardly anything is known about ASEAN as an actor and negotiator in global forums such as the United Nations, the World Trade Organization (WTO), the International Monetary Fund (IMF) or the climate change and non-proliferation regimes. The association's global role is a theme thus far largely ignored by scholarship on ASEAN.[3] Yet this is hardly surprising, as for a long time ASEAN itself did not prioritize its global role in any noteworthy sense. It was the Indonesian chairmanship in 2011 that for the first time devoted greater attention to global affairs, as the chairmanship's motto "ASEAN in a Global Community of Nations" suggests. This makes exploring ASEAN's role in global forums a pioneering endeavor, though one that will still be preliminary, tentative and incomplete in many respects. In fact, this study can only be the beginning of a more comprehensive and systematic research agenda that examines ASEAN's international behavior from a single case perspective as well as through a comparative lens. The latter would certainly deepen our understanding of ASEAN's international role as it would place it in perspective with the performance of other (non-Western) regional organizations.

The performance of a regional organization as an actor and negotiator in international forums is affected by a

[3] For two tentative pieces, see Tan (2012) and Tay (2013).

range of factors. Structurally speaking, these factors include the organization's normative underpinning (cognitive structure), its level and design of institutionalization (internal structure) and how embedded it is in the global power distribution (external structure). In order to become an effective actor, regional organizations must possess a capacity to perform various functions including agenda-setting, norm entrepreneurship and the ability to mobilize support for their positions, and, ideally through their actions, must be able to influence the structure that imposed constraints upon them. With regard to ASEAN, the organization has sought to act for and coordinate the member states' positions through various mechanisms. However, it has thus far failed to become an effective collective actor and negotiator in global forums. In fact, in key issues of the current world order, such as the reform of the United Nations, trade liberalization, the reform of the global financial architecture, climate change and non-proliferation ASEAN has failed or has only intermittently been able to muster collective strength and to speak with one voice (Wouters and Burnay 2011: 3). While ASEAN has often been celebrated as one of the most successful non-Western regional organizations (Martin 1987; Dosch 1997; Acharya 2001) and is rightfully regarded as a central organization in the East Asian region, it has not been able to translate the prestige it has gained as a "manager of regional affairs" (Haacke 2006: 130) into global influence.

In this book we seek to explore ASEAN's cohesion in global negotiations. We argue that in global forums ASEAN has to contend with four constraining factors: first, the ASEAN Way as the grouping's repository of shared cooperation norms and, second, as a direct outflow of the former, ASEAN's organizational structure. Neither ASEAN's value system nor its internal structure is overly conducive to collective action in the global political arena. Both are the legacies of a "cognitive prior" (Acharya 2009) shaped by centuries of conflict, threats, instability and political uncertainties that have deeply ingrained suspicion, distrust and a sense of vulnerability towards the external world in the minds of decision-makers and major parts of the public. These legacies are reflected in the strong emphasis of the ASEAN Way on sovereignty norms. The seemingly cosmopolitan liberal norms ASEAN adopted with the Bali Concord II of 2003, elevated to quasi-constitutional status in the ASEAN Charter, may have eased external normative pressures on ASEAN, but have so far done little to overcome ASEAN's cohesiveness dilemma. On the contrary, they have, and this is our third point, exacerbated the association's collective action problems by creating a value base that is contradictory below the surface of rhetorical unity (Rüland 2009; Desierto 2010–11).[4] Fourth and finally we argue that Southern regional organizations such as ASEAN also have to cope with an uneven institutional playing field. While it is true that emerging powers such as Brazil, Russia, India, China and South Africa (the BRICS states), and other rising powers, including Indonesia, increasingly challenge the legitimacy of the established international institutional order, including its representativeness, decision-making procedures and normative underpinnings (Hurrell 2006; Prys 2010; Rüland 2012b), the

[4] See also Wanandi, *Jakarta Post*, 19 March 2009.

institutional power of the mainly Western creators of this order is only gradually eroding and thus markedly restricts the scope for effective collective action of Southern regional organizations.

The subsequent chapters of this book address ASEAN's performance as an actor and negotiator in global forums in greater detail. More specifically, we seek to provide at least preliminary answers to the questions of to what extent, why, how and when ASEAN member governments coordinate their positions in international forums. We seek to assess the intensity, formats and strategies ASEAN employs in its collective actions at different stages of negotiation and in different issue areas and negotiating forums.

Following this introduction (Chapter 1), we start with the design of an analytical framework (Chapter 2), which comprises three parts, namely: (1) a theoretical discussion of the concept of externalization; (2) a typology of regional cohesiveness; and (3) theory-guided reflections of actors' negotiation capacities, stages of negotiations and pertinent negotiation strategies. This analytical framework is a constructivist reinterpretation of the neo-functionalist externalization thesis, but making theoretical eclecticism a virtue (Katzenstein and Sil 2008) also takes into account rationalist arguments informed by negotiation theory and the general literature on the bargaining behavior of collective actors.

In Chapter 3 we explore ASEAN's "cognitive prior" and repository of cooperation norms, which are major factors determining ASEAN's actor capacities in international forums. We contend that the region's historical legacies have strongly shaped the association's sovereignty-based cooperation norms, creating a cognitive disposition among ASEAN members in which national interests trump regional concerns. In this chapter we also investigate ASEAN's negotiation capacities from both a national and a regional perspective. Next, in Chapter 4, we examine the cohesion of ASEAN members at different stages of negotiations in international forums and scrutinize ASEAN's behavior as an actor and negotiator in major global forums. In Chapter 5, we review ASEAN's negotiating strategies and locate ASEAN's joint action on the typology of cohesiveness developed in Chapter 2 that ranges from bowling alone and non-cooperation to action as a bloc. Chapter 6 traces the negotiations on agriculture in the WTO and on the Myanmar issue on forced labor in the International Labor Organization (ILO) and the United Nations. While the first case examines negotiations over material values, the second focuses on the negotiation of norms and ideas. Finally, in Chapter 7 we summarize our examination of ASEAN's role as an actor and negotiator in global forums and provide suggestions for more effective coordination and collaboration in such venues.

Chapter 2

Analytical framework: a cognitive approach of externalization

2.1 Externalization and international negotiations

Neo-functionalist scholarship has made one of the first systematic attempts to explain why and under what circumstances regional organizations act cohesively in global forums. Known as the externalization hypothesis, Schmitter (1969; 1971) and Nye (1967; 1971) have argued that with progressive regional integration member states of a regional grouping tend to develop an interest in becoming a cohesive actor vis-à-vis third states. The motivation to centralize policies towards the extra-regional world is largely defensive: to safeguard the economic benefits reaped from closer regional cooperation (Haas and Rowe 1973: 4), to reduce external dependence of member states and, at the same time, protect their foreign policy autonomy (*ibid.* 5). In a mutually reinforcing relationship, externalization is also believed to foster regional integration insofar as developing joint positions towards outsiders creates a need for increased internal consultation, communication, coordination, harmonization and, hence, institutionalization (*ibid.* 6). Externalization, in other words, has a dual effect: it helps to curtail the "exogenous determination of the external conditions of regional organizations" and, vice versa, creates conducive conditions for deepening regional integration (Schmitter 1971: 244; Jorgensen-Dahl 1977: 36).

In an empirical study Haas and Rowe tested eighteen regional organizations on externalization (Haas and Rowe 1973). In their research design they posited that primarily the material institutional properties such as functional specificity, homogeneity and autonomous central authority would influence the cohesiveness of regional organizations in global forums. The more functionally specific, the more homogenous the membership and the more centralized the organizational structure, they argued, the greater the likelihood is that a regional organization will act cohesively in global forums. By contrast, regional organizations with a broad functional scope, a diverse membership and a decentralized organizational structure are expected to be less united in global institutions. As the measure for cohesiveness they used the voting behavior of regional organizations in the United Nations General Assembly (*ibid.*).

Haas and Rowe's assumption of a strong causal relationship between material institutional factors and the cohesiveness of regional organizations in global forums appears intuitively plausible. However, closer scrutiny suggests that material institutional properties are only epiphenomena shaping the behavior of regional organizations in global forums. Functional specificity, for instance, may mask conflicts and severe disagreements in the policy field selected for regional cooperation. If regional organizations, like ASEAN in its early years (despite other pronouncements in its founding document, the Bangkok Declaration of 1967), start cooperating in the field of security, the depth of this cooperation has its limits if member states grapple with memories of war and hostile encounters. Surely such historical legacies may be overcome as a result of external shocks and/or interventions of a hegemon (Legro 2000), as in Europe after the Second World War with American midwifery, but under normal circumstances they create rather stable cognitive patterns that tend to reproduce suspicious and distrustful behavior.

Homogeneity, too, does not necessarily facilitate a deepening of regional cooperation. If, for instance, member states of similar size and similar resource endowment fiercely compete for leadership, even a common (democratic) value base may not help overcome national egoism, nor pave the way towards joint regional action. Vice versa, great diversity in terms of size, population, culture, political system, economic performance and military power may be less an obstacle to the deepening of regional integration than assumed by Haas and Rowe in cases where member countries have encountered a history of good neighborliness, peaceful dispute settlement and mutual respect. Then even major ideological differences may not stand in the way of a deepening of regional integration. The pooling of sovereignty and centralization may be more decisive factors in strengthening the cohesion of a regional association, but they, too, would hardly occur if they did not rest on a modicum of mutual trust, recognition and solidarity.

Finally, the neo-functionalist externalization thesis neglects the institutional environment in which regional organizations are embedded. For instance, it does not account for the distribution of power in global forums. Yet the persistent experience of acute power asymmetries in global forums may exacerbate pre-existing notions of a hostile external world and feelings of vulnerability among the member governments of Southern regional organizations. While such circumstances may indeed strengthen their inclination towards collective action, they may also affirm extant beliefs that national interest is best served if they keep their options open and respond pragmatically to the exigencies of international relations and the dynamics of negotiation processes.

More recent studies using game theory, inspired by Putnam's two-level games (Putnam 1988) and Tsebelis' "nested games" approach (Tsebelis 1990; Coleman and Tangerman 1999; Collinson 1999; Alter and Meunier 2006), proceed from the assumption that as utility maximizers negotiation behavior of governments is determined by win-sets reflecting the political preference structures in the domestic, the intra-regional and the global political arenas (Putnam 1988; Tsebelis 1990). Similar cost-benefit calculations underlie (liberal) intergovernmentalist approaches (Moravcsik 1998) applied to the study of the negotiation behavior of regional organizations in global forums (Smith 2006: 116).

However, all these approaches tend to underestimate ideational and cognitive factors. We therefore opt in this study for a constructivist reinterpretation of the neo-functionalist externalization hypothesis. Constructivism holds promise for our research in several ways (Hopf 1998; Acharya 2012: 9). Not assuming that regional organizations behave identically or similarly across time and space, as rationalist approaches would seek to show, constructivism is more amenable to the contingencies of social reality and hence entails greater context sensitivity. "While not entirely negating the relevance of material factors, constructivism, with its emphasis on ideas, norms, beliefs, knowledge and discursive practices," gives meaning to material facts (Johnston 1996: 22) and opens avenues for an analysis that properly takes into account region-specific or country-specific historical legacies as well as collective memory fed by representations of the past (Halbwachs 1985). In other words, history and the way it is socially constructed matters. This means that constructivism is less likely to fall into the Euro- or Western-centrism trap than rationalist approaches, even though it is by no means immune to such misperceptions, too.

Seen in this light, the externalization of regional organizations may be conceived of as a path-dependent process, albeit not a deterministic one. Path dependence means that choices or decisions made at critical junctures in a historical process can influence subsequent decisions even though circumstances have changed markedly (Schmidt 1995: 718; Mahoney and Thelen 2010). Yet, as constructivism posits an endogenous constitution of actor preferences, path dependencies do not exclude that regional organizations may change their behavior, identity and interests as a result of discursive processes (Schmidt 2010) or at critical junctures that may be caused by crises, external shocks, dramatic shifts in the regional or global power equation or also marked improvements of contextual conditions (Legro 2000; Acharya 2004).

In our study, we argue that ASEAN's actions in global forums are largely a function of the member states' "cognitive prior" (Acharya 2004; Acharya 2009). By "cognitive prior" we mean, hereby following Acharya, "an existing set of ideas, belief systems, and norms, which determine and condition" current world views and behavior of individuals, groups, states and even regional organizations (Acharya 2009: 21). This "cognitive prior" has become part of Southeast Asians' "cultural memory" (Assmann 2002) and tells us what is considered appropriate, legitimate and, hence, feasible. The more resilient these locally established ideas, norms, causal beliefs and world views are, the more likely it is that, despite growing pressures for ideational change, they will persist in informing the thinking of policymakers and the wider public.

In this book, we posit that ASEAN's cognitive prior has a decisive influence on the grouping's mode of cooperation, its institutional development and, hence, its actorness. It informs us about the experiences of ASEAN countries in their interactions among themselves. Even more importantly, it gives evidence about how these experiences have been translated into norms and behavioral dispositions, which guide ASEAN decision-makers in their dealings with third states and the external world. In other words, the historically entrenched notions of mutually ascribed identities among regional partners, extant cultural norms, statecraft and diplomatic interaction patterns determine ASEAN's depth of integration and the way member governments perceive the extra-regional world. The historical experiences with each other, especially if reinforced by similar encounters with the extra-regional world, create path dependencies that persistently reproduce members' perceptions of cooperation and strongly shape their actual cooperative behavior.

Central to this book is the assumption that ASEAN member governments externalize their regionally constructed and socialized internal norms and practices of cooperation.

These regionally established practices also markedly shape the way and the degree to which the grouping interacts in global institutional settings. We thus expect, in other words, that the association's world views and causal beliefs determining the degree, intensity, scope and depth of its internal cooperation also shape its behavior towards non-members and in global forums. A turbulent history, experiences of vulnerability, insecurity and victimization have markedly shaped the region's and its foreign policy elites' world views, which are not conducive to a deeply institutionalized regional cooperation. As a result, even after the formation of ASEAN, distrust towards partners lingers, resulting in a regional cooperation in which national interest comes first. We thus expect that in global forums ASEAN's cohesion will also be limited, giving rise to a pragmatic policy with a proclivity to defect when national interest seems to dictate.

2.2 Regional organizations in international fora: a typology of cohesion

In this study we assume that a necessary condition for effective negotiation by regional organizations in international fora is a high degree of regional cohesion. Cohesiveness increases the bargaining power and the actorness of regional groupings in global fora that may result in favorable (material) pay-offs, but may also influence the agenda, the institutional design and the norms under which international organizations operate. In order to assess the cohesion of regional organizations, we propose a four-scale typology of regional cohesion derived from the theoretical literature

Table 2.1 *Typology of actor cohesion*

Type of cohesion property	Bloc	Quasi-bloc	Caucus	Bowling alone
world view	optimistic	more optimistic than pessimistic	more pessimistic than optimistic	pessimistic
trust	very high	high	low	none
regional identity	very high	high	low	none
defection from collective action	never	rarely	frequently	always
power-sensitivity	low	low	high	high
capacities of knowledge generation	very high	high	low	very low

on international cooperation (see Table 2.1). We thereby distinguish between regional organizations acting as a bloc, a quasi-bloc, a caucus or groupings in which members tend to act alone.

We speak of a *bloc*, when members of a regional organization share an optimistic outlook on the external world. This means that they regard their neighbors as friends and partners rather than as potential foes. Such a generally optimistic world view is the result of positive historical experiences based on long periods of peaceful coexistence and the perception of partners as reliable. Reliable partners normally comply with agreements and do not engage in free-riding or cheating. Neither do they defect from collective action when circumstances tempt them to do so. The more members of a regional organization share such experiences, the greater is their mutual trust. Shared regional identities may further deepen mutual trust and the willingness to solve global and regional problems through coordination, compromise and cooperation. Under such conditions, we expect higher levels of regional institutionalization, a relaxed attitude towards the sovereignty norm, concern for the welfare of members and a more principled and less power-conscious behavior vis-à-vis fellow members as well as outsiders. Members have developed a high capacity for knowledge generation and they share know-how with their peers. Cohesion in global fora is high and reflected in intense communication and policy coordination, a high degree of solidarity, as well as routinely engaging in joint negotiation and common voting.

Actor cohesion in global fora tends to be low or non-existent if member states of a regional organization share a history of conflict and violence prior to joining a regional grouping and if, as a result, distrust, suspicion and ill-feelings towards each other and towards non-members linger. International relations are then perceived as anarchical, an arena in which contingent, cunning and strategic behavior predominates. Perceptions of the external world are under these conditions pessimistic and guided by a high degree of power-sensitivity. In fact, actors respond seismically to actual or seeming shifts in the global or regional power equation. In such contexts of turbulence, uncertainty and unpredictability, governments tend to act along established norms (Goldstein and Keohane 1993) and, hence, reproduce entrenched pessimistic world views and power-sensitive behavior. Such essentially negative notions of the external world normally do not completely rule out cooperation but tend to confine it to short-term activities and shallow integration. If practiced at all, cooperation is highly contingent and relative gains oriented. Institutionalization is low and behavior towards fellow members is characterized by pragmatism, even opportunism, and a penchant for free-riding and non-compliance with agreements where they do not seem to coincide with national interests. Knowledge-generation capacities are either low or not shared with peers. In its most extreme form, such behavior may lead to *bowling alone* or *non-cooperation* in international fora.

Bloc-building and *bowling alone* are the extremes of a continuum of cohesion displayed by regional organizations in global fora. Yet working with such a binary typology of cohesion fails to capture the complexity of international negotiations. We therefore introduce two additional intermediate degrees of cohesion: *quasi-bloc* and *caucus*. The first type is closer to the bloc pole, the second type closer to the non-cooperation pole.

A regional organization acts as a *quasi-bloc* if member states share a more optimistic than pessimistic world view even though there may have been occasional conflicts among them in the past. Yet there exists a relatively high level of mutual trust as these conflicts have been effectively settled and in the collective memory frequent experiences of goodwill towards each other have negated reminiscences of disputes. As a result, over time, a tangible regional identity has developed that strengthens regional cohesion. However, since there have been experiences of previous conflict among members and with external parties, members of a quasi-bloc have nevertheless retained a modicum of power-sensitivity that influences their cooperative behavior. Knowledge generation capacities are substantial and know-how relevant for international negotiations is often shared with fellow members. Members of a quasi-bloc tend to coordinate their policy preferences and voting behavior in international fora, although they do not *always* vote jointly. While individual members feel bound by regional solidarity, there remains a residual likelihood that, depending on their national interests and their cognitive dispositions, they may defect from collective action. Quasi-blocs leave individual members some flexibility to articulate and pursue their own policy preferences where they do not coincide with the majority of the regional grouping, despite a strong proclivity for finding compromises.

Acting as a *caucus*, we would expect a regional organization to display a markedly lower and less binding degree of policy coordination than a quasi-bloc. The region's past is here perceived in more critical terms than in a bloc or a quasi-bloc and distrust of partners persists to varying degrees. Yet a precondition for a caucus is that members have nevertheless developed a regional identity based on a modicum of normative affinities and that they share material interests. In the process of international negotiations, we would expect members of the regional organization to meet regularly, often in an informal capacity, in order to exchange information and to coordinate bargaining strategies on the basis of the lowest common denominator. This entails the avoidance – or at least minimization – of actions that would work to the detriment of other members of the regional organization, but a considerable degree of national autonomy is retained in the negotiation process. Knowledge-generation capacities are limited and inequitably distributed among members and there is no established practice of sharing know-how with members suffering from inadequate capacities for knowledge production. Acting as a caucus, a regional organization would less frequently act in concert than a quasi-bloc. There may even be constellations where individual members of a regional association join other coalitions, irrespective of the fact that the latter's interests may be at variance with those of their regional grouping's fellow members.

These four types of cohesion are ideal types. In the reality of negotiation processes they rarely or perhaps even never appear in pure form. We expect that negotiation processes often exhibit cohesion properties of types adjacent on the continuum of cohesiveness outlined above. Moreover, while world views of negotiators and political elites may be deeply entrenched and may markedly shape their cooperation behavior, there is nevertheless space for some variation. World views may vary according to policy field, the type, phase and strategy of negotiation depending on the context of negotiations and their previous history. World views may also change if a new generation of diplomats, socialized differently than their predecessors, emerges onto the scene. In Chapters 4 and 5, we try to take such variation into account.

2.3 Capacities, stages and strategies in international negotiations

Capacities

We expect a regional association to act as a successful negotiator in global fora if it is able to nurture negotiation capacities at the national and the regional levels (Panke 2013a; Panke 2013b). National capacities in the first place refer to the expertise of the government bureaucracy, including its level of legal and technical training, its analytical abilities and its capability and willingness to tap extra-bureaucratic centers of knowledge. The last presupposes that such centers of knowledge exist outside the government bureaucracy. Intellectual, analytical and technical input may be provided by specialized research institutes, universities and think tanks, but also by intermediary organizations like economic interest groups, civil society groups, with or without assistance from bilateral and multilateral donor organizations and other foreign aid providers. The extent to which these centers of knowledge have developed and the degree to which they are integrated into epistemic networks have a bearing on the ability of governments to respond to new challenges effectively, to contribute in an informed way to the negotiation of joint regional positions and to participate meaningfully in global negotiations.

The cognitive dimension comes in when questioning the extent to which these national capacities can be transferred to the regional level (a) in order to develop robust common positions in international negotiations and (b) to support those member governments that have weak or non-existent domestic capacities for generating and tapping expert knowledge. Both actions require member governments to abstain from pursuing strong national negotiation positions at the expense of other member states and to develop a certain degree of regional solidarity by transferring know-how from countries endowed with more expertise to those with less epistemic resources. Moreover, for collecting, coordinating, integrating and processing knowledge resources, a regional organization must develop a modicum of centralization. In other words, there must be an organizational entity, a secretariat, which performs these functions competently. As outlined in Table 2.1, we expect such attitudes mainly from regional organizations acting as blocs or quasi-blocs in international fora.

However, in a regional organization where distrust and rivalry shape the relationships of member countries, we expect that the regional level will play only a limited role in capacity building in international negotiations. Under such conditions, member states may be willing neither to create a centralized organizational unit nor to share costly expertise with fellow members. Rather than regarding the sharing of knowledge as an act of empowering their weaker members, more-affluent and stronger members tend to make the weaker partners dependent on their superior capacities and the leverages that the latter give them in international negotiations. This deprives less-resourceful partners of ownership of the negotiation positions promoted by those better endowed and it may deepen pre-existing notions of distrust. We thus assume that failure to share knowledge among members of a regional grouping will have repercussions on a regional association's ability to develop common negotiation strategies and positions. Such behavior is most likely for caucuses and groupings with a tendency among members for bowling alone.

Stages

Negotiation is a "decision-making method used by actors to reconcile their respective policy positions when they disagree about preferred outcomes" (Conceição-Heldt 2006: 146). Usually, it involves two or more parties and a sequence of actions, including demanding, arguing and proposing (Odell 2010: 620). As a staged process, it normally begins with a *pre-negotiation* phase in which interested parties agree that there is a problem or an issue that needs to be addressed collectively. They seek to define the problem to make it conducive for negotiations and then to explore the possibilities of the negotiation. Actors that identify such problems display a certain capacity to assume an early-warning role and to adopt opinion-leadership. This initial stage might be followed by the *main negotiation phase* that is characterized by the setting of guiding principles, norms and rules of the negotiation and the search for concessions and compromises – in short: an approximation of positions – and, finally, an attempt to work out the details of an agreement, including its normative content. A third and *final phase* may include the agreement of mutual obligations, the determination of dispute settlement procedures, the elaboration of compliance mechanisms and voting (Spiller 2008: 54).

In negotiations on matters of significance the voting procedure may have a bearing on the preceding negotiation process. Negotiation strategies may differ depending on whether decisions are made by majority voting or on the basis of consensus. Under the latter, like in the WTO or the climate regime, individual members of regional organizations may regard coherent behavior to be less urgent, as consensual decision-making allows them to obstruct negotiations, either for principled reasons or in the expectation of greater individual pay-offs. By contrast, under majority voting, regional organizations may be more inclined to act cohesively, as obstruction does not pay because a recalcitrant minority may easily be overruled by a simple or qualified majority without having extracted gains for itself. However, the larger the membership of a cohesive regional organization and the more it is part of a larger coalition, the more difficult it is to overrule the grouping and the greater the concessions and the side-payments it may obtain for its consent.

Strategies

In the process of negotiation, protagonists employ a variety of strategies in order to achieve their goals. The most important of them include exerting leadership, framing, agenda-setting, coalition-building, image-projection and creation of soft power. It must be noted that in the absence of bloc-type cohesiveness, members of a regional organization may employ these strategies for the benefit of the regional organization, for their own interests, or both. All of these strategies cut across all three stages of the negotiation process, but some may be applied to a greater extent at a specific stage. Framing techniques, for instance, may be of a greater significance in the early stages of negotiation during the agenda-setting process, but they may also reappear when it comes to finding common ground in the process of defining the principles, norms, rules and procedures of a negotiation process. Moreover, these strategies are as much relevant for the internal process of sorting out a common negotiation position as for the interaction with third states.

Exerting leadership is one of the most significant strategies negotiators can apply. Two types of leadership may be considered relevant here, namely *formal* and *entrepreneurial* leadership. The first type denotes agenda-management and brokerage responsibilities to facilitate negotiation, such as structuring bargaining around negotiating texts (Tallberg 2008: 10). Specific roles, functions and authority of *formal* leadership, however, may vary, depending on the rules and norms of the institution within which the negotiation takes place. In the case of the EU Council Presidency, Tallberg (2008) argues that the presidency possesses agenda-shaping power, despite its limited role in initiating policy, which falls under the mandate of the EU Commission. According to him, the President may exert influence by deliberately emphasizing or barring certain issues that are already on the agenda. Instead of being an office without power, the Presidency provides opportunities for the country occupying the position to influence policy outcomes (*ibid*). Entrepreneurial leadership is more *informal*, but may also play an indispensable role in international negotiation. Young defines entrepreneurial leadership as "the ability of an actor to foster integrative bargaining and to put together deals that would otherwise elude participants" (Young 1991: 293). The functions of this type of leadership include agenda-setting, popularizing the issues at stake, the inventing of policy options to overcome bargaining impediments and arranging support for options (*ibid.* 294). Entrepreneurial leaders can thus be seen as (informal) brokers in international deal-making.

Deliberate moves of regional organizations to capture executive posts thus take into account the considerable power the chair of a forum or organization may convey. Successful chairs may also accumulate "soft power" for their country or their region, especially if they gain recognition as not only honest but also effective brokers and competent moderators of the negotiation process, thereby markedly increasing their authority and influence on the outcome of negotiations. A side-effect may be a reputational "spill over" in the sense that successful chairs benefit from the acquired social capital in future negotiations and in other policy fields.

Another strategy often employed in negotiations is *framing*, a concept, though, that is contested in social sciences and the meaning of which varies between academic disciplines (Benford and Snow 2000; Druckman 2011: 280). According to one definition, frames "are interpretative structures embedded in political discourse" (Kinder and Sanders 1996: 164, quoted in Druckman 2011: 282). In political science Druckman has distinguished two types of framing that are of relevance for our analysis. One is what he calls the "frame of communication," the other he categorizes as the "frame of thought." While both "concern variations in emphasis or salience" (Druckman 2011: 282), they differ "with the former usage focusing on what a speaker says [. . .] and the latter usage focusing on what an individual thinks" (*ibid.* 282). In international negotiations, we expect (collective) actors primarily to rely on "communicative framing," which has been likened to a "rhetorical weapon" (Kinder and Sanders 1996: 164, quoted in Druckman 2011: 282). Actors in international organizations use it primarily for agenda-setting, but also resort to it at other stages of negotiation. They strategically choose their frames in order to highlight the salience of an issue and to change the preferences and priorities of other actors by making an issue semantically congruent with the latter's belief systems and preference structure. Besides, skillful framing is a strategy to delegitimize the arguments of other negotiators, to delegitimize competing paradigms, to build, rebuild or leave coalitions and to generate soft power. On a more cynical note, negotiators also rely on framing techniques to spread disinformation (Jayakumar 2011: 58). In their framing strategy they set out from a pre-given mindset, that is, certain "cognitive structures that make sense of the issues" (Kinder and Sander 1996: 164, quoted in Druckman 2011: 282). In other words, communicative frames may be strongly influenced by the ideological bias of actors or their experiences in earlier negotiation rounds.

Coalition-building is a strategy that smaller states and middle powers especially, as well as weaker regional organizations, frequently apply in negotiations and institutional politics. It is a form of institutional balancing that they view – in the absence of sufficient resources for internal balancing (Narlikar 2003: 10) – as a viable strategy for curtailing the superior bargaining power of hegemons and large players through resource pooling and the strength of great numbers. It increases the bargaining power of states that, if acting individually, would have little chance to influence the outcome of negotiations. Yet coalition-building requires compromises with partners, as it is hardly conceivable that their preferences and interests would be fully identical. Still, with the win-sets large enough, states or regional organizations joining a coalition can hope for a better deal than if they had decided to act alone. Coalitions are often, but by no means always, issue-based. That is, they are formed around a certain issue under negotiation. Issue-based coalitions tend to be short-term strategies, essentially following pragmatic considerations, even though there are also long-term coalitions such as in the United Nations, the G77 or the Forum of Small States (FOSS) and in the WTO the Cairns Group, the Like-Minded Group or the Café au Lait Group (Desker 2009). They respond to the issue structure, but more often to the exigencies of a negotiation process. In the latter case, they sometimes disband or members defect even before the negotiations have ended. Actors in global fora often join two or more coalitions at the same time. Such multi-membership in bargaining coalitions weakens the coalitions if they pursue contradictory objectives or if they fail to make their goals reasonably compatible.

Regional organizations are coalitions by definition, but in order to strengthen their bargaining position in global fora they may seek alliances with non-members. The credibility and effectiveness of a regional coalition within a larger alliance chiefly depends on the level of the cohesiveness the respective regional organization is able to muster. In other words, if the regional organization enters the coalition with non-members as a bloc or quasi-bloc, its bargaining position tends to increase. Thus, it is essential, at least in theory, that all member countries support the coalition and do not defect from it. However, if the conditions for bloc-building do not exist, the individual members of the regional organization will be less likely to join the coalition and may get involved in other coalitions that may pursue non-complementary or even contradictory objectives. In such a situation, the credibility and effectiveness of the coalition will suffer. Regular and effective intra-regional consultation and coordination may be a second best option, compensating for the actorness deficit and other adverse effects resulting from limited cooperation, but in general caucuses reduce regional organizations' bargaining power.

Actors using *forum shopping* as a negotiation strategy "pick and choose" from the forums or the organizational venues that best fit their individual political agenda (Forman and Segaar 2006: 213). Governments and collective actors such as regional organizations are expected to turn to forum shopping if they do not succeed in achieving their negotiation goals in a specific forum or if they seek to "soft balance" institutional power shifts elsewhere (He and Feng 2008). They may then either turn to other fora or – if suitable alternative fora do not exist – establish new institutions. If a regional organization is able to shift issues to a forum where its bargaining power is greater – for instance, due to another membership composition, greater "voice opportunity," more favorable issue-linkages and more favorable decision-making procedures – the grouping's influence on the outcome of decisions increases. Bargaining may result in a better outcome in an alternative forum, but even if an outcome considered detrimental for the grouping's collective interests and those of its individual member governments is prevented through forum shopping, the ability to transfer the issue to another forum represents a certain degree of actorness. This kind of actorness will certainly be noticed by third parties and contributes to the perception of non-members that the respective regional organization must be regarded as a fairly cohesive actor. If only individual members of the regional organization try or even succeed in forum shopping exercises, this will most likely weaken the cohesion of this grouping and negatively influence its perception by others as an entity to be reckoned with.

Image projection and creation of "soft power" are additional strategies that states may employ to create a comfortable and facilitating environment for negotiations and to increase their influence on the outcome of negotiations. Images that international negotiators may want to project are those of a knowledgeable and professional actor, an effective agenda-setter, honest broker, mediator and bridge-builder. Image-projection activities serve to enhance the legitimacy of actors, the creation of trust and confidence of others in the abilities and objectives communicated by a negotiator. A positive international image may strengthen the "soft power" of negotiators. Soft power denotes the ability of actors to co-opt others rather than using compulsory, structural or institutional power to persuade others to do something they otherwise would not (Nye 1988). It comes close to the concept of "productive power" or "power to," denoting the power to influence the behavior and interests of others through discursive means (Barnett and Duvall 2005). Frequently providing the venue for meetings of major international organizations and the ensuing display of superior organizational, agenda-setting and leadership capabilities, all this converges in the expectation that the positive image conveyed by these capacities translates to more accommodating behavior by others in the negotiation process and eventually more positive bargaining outcomes. Members of a regional organization pursuing "soft power" strategies may help to extend the benefits of this strategy to other members of a regional association. This is the case if the strategy is the outcome of intra-group processes of coordination and third parties perceive such strategies as a regional strategy.

2.4 Methodology

Methodologically, the subsequent analysis is a single case study with diachronic and synchronic in-case comparisons. The selection of ASEAN for a single case study was pre-given as the study is part of a larger research project exploring a broad range of issues related to the overarching question of how law facilitates regional integration. Yet ASEAN is certainly a typical case (Gerring 2008: 91) for such a study as it shares with other non-Western regional organizations key characteristics of what is known as the "new regionalism." Among the traits shared is the intergovernmental structure, the comparatively low level of legalization and institutionalization and the great heterogeneity of member countries with regard to political system, economic development, size, population, resources and culture. Single case studies allow for an in-depth exploration of a topic, but have their limitations as far as the generalization of the findings is concerned. While they may be conducive for the building of preliminary hypotheses or testing existing theoretical approaches, deriving from them more general insights necessitates further exploration through medium-n or large-n studies (George and Bennett 2005).

Within-case comparisons may strengthen preliminary hypotheses based on the findings of a single case study. Such within-case comparisons can take the form of diachronic and synchronic comparisons. In this study we operate with both types of comparison.

In the theoretical section we have claimed that, more than material institutional properties, cognitive factors influence the degree of cohesion of regional organizations in their interactions with third states and as actors in international forums. In other words, ASEAN's organizational structure is the result of world views largely shared by the region's foreign policy elites that are not conducive to a deepening of regional integration and increasing cohesion in international forums. In our study we must therefore examine the extent to which such world views have changed over time and whether the ideational path dependencies, which in the theoretical section we expected tangibly to shape ASEAN's behavior in international fora, persist. Moreover, such a longitudinal perspective or diachronic dimension of comparison also tells us whether ASEAN acted more cohesively in international fora when it had only five or six members than with ten members after enlargement in the 1990s (Than and Gates 2001).

Enlargement would imply that the grouping has become more heterogeneous than it used to be before. It would also inform us whether there were changes of behavior when ASEAN was functionally more specific and less centralized than today.

Synchronic comparisons refer to ASEAN's behavior in different international organizations. Owing to time constraints and limited resources we had to make choices in this respect and decided to concentrate on two organizations that ASEAN member countries have always valued as highly significant: the United Nations and the World Trade Organization. Also synchronic are occasional comparisons between ASEAN and other regional organizations in the Global South such as the Mercado Común del Sur (Mercosur), the Andean Community, the South Asian Association for Regional Cooperation (SAARC), the South African Development Council (SADC) and the Economic Community of West African States (ECOWAS). Again, limitations of time and resources account for the fact that these comparisons may be more eclectic than we wished them to be.

Yet these methodological shortcomings may be compensated to a certain extent by our decision to conclude the study with two carefully selected in-depth case studies. These trace ASEAN's behavior through all stages of negotiation in two major issues. Both cases show variation along all relevant dimensions and may hence provide useful insights into the mechanisms of ASEAN coordination and cooperation in major international fora (Gerring 2008: 97). In the first case, we examine the role of ASEAN in agricultural negotiations in the WTO, tracing negotiations on the distribution of material values. In the second case, we explore ASEAN's negotiation in the International Labor Organization on forced labor in Myanmar and, hence, an issue where norms and ideas were contested. In both cases, we examined ASEAN's degree of cohesiveness and sought to determine the conditions under which cohesion changed. Both cases constitute a genuine test for ASEAN's actorness as both were of considerable significance either for the material well-being of the region or the grouping's and its member states' identities.

The few studies exploring what makes regional organizations cohesive in international organizations have so far mainly concentrated on voting behavior in the UN General Assembly (UNGA). Burmester and Jankowski are right in claiming that owing to the fact that many UNGA resolutions "are passed (nearly) unanimously," UNGA voting "tells us very little about the (possible) coordination of foreign policy in a regional organization" (Burmester and Jankowski 2013: 4). Indeed, the fact that some 193 member countries could agree on a resolution merely suggests that the issues at stake were either insignificant or the resolution's text was boiled down to the lowest common denominator. While not ignoring voting behavior in the UN, we nevertheless decided to explore the extent to which ASEAN members agree on *crucial* issues in the UNGA such as Security Council reform or the democratization of the UN. That is, issues that did not necessarily end with a vote. Moreover, as behavior of regional organizations may vary significantly across policy fields, we scrutinized ASEAN's behavior in another major international forum, the WTO, in the field of trade negotiation.

While our research is theory-guided and deductive, it also entails inductive and interpretive elements. This has consequences for the research techniques we employ. Although we make use of statistical data, for instance, on leadership positions in the WTO and UN bodies (see Chapter 5), we rely heavily on qualitative data analysis.

Owing to the virtually non-existent literature on the role of ASEAN as an actor and negotiator in global forums, our research required data collection from many sources and a high degree of data triangulation. The time frame covered ranged from the mid-1990s to 2013. Through access to electronic databases such as LexisNexis and online news archives, we collected hundreds of newspaper reports, including those from international media as well as major Southeast Asian newspapers such as *Straits Times* (Singapore); *New Straits Times* and *Star* (Malaysia); *Jakarta Post*, *Jakarta Globe* and *Kompas* (Indonesia); *Philippine Daily Inquirer* (Philippines); and *Bangkok Post*, *The Nation*, *Matichon* and *Thai Rath* (Thailand). These reports have been supplemented with official documents from the websites of ASEAN and individual ASEAN governments as well as from online databases of the WTO and the UN, such as the Bibliographic Information System (UNBISNET).[1] The last includes official statements, reports and minutes of meetings, voting records and discussion papers. Others were acquired either directly from members of the ASEAN Committees in third countries or from the websites of the Indonesian, Vietnamese and Singaporean

[1] Data for the statements from the countries in the General Assembly plenary session and sessions of the 1st committee were obtained from the verbatim meeting records held by the Dag Hammarskjöld Library at www.un.org/depts/dhl/.

Permanent Missions to the UN in New York. With the selection of these three countries, we have scrutinized activities in the UN General Assembly (UNGA) of a large member state, a small member state and a new member state of ASEAN. Other official documents come from the main UN bodies, namely the UNGA, the Human Rights Council, the Security Council and the Economic and Social Council (ECOSOC). Because of the large amount of data, we concentrated on official documents between 2010 and 2012. We have coded these documents and interpreted them in accordance with our research questions. Also, political autobiographies, collections of speeches by ASEAN foreign policymakers and key negotiators, as well as self-reflections of diplomats served as important sources for our study. Most valuable in this respect were the published political autobiography of Singapore's former Permanent Representative to the United Nations and Minister of Foreign Affairs, S. Jayakumar, the speeches of the late Indonesian Foreign Minister Ali Alatas and the volume on Singapore's diplomatic service edited by Tommy Koh and Chang Li Lin.[2]

In addition, we acquired information through email inquiries and twenty-nine semi-structured interviews in Bangkok, Jakarta, Singapore, Geneva, Freiburg, Frankfurt and Berlin between February 2010 and March 2014. This includes telephone interviews with diplomats based at the ASEAN Committees in New York and Geneva and in ASEAN capitals. We also interviewed former and incumbent officials of the ASEAN Secretariat and scholars. A few interviews with

[2] See Jayakumar (2011); Alatas (2001); Koh and Chang (2005).

non-ASEAN diplomats served to obtain a better understanding of how ASEAN activities in international organizations are perceived from an external perspective. The interviews gave us access to information that is not recorded elsewhere. The questions asked concern (1) the negotiating capacities and strategies of the ASEAN member states (human resources, training, policy inputs from think tanks and civil society organizations, etc.); (2) negotiating positions of the individual countries in specific issue areas; (3) how, under what conditions and to what extent ASEAN members coordinate in international organizations and negotiating fora such as the UNGA, WTO and G20; and (4) prospects and challenges for ASEAN coordination. Because of the sensitivity of some of the information provided in this book and requests of interviewees not to be named, all interview sources are anonymous.

The information acquired from the interviews took the form of both facts and opinions. For increased accuracy, we practice data triangulation, that is, cross-checking information from various sources whenever possible. For instance, information acquired from interviews was double-checked in other interviews and by information obtained from documents, newspaper reports and the published literature (Devies 2001: 73–80). And although much of the information provided here is the interview respondents' personal opinion, it elucidates the actual problems and challenges ASEAN negotiators face and thus constitutes valuable information for our analysis.

In our two in-depth case studies we operated with process tracing, a research technique that is based on extensive description and historical narratives (see Chapter 6). It must be noted that our approach is different from the standard use of process tracing in that we do not seek to identify the causal chain or causal mechanism between independent and dependent variables (Schimmelfennig 2006), but to capture the mechanisms by which ASEAN's actorness is either strengthened or undermined during the negotiation in specific issue areas.

Chapter 3

ASEAN's cognitive prior and negotiating capacities

In accordance with our theoretical assumptions, this chapter explores the extent to which the world views of Southeast Asian foreign policy elites are conducive for regional integration and a cohesive stance in global fora. We therefore scrutinize the ways in which historical experiences and extant ideas have influenced the contemporary political decision-makers' outlooks on the external world and how the latter have shaped the region's shared repository of cooperation norms. These norms are pivotal for ASEAN's organizational structure and the degree of cohesion it is able to develop. To avoid misunderstandings: this is not a section providing a comprehensive narrative of Southeast Asian history and the evolution of ASEAN.[1] It is merely a section depicting in broad brushes the ideational path dependencies in which Southeast Asian political elites have been socialized.

The ideational and normative underpinnings of regional integration also have a bearing on how much member governments are willing and able to tap domestic and regional sources of knowledge and thereby strengthen ASEAN's actorness. The second part of the chapter therefore explores ASEAN's actor capacities. It examines the kind of resources

[1] For comprehensive overviews, see Dosch (1997); Acharya (2001); Narine (2002; 2008); Haacke (2003).

member governments may draw from in order to generate and tap the knowledge needed to participate successfully in international negotiations. The first section of this part of the chapter primarily investigates domestic epistemic resources, while the second section seeks to assess the extent to which regional centers of knowledge exist and to what extent domestic sources of know-how have been "ASEANized." This addresses the question whether the respective expertise is made available to fellow ASEAN members in an attempt to strengthen the region's cohesion and solidarity in international negotiations and, if so, to what extent this is the case.

3.1 Cognitive and institutional dimensions of ASEAN's actorness

Southeast Asians' world views have been strongly shaped by an unusually turbulent history (Kasetsiri 1976; Wyatt 1984; Taylor 1987; Ricklefs 2001). The experiences of war, insurgencies, rebellions, secessions and foreign invasions, conquest and dominance can be traced back as far as the pre-colonial period. The memories of devastation and depopulation caused by wars and endemic violence have become deeply ingrained in the mental maps of the region's rulers and decision-makers. The instability of Southeast Asia's pre-colonial empires and kingdoms was proverbial. Even though some of these empires, such as Champa, Pagan, Majapahit or Ayudhaya flourished for centuries, all of them went through severe crisis and near collapse. In the end, none of them survived. Some, as for example Ayudhaya, were virtually annihilated through conquest. Internal strife, the rise of new powers inside and outside the region, or combinations of both brought them down.

This waxing and waning of empires, the persistent insecurity and vulnerability of kingdoms and their rulers, found their expression in the political literature long before the advent of the colonial powers. Hindu-Brahmanic political thought reaching Southeast Asia from the Indian subcontinent through traders spread widely at the region's courts. In the process, Southeast Asia's rulers became familiar with these ideas, including those of the Kautilya's *Arthasastra*, an Indian political guidebook for rulers. These thoughts were localized in poems celebrating kings and their empires, such as the fourteenth-century Javanese poem *Negarakretagama* of the Majapahit era (Reid 1998; Nguitragool 2012). The poems familiarized elites with the concept of geometric politics (Zimmer 1976) and a holistic concept of power, which also included the obligation of the rulers to ensure prosperity in their perimeter of influence.[2] In simplified terms, notions of the external world rested on the assumption that a king and his realm are surrounded by concentric circles (*mandalas*) of foes and allies (*ibid.*). The foes are to be found in an immediately adjacent circle of neighbors, while the allies are located in the next concentric circle. In other words: the neighbors of the neighbor are potential allies of a ruler and, hence, the enemies of the enemy (*ibid.*).

As pre-colonial empires and principalities were usually organized as layers of suzerainty relationships, the

[2] The following paragraphs draw strongly from Jetschke and Rüland (2009: 438–439) and Nguitragool (2012).

cohesion of the empire declined with increasing distance to the court. With the power of the overlord fading at the empire's peripheries, the likelihood increased that vassals would shift their loyalties to rival overlords should opportunities occur or conditions dictate. This gave the *mandala* concept an inherently expansive and aggressive dimension: in a world of Hobbesian anarchy, rulers can only survive and maintain the welfare of their subjects if they pre-emptively attack their neighbor's territory and by conquest enlarge their empire. Otherwise, sooner or later, they will be attacked themselves, with their survival at stake. Moreover, a large perimeter of influence bestows legitimacy; it is testimony to the divine origin of the ruler who may claim to be a *cakravartin* or world ruler (McCloud 1995: 73).

In order to remain in power under these highly volatile conditions, the ends justify the means. Put differently: the ruler is allowed to resort to all means that help him or her in averting challenges. War, murder, treason, lies, espionage, deception and other actions that in idealist notions of politics may appear morally reprehensible thus constitute legitimate means to ensure political survival (Zimmer 1976). In the extant belief of local elites, power is therefore amoral. It is considered as finite and hence indivisible (Anderson 1972: 7). Power sharing, a virtue in liberal political theory, thus heralds the decline and ultimately the loss of a ruler's charisma; it is the precursor of chaos and turmoil.

These political ideas have been popularized in Indian-origin art genres that reached Southeast Asia together with the *Arthasastra*. Ancient Indian epics such as the *Mahabharata* and the *Ramayama* have been deeply internalized by Southeast

Asian audiences up to the present day. They are still part of the school curriculum and their episodes reappear in paintings, sculptures, architecture, music, theatrical plays, folklore and even comics, pop-art and internet blogs (Jetschke and Rüland 2009; Kasetsiri 1976: 133; Thongthep 1993: 5; Weintraub 2004). Broadly speaking, they convey the message that even the good and virtuous is persistently threatened by villains and demons.[3] Warfare, violence, intrigue, insecurity and tragedy are thus depicted as unavoidable facts of life. Such skeptical world views do not only persist in the culturally Indianized parts of Southeast Asia, but also the region's Sinicized parts, here mediated through the teachings of Chinese strategic thinker Sun Tze or in literary form through the "Romance of the Three Kingdoms" (*Sam Kok*).

The ideas of the *Arthasastra* have also been sustained in the nationalist discourse that, by constructing a collective identity drawing from a glorious past, frequently makes references to the Indianized empires of the pre-colonial era such as Sukothai in Thailand or Sri Vijaya and Majapahit in Indonesia (Smith 2000: 500). By doing so, nationalist ideology revalidates political ideas associated with these great eras. In Indonesia, notions of the *mandala* concept have inspired Sukarno's "Guided Democracy" as well Suharto's *Orde Baru* (Anderson 1972). The Indonesian military still relies on the concept of concentric circles as the foundation of a security doctrine (Anwar 1994; Smith 2000; Perwita 2007; Widjajanto 2008) developed during the Suharto era that regards the

[3] See also *Jakarta Post*, 21 September 2000; 25 November 2001; 1 May 2003; 11 April 2005; 7 September 2005; 4 September 2007 and 28 February 2008.

immediate neighborhood as the most crucial region for the country's security. However, in contrast to *Arthasastra* logic, it seeks to pacify the adjacent region not by military conquest but by nurturing cooperative relationships designed to serve the national interest. How much the *mandala* concept continues to permeate everyday political discourses is highlighted in numerous commentaries by scholars and politicians. Soedjati Djiwandono, a well-known Indonesian political analyst, for instance, argued with regard to tense Indonesian–Malaysian relations that "geographic proximity does not ensure easy relations between neighboring countries. On the contrary, it may precisely be a hindrance to good and friendly relations."[4] Lee Kuan Yew, Singapore's former Prime Minister, was even more straightforward, stating that "the immediate neighbors are not always the best friends" (quoted by Hänggi 1992: 284 and in similar terms by Ba 2009: 51).[5] Such statements are reflective of historically

[4] See J. Soedjati Djiwandono, *Jakarta Post*, 6 March 2002. For Indonesia, see also a commentary in the *Jakarta Post*, 15 November 1999 and comments of diplomat Siswo Pramono, *Jakarta Post*, 4 March 2010 and scholar Hadianto Wirajuda, *Jakarta Post*, 2 February 2009 and 4 April 2011. The concept played a particularly prominent role under the presidency of Megawati Sukarnoputri. See "Indonesia's Evolving Foreign Policy and ASEAN Leadership," Center for Strategic and International Studies (CSIS), 22 April 2002, available at: http://web.archive.org/web/20070812000137/http://www.csis.or.id/feature_view.asp?id=27&tab=0 (accessed 6 November 2014).

[5] Slightly varying the theme, former Singaporean Foreign Minister Jayakumar wrote: "There is a cliché in diplomacy that there are no permanent friends, only permanent interests" (Jayakumar 2011: 112). For Indonesia, see J. Soedjati Djiwandono, *Jakarta Post*, 6 March 2002.

hostile relations between neighbors who have long regarded themselves as arch enemies. Cases in point are Burma and Thailand, Thailand and Vietnam, Cambodia and Vietnam and Cambodia and Thailand. Western versions of geopolitics serve further to perpetuate these "frozen" ancient geopolitical world views.[6] At least in Indonesia, the writings of Mackinder, Ratzel and Haushofer are still part of military training, as are strategists such as Clausewitz (Sunardi 2004: 157–166; Anggoro 2005: 62–66; Laksmana 2008). They have, in fact, relegitimized and modernized prior geopolitical strategic thinking.[7]

Summing up, the cognitive legacy of Indian and, to a lesser extent, Sinic political thoughts for the region's cooperation culture is sixfold. First, and perhaps most importantly, it conveys a skeptical anthropology, a world view of political realism (Weinstein 1976: 61; Boesche 2002; Novotny 2010; Nguitragool 2013),[8] in which trust is in short supply and

[6] The ongoing significance of geopolitics in the Indonesian approach to international relations is also underscored by the fact that Universitas Indonesia has established a professorship of international relations and geopolitics which is held by former Defense Minister Juwono Sudarsono, *Jakarta Post*, 9 November 2011.

[7] But also in other ASEAN countries we often find references to "fundamental geopolitical realities." For Singapore, see, inter alia, Mahbubani (2005: 95).

[8] In a survey of 277 Indonesian international relations students, Nguitragool found that, with 39.9 percent, political realism received by far the most responses, even though the percentage might be markedly lower than forty years earlier when Weinstein (1976) conducted his fieldwork (Nguitragool 2013: 10).

power is the dominant factor in interstate relations.[9] This entails, second, the view that in a world where power is pervasive, the international order is highly unstable, fluid and precarious. Guspiabri Sumowigeno, the director of the Centre for Indonesian National Policy Studies (CINAPS), argues that in international relations "there are neither real friends, nor eternal enemies."[10] Governments thus place a premium on a foreign policy that guarantees stability and state survival, which they feel is best guaranteed by the "para bellum" doctrine: "If you want peace, prepare for war."[11] Third, the notion of power as a finite quantity inculcates in political actors relative gains thinking: one person's gains are necessarily someone else's losses. Fourth, where the belief prevails that power needs to be concentrated and centralized, formal political institutions, in particular power-sharing decentralizing arrangements, are viewed as a dilution of authority. This may have limiting repercussions on cooperative arrangements that always entail compromises and trade-offs. Fifth, the ethnocentric perceptions inherent in the centralized world views of the *mandala*

[9] This is corroborated by an opinion poll commissioned by the German Friedrich-Ebert Foundation, which found that an appalling 59.8 percent of the surveyed regional elites do not trust other countries in Southeast Asia to be "good neighbors" (Roberts 2007).

[10] Guspiabri Sumowigeno, "Mempersoalkan Politik Luar Negeri Presiden SBY," 21 August 2010.

[11] See *ibid.* For similar statements, see Indonesian President Yudhoyono during one of the Ambalat crises, *Tempo Interaktif*, 26 February 2009; Muladi, the governor of Lemhannas, an Indonesian military think tank, *Tempo Interaktif*, 28 May 2009 and *Kompas*, 2 June 2009; and for Indonesian legislators, see, inter alia, *Suara Pembaruan*, 5 March 2005 and *Tempo Interaktif*, 5 March 2005 and 1 September 2010.

concept have set limits to regional cooperation by stressing exceptionalism and hierarchy. They are thus – even as diffuse cognitive remnants – still an impediment to "deeply" institutionalized regional cooperation. Sixth, and finally, these ancient political ideas entail strong collectivist and paternalist notions of society (Solidum 1974: 85). The latter have been re-invented, modernized and re-legitimized by imported nineteenth-century European organic state theory and its concomitant state-corporatist arrangements of state–society relations (Reeve 1985; MacIntyre 1994; Bourchier 1999; Rüland 2012a). The strong influence of organic state theory fuels state-centric notions of regional cooperation (Sukma 2000: 90), as only governments are believed to dispose of or to build up the capacities needed for protecting and maintaining national sovereignty and autonomy. The vestiges of this organicism are still ubiquitous in ASEAN discourses. They can, for instance, be found in references to ASEAN as a "family," a concept that in addition to the rhetorical use in the quest for unity, consensus and harmony,[12] also helped privatize intramural interactions, appropriating the practice of closed-door diplomacy and policy of keeping external powers out of the region.

It is not only a broad array of cultural media that have perpetuated ancient views of the external world. More recent history has also served as persuasive and powerful evidence for the plausibility of these age-honored perceptions.[13] Nearly

[12] For an analysis of ASEAN's regional corporatism, see Rüland (2012a).

[13] Former Singaporean Foreign Minister S. Jayakumar speaks in his political autobiography of a "fractious history": Jayakumar (2011: 100).

all of Southeast Asia was colonized except for Thailand, which nevertheless suffered severely from Western imperialism in the second half of the nineteenth century and the first decades of the twentieth. During the Second World War large parts of Southeast Asia had been occupied by Japanese military forces and in the process became a major war theatre. The atrocities committed against civilians and the physical destruction are deeply ingrained in the memory of the peoples of the region. The post-war return of the Dutch and French colonialists to Indochina and the Indonesian archipelago, the subsequent wars for national independence with hundreds of thousands of casualties, and the lack of support – and in the case of Vietnam even enmity – from the USA, their anti-colonial rhetoric notwithstanding, did little to increase the trust of Southeast Asian elites in Great Powers and the international community (Ricklefs 2001). The vagaries and exigencies of the Cold War, neo-colonialist ploys, Great Power intervention, discrimination and marginalization in international institutions and economic dependence further inculcated in the minds of Southeast Asian political elites the belief that the external world is hostile and systematically working to the disadvantage of smaller and weaker countries (Weinstein 1976: 364). The unfolding second Indochina war, transforming Southeast Asia into a frontline region in the confrontation between the West and the socialist camp, further deepened these sentiments of insecurity.

With these historical and ideational legacies it is hardly surprising that despite an intensifying will to overcome tensions with neighbors and to create a more peaceful political environment conducive for economic growth, suspicion and distrust towards neighbors continued to linger (Weinstein 1976: 364). The founding of ASEAN on 8 August 1967 sent a strong signal, expressing the intention to overcome regional strife and to achieve regional prosperity (Kivimäki 2008). ASEAN followed two earlier failed attempts at regional cooperation, that is, the Association of Southeast Asia (ASA) and Maphilindo (Malaya, the Philippines and Indonesia) (Gordon 1966; Solidum 1974). It ended years of tension and hostility among the association's founding members, climaxing in the Indonesian confrontation policy (*konfrontasi*) against neighboring Malaysia (1963–1966).[14] Through its leadership in establishing ASEAN, Indonesia sought to shed its image of a revisionist firebrand power, rebuild forfeited international trust and at the same time curtail Great Power influence in Southeast Asia (Weinstein 1976; Leifer 1983; Ba 2009).

The newly formed regional organization began as a functionally quite specific organization. Although the founding document, the Bangkok Declaration, named economic and social cooperation as key objectives, it was in fact security cooperation that served as the glue for the grouping for much of the time until the end of the Cold War. Economic cooperation started in the mid-1970s, but did not reach a noteworthy level before 1992 when, in its fourth Summit in Singapore, ASEAN agreed to create an ASEAN Free Trade Area (AFTA). In the 1990s, as ASEAN decision-makers realized that political and economic issues of cooperation cannot be isolated from

[14] Other issues creating tensions in the region were the Philippine claim for the Malaysian state of Sabah, the former British North Borneo, and the withdrawal of Singapore from the Federation of Malaysia in 1965.

other policy fields such as social development, environment, labor, migration and education, to name a few, they embarked on what in ASEAN jargon was called "functional cooperation." In the process functional specificity gave way to a multifunctional cooperation scheme.

Although the five founding members - Indonesia, Malaysia, the Philippines, Thailand and Singapore - were already quite diverse in terms of political system, economic development, population, size, culture and relations with external powers, this diversity markedly increased with the grouping's enlargement in the 1990s. After the accession of tiny Brunei in 1984, Vietnam (1995), Myanmar and Laos (1997) and Cambodia (1999) became members of ASEAN, thus bringing the grouping's membership to ten.

ASEAN's level of centralization was strongly informed by the repository of cooperation norms that the association developed over the years. The cognitive legacies of centuries discussed above and also the self-image of a community of non-equals were pivotal for establishing a normative regional order in which Westphalian sovereignty norms figured prominently and that became a formidable obstacle for the deepening of regional integration.[15] The Treaty of Amity and Cooperation (TAC) of 1976, the document establishing what later became known as the ASEAN Way, devised ASEAN as a strictly intergovernmental regional cooperation scheme without any ambitions of developing EU-type supranational institutions, irrespective of the persistent mimicking of European integration rhetoric and institutional nomenclature

[15] See also authors' interviews, 11 April 2012.

(Jetschke 2009). National sovereignty and autonomy, territorial integrity, equality and, in particular, non-interference into the internal affairs of fellow members thus became key norms of the grouping (Narine 2002; Haacke 2003; Jones 2012; Beeson and Stone 2013). As a result, regional cooperation was less functionally driven as a response to concrete collective action problems caused by pressing cross-border problems, but rather a defensive institutional device to increase national resilience (*ketahanan nasional*) of member states. National resilience denotes "the ability of a nation to cope with, endure and survive any kind of challenges or threats she meets in the course of her struggle to achieve her national goals" (Anwar 1992: 13).

The quest to maximize national autonomy as one of the key rationales for regional cooperation entailed a low level of legalization, institutionalization and centralization. Most of ASEAN's decisions have been non-binding and may be best characterized as "soft law." In the past, ASEAN governments and ASEAN officials often celebrated the concomitant informality and pragmatism as a virtue of Southeast Asian regionalism that allows for swift and flexible responses to changing circumstances. For a long time, however, they played down or completely ignored the flipside of shallow institutionalization so that only a fraction of decisions and agreements – in fact, less than 30 percent – have been actually implemented.[16]

Consensual decision-making is another dimension of ASEAN's intergovernmentalism. In the light of conflictive

[16] *Jakarta Post*, 22 November 2007.

relations among member states prior to the formation of ASEAN, creating a semblance of harmony was more important than negotiated agreements. Members eschewed intensive bargaining and acrimonious negotiation and litigation as practiced in the European Union, fearing its potentially divisive and harmful effects on the still fragile spirit of cooperation. Rather than accentuating what divides them, ASEAN member countries sought to establish decision-making processes that would foster unity. In many cases, however, by *de facto* endowing member countries with veto power, consensual decision-making was little more than a persistent search for the lowest common denominator and the bracketing of contentious issues. This made it difficult for the grouping to act jointly in other forums,[17] although there were certainly instances in which ASEAN authoritatively spoke with one voice – ASEAN's Cambodia policy in the UN in the 1980s (Snitwongse 1989; Haacke 2003; Narine 2008; Ba 2009) and its cooperation during the GATT's Uruguay Round (1986–1994) may serve as shining examples (Sally 2004; Sally and Sen 2005).

Consensual decision-making became an even greater constraint for joint action in global forums with the grouping's enlargement in the 1990s. The strengthening of international bargaining power and greater protection from Great Power interference in the region may have been plausible motivations for the creation of a Southeast Asia-10 (Rüland 2000). But without a carefully managed accession process it soon turned out that the history of hostile relations with neighbors, which the new members brought into the

[17] See also *Jakarta Post*, 29 October 2010.

association, further cemented their diehard adherence to the intergovernmentalist core values of the ASEAN Way, making it even more difficult to act cohesively.

Thus, unsurprisingly, consensual decision-making became one of the key issues in ASEAN's more recent institutional reform debates. The Eminent Persons Group (EPG), mandated at the grouping's 2005 summit in Kuala Lumpur with the task of devising ideas for an ASEAN Charter, a quasi-constitutional document, was encouraged by ASEAN leaders to submit a bold and visionary blueprint. It did so by proposing to replace consensual decision-making by a majority voting system (Report of the Eminent Persons Group, 2006),[18] a proposal strongly supported by the Indonesian government and several regionally organized civil society networks. However, ultimately, the charter-writing High-Level Task Force (HLTF), faced with strong reservations of the majority of ASEAN governments, only provided for a more flexible decision-making process in the implementation of economic commitments, for which it introduced the Ten Minus X formula (Article 21, 2). In all other areas it retained consensual decision-making (Article 20, 1). The ASEAN Charter thus contributed little to transforming ASEAN into a bloc or quasi-bloc in its dealings with the external world. In fact, the Charter reforms retained features of the organization that confine its cohesion in international negotiations to a caucus.

But ASEAN's much cherished equality norm also had repercussions on the association's institutional trajectory. The decision that all member states should contribute equally to

[18] *Jakarta Post*, 14 July 2007.

the ASEAN Secretariat's budget was a deliberate symbolic act highlighting ASEAN as a group of equals, albeit with the consequence that the limited financial capacities of the poorer member states tightly circumscribed the Secretariat's funding support and, consequently, its professional capacities.[19] As a result, ASEAN has only a small Secretariat established in 1976 in Jakarta following the grouping's first summit in Bali. For most of the time since then, and despite repeated reforms of the Secretariat, ASEAN justified its lean institutionalization with the argument that it seeks to avoid the emergence of a bureaucratic juggernaut, or in somewhat more polemic terms, the "Brusselsization of ASEAN" (Dosch 2003: 38).

The discovery of analysts and some ASEAN governments that the association is in need of a more robust institutional infrastructure is of quite recent origin and a consequence of the Asian financial crisis. Today some ASEAN officials openly propagate the development of Jakarta into the "Brussels of the East," a metaphor for a more institutionalized ASEAN.[20] However, despite mounting criticism of ASEAN's weak capacities for policy preparation, coordination and implementation, and calls for a funding of the Secretariat reflecting the economic status of member countries,[21] the ASEAN Charter retained equal annual contributions (Article 30). How much and in what way the under-financing of the Secretariat impacts on ASEAN's capacities to coordinate

[19] See also authors' interviews, 11 April 2012.

[20] ASEAN Deputy Secretary General Bagas Hapsoro, *Jakarta Post*, 23 January 2010; similarly, *Jakarta Globe*, 17 December 2010.

[21] *Kompas*, 29 February 2008; *Jakarta Post*, 6 May 2008.

policies and to provide much needed technical expertise for policy options will be discussed in greater detail later in this chapter.

Given the region's historical legacies, which have decisively shaped ASEAN's cooperation norms and organizational set-up, and the continued experience of an asymmetric world order, the grouping failed markedly to deepen regional integration. Although varying across member countries and within foreign policymaking elites, power sensitivity, notions of an essentially hostile international environment, an awareness of vulnerability,[22] victimization[23] and insecurity, and concerns over the fragility of the international order continue to be deeply ingrained in the region's collective memory even after the ASEAN Charter took effect. A survey conducted by the Jakarta-based Center for Strategic and International Studies, for instance, found that most respondents – and in particular those from ASEAN's larger powers, but also those from

[22] For Singaporean examples, see Jayakumar (2011); for Indonesia, diplomat Siswo Pramono, *Jakarta Post*, 4 March 2010 and scholar Cornelius F. Luhulima, *Jakarta Post*, 6 August 2010. For a Cambodian example, see Prime Minister Hun Sen, "ASEAN Still Faces Many Challenges: Hun Sen," 9 July 2012, available at: www.asianewsnet.net/home/news.php?id=33139 (accessed 12 July 2012); for Malaysia, see Prime Minister Tun Najib Razak, as quoted by *Tempo Interaktif*, 31 August 2010.

[23] On victimization, see also *Jakarta Post*, 23 March 2005. In a more recent article in the *Jakarta Post*, two Universitas Indonesia scholars write: "Indonesian people (including political parties, civil society groups, the media) still feel that they are actually the systematic victim subject of the world economic system arranged by conspiracy of the external forces (in popular terms 'The West')," *Jakarta Post*, 19 April 2010.

Singapore – are hesitant to rely on regional cooperation as a means to overcome cross-border problems. They tend to rely much more "on military self-sufficiency or bilateral alliances to prevent or to respond to pandemics, humanitarian crises, or terrorism" (Gill et al. 2009: 12–13).[24]

The pervasive survivalist discourses surrounding foreign policymaking in virtually all countries of the region are testimony to the widespread reservations towards deepened regional integration.[25] They suggest that little has changed since Weinstein's seminal study of Indonesian foreign policy elites in the late 1960s and early 1970s (Weinstein 1976: 362). Former Singaporean Foreign Minister Jayakumar, for instance, fears that the international arena degenerates into "the law of the jungle" in which the lives of small nations may be – quoting Hobbes – "nasty, brutish and short" (Jayakumar 2011: 76).[26] The big swallow the small: "The bigger and more

[24] See also PacNet #12, "Strategic Views on Asian Regionalism: Survey Results and Analysis," *PacNet Newsletter*, 18 February 2009.

[25] For examples, see the frequent references of Indonesian President Susilo Bambang Yudhoyono to Indonesia's sailing in a "turbulent sea," *Jakarta Post*, 2 February 2009; former Singaporean Foreign Minister Jayakumar in his political autobiography (Jayakumar 2011: 23); or Malaysian Prime Minister Tun Najib Razak, *Jakarta Post*, 18 November 2011. See also comments of political analyst Soedjati Djiwandono, *Jakarta Post*, 6 March 2002; an editorial on Indonesia's foreign policy, *Jakarta Post*, 19 August 2008; and *Straits Times*, 20 May 2010.

[26] For a similar description of the world, see former Indonesian Foreign Minister Ali Alatas in a speech held at the United Nations General Assembly, stating that "ours is still an essentially brutal world. In many places, wanton violence and armed conflicts persist, often bringing about humanitarian disaster." In the speech Alatas goes on to deplore the persistent abuse of power in world politics and the devastating

powerful a country is, the greater its clout" (*ibid.* 22).[27] As a small state "you are either at the table or you are on the menu!"[28] Indonesian President Yudhoyono shares this skeptical world view, albeit expressing it less stridently, when arguing in a speech before the UN General Assembly: "Let's face it: the remnants of Cold War mentality still persist in parts of the geopolitical landscape – not least our own United Nations, where rigid, dogmatic, zero-sum calculations sometimes still come into play."[29]

What thus counts – even in multilateral institutions such as the UN – is "the national interest,"[30] which in the view of Yudhoyono's Foreign Minister, Marty M. Natalegawa, denotes "the capacity for independent decision-making."[31] Jusuf Wanandi, the dean of Indonesia's political think tank community, opened an opinion piece in the *Jakarta Post* in which he raised strong doubts about the wisdom of Indonesia ratifying the ASEAN Charter with the following words:

consequences this has had, especially in the twentieth century (Alatas 2001: 602).

[27] Similarly, in his Rajaratnam Lecture of 19 May 2010: "History is replete with stories of small nations which have come and gone. Independent city-states – for example, in ancient Mesopotamia, Greece and Italy – flourished for a time only to be swallowed up by larger, more enduring empires." See *Straits Times*, 20 May 2010.

[28] Jayakumar, quoted by the *Straits Times*, 20 May 2010.

[29] Speech by HE Dr. Susilo Bambang Yudhoyono, President of the Republic of Indonesia at the General Debate of the 67th Session of the United Nations General Assembly, New York, 25 September 2012, available at: www.presidenri.go.id/index.php/eng/pidato/2012/09/26/1970.html (accessed 4 February 2014).

[30] *Ibid.* [31] *Jakarta Post*, 21 December 2009.

> It is an accepted wisdom that in international relations every nation pursues its own national interest. This notion is based on state sovereignty, the basis of relations between states since the Treaty of Westphalia in 1648.[32]

These views hardly differ from policy discourses elsewhere in the region where the "national interest" is likewise omnipresent. For former high-ranking Singaporean diplomat Bilahari Kausikan these interests are simple: "to survive - because in international relations, survival is the prime value without which no other value can be realized - and to contribute to a better life for our people" (Kausikan 2005: 103). Ultimately, Jayakumar summarizes his experiences as Singapore's Permanent Representative in the UN by stating that "politics and national interests really dominated all decision-making in the UN" (*ibid.* 57). Tellingly, the "nationalist interest" is the dominant concept in his political autobiography. To preserve the national interest, persistent power balancing is the key imperative.[33]

Similar comments were aired in Malaysia. Malaysia's former Foreign Minister Y. B. Dato Seri Utama Dr. Rais Yatim opined in the Strategic Plan 2009–2015 that his country's foreign policy must be "guided by the fundamental principles of promoting and protecting the national interests" (Wisma Putra 2009: vii). This idea was translated into the Ministry of Foreign Affairs' first foreign policy objective, that

[32] See Wanandi, *Jakarta Post*, 6 May 2008. Similarly, Indonesian diplomat Siswo Pramono, *Jakarta Post*, 4 March 2010.

[33] This is a key conclusion we derive from Jayakumar's political autobiography.

is to safeguard and protect "national sovereignty in the international arena" (*ibid.*). Also, in Thailand, nationalist sentiments are deeply rooted, as Sunait Chutintaranond confirms, deploring that such attitudes have "dehumanized our neighbors" and "built up the idea of neighbors as enemies and threats to our nation."[34]

In the view of the region's foreign policy elites, the best way to cope with adverse circumstances in the international arena is to build up "national resilience" (*ketahanan nasional*). While it is foremost the duty of foreign policymakers to pursue the national interest, the latter may entail regional cooperation as long as it facilitates resource pooling in policy areas with common interests. Beyond this, member states may chart their own course of action that might not necessarily be compatible with another of their fellow ASEAN members. Nothing explains this motivation better than Indonesia's longstanding and overriding foreign policy doctrine of "*bebas dan aktif*" – free (or independent) and active.[35] But the essence of "*bebas – aktif*" has not evaded other member countries. Singapore, writes former Foreign Minister Jayakumar, pursues "the goal of broadening our linkages with the world so as not to be constrained solely within ASEAN" (Jayakumar 2011: 23–24). "We make common

34 "Nationalism Undermines Prospects for a Caring and Sharing Community Say Thai Civil Society Representatives," 18 October 2009.

35 For the unabated relevance of the "*bebas dan aktif*" doctrine for Indonesian foreign policy, see a government directive: Direction of Indonesian Foreign Policy, 6 September 2009, available at: http://web.archive.org/web/20100521170742/http://www.deplu.go.id/Pages/Polugri.aspx?IDP=21&l=en (accessed 4 November 2014).

cause with others," he adds later, "when our interests coincide. [But] even then, there is no guarantee of support when the crunch comes" (*ibid.* 112). And Bilahari Kausikan almost pre-empts Indonesian scholar Rizal Sukma's concept of a "post-ASEAN" policy when he writes that "we [referring to Singapore] are inescapably and forever part of Southeast Asia. But we must also never be limited to or be trapped by Southeast Asia" (Kausikan 2005: 105).

These beliefs may have been challenged in recent times by more liberal notions of the international order and their ideational origins may be more diffuse today; yet, as shown above, they are still widely present and shape state behavior. This sense of erstwhile marginalization and victimization through Great Powers and the external world, as well as justified pride over post-independence achievements, have given rise to strong aspirations for international recognition and reputation.[36] ASEAN states want to be seen, as Katsumata emphatically argues (Katsumata 2009), as on a par with the economically advanced countries of the West. In fact, one may liken their behavior to upwardly mobile members of lower social classes who, after having risen through merit and hard work to upper middle class status, display a particularly strong desire for social recognition.

3.2 Negotiation capacities

While the previous section has depicted the cognitive background against which ASEAN's behavior in international

[36] For examples, see *Straits Times*, 17 January 1999.

organizations must be gauged, the subsequent sections discuss in greater detail how this "cognitive prior" affects the association's negotiation capacities and their national and regional institutional underpinnings. We thereby depart from the observation that, like many other regions of the Global South, ASEAN must operate in a global institutional environment in which the economically advanced countries of the West control access and membership, dominate decision-making and strongly influence the normative order.[37]

It is thus hardly surprising that Southeast Asian governments had realized early on that smaller and weaker developing countries would only have a chance to influence international decisions if they spoke with one voice. The Declaration of ASEAN Concord signed in Bali in 1976 (Bali Concord I), for instance, expresses an early commitment of ASEAN member states to unite for

> the reform of [the] international trading system, the reform [of the] international monetary system and transfer of real resources, in the United Nations and other relevant multilateral fora, with a view to contributing to the establishment of the New International Economic Order.

More recently, the ASEAN Charter reiterated the calls for more coordinated external policies. The Charter promoted "regional resilience" (Article 1, 2) and called for "enhanced consultations on matters seriously affecting the common interest of ASEAN" (Article 2, 2g). Article 41(4) was even more specific, demanding that

[37] For details, see Rüland (2012a).

> In the conduct of external relations of ASEAN, Member states shall, on the basis of unity and solidarity, coordinate and endeavor to develop common positions and pursue joint actions.

Moreover, Article 41(6) urges ASEAN countries to pursue "consistency and coherence in the conduct of ASEAN's external relations." More specifically, the Bali Concord III, adopted in April 2011, urged the members to develop

> a more coordinated, cohesive and coherent ASEAN position on global issues of common interest and concern, based on a shared ASEAN global view which would further enhance ASEAN's common voice in relevant multilateral fora

and an

> enhanced ASEAN capacity to respond to key global issues of common interest and concern which would benefit all ASEAN Member States and its people.[38]

Finally, in January 2012, the enactment of "Rules of Procedure for the Conclusion of International Agreements by ASEAN" sought to strengthen ASEAN as a negotiator not *in* but *with* international organizations, although the new rules did little – as critics complained – to transcend the grouping's intergovernmental structure.[39]

[38] Available at: http://web.archive.org/web/20120502235821/http://www.aseansec.org/documents/19th%20summit/Bali%20Concord%20III.pdf (accessed 4 November 2014); see also *Jakarta Globe*, 7 June 2012.

[39] "ASEAN Adopts International Negotiating Procedures," available at: http://aseanec.blogspot.com/2012/01/asean-adopts-international-negotiating.html (accessed 1 February 2012).

The increasing attention ASEAN recently paid to developing common positions and a quasi-bloc cohesion in global forums is a vital precondition if Indonesian ambitions to strengthen the association's global role are to be more than cheap talk. In 2011, the Indonesian government placed its presidency of the grouping under the slogan "ASEAN Community in a Global Community of Nations."[40] For Indonesian Foreign Minister Marty M. Natalegawa ASEAN should intensify its contributions to creating greater stability in the world[41] and, as President Susilo Bambang Yudhoyono added, to "tackling global problems."[42] Vice President Boediono proposed "a post-2015 vision for ASEAN" with "a more cohesive ASEAN role in addressing global issues,"[43] a goal – we have seen – Indonesia was able to enshrine in the Bali Concord III.[44]

Taking the quest for a more assertive ASEAN in global issues seriously, the subsequent paragraphs focus on the internal dimension of ASEAN's negotiation capacities. This entails, first, that non-state resources of expertise exist, that, second, they are tapped, that, third, the more developed member countries support the negotiating capacity of less advanced ASEAN member countries and finally that conflicts of interests are reconciled among member governments. In

[40] *Jakarta Post*, 17 November 2011.

[41] *Bernama*, 17 December 2010. For a similar statement of Marty, see *Jakarta Post*, 13 January 2011.

[42] *Jakarta Post*, 5 January 2011. For similar quotes, see *Philippine Star*, 8 August 2011, which quotes Yudhoyono as saying that "We [ASEAN] have to contribute to the world's governance."

[43] *Jakarta Post*, 26 April 2011. [44] *Jakarta Globe*, 7 June 2012.

this section we argue that, even though at a rhetorical and declaratory level ASEAN seeks to strengthen its cohesion in global forums, it continues to struggle with institutional weaknesses resulting from its cooperation norms. The rhetoric-action gap permeating many areas of ASEAN cooperation (Jones and Smith 2007; Jetschke 2009; Jetschke and Rüland 2009) is thus also visible in the conduct of its external affairs.

National negotiation capacities

As in a globalized and rapidly modernizing world policy issues increase in complexity, generalist bureaucrats no longer have the expertise to appraise with sufficient competence policy alternatives in terms of effectiveness, costs and long-term benefits. This is particularly true for policy areas such as trade, finance, climate change and nuclear non-proliferation. To cope with the growing technicality of policy matters, governments must thus increasingly rely on epistemic communities that provide them with the knowledge needed to set agendas and to negotiate favorable agreements in international forums. Such epistemic communities and advisory capacities may be an integral part of the government apparatus, but normally extend to the expertise of academic institutions, economic interest groups and non-governmental organizations (NGOs).

Not surprisingly, given the deeply entrenched ideas of government paternalism and the executive dominance we had identified as one of ASEAN's cognitive dispositions in the previous section, the size, influence and ability of the non-governmental elements of epistemic communities to generate knowledge are limited, although they vary across Southeast Asian countries. Crucial factors for them to flourish are the level of economic development and the degree of academic liberty in a country as essential elements of an enabling institutional environment. More-affluent countries can afford to finance more, better-staffed and better-equipped universities and think tanks than poor countries, whereas a modicum of political pluralism and, as a consequence, academic liberty is a precondition for free-flowing policy discourses and "arguing"[45] without taboos. The strength of a national epistemic community, of course, also depends on the extent to which it is embedded in international scholarly debates and in how far its members are aware of cutting-edge research in the respective policy field.

Government ministries are a first, albeit – as stated above – often insufficient resource for the generation and management of knowledge needed for the successful conduct of international negotiations. This entails the availability of government personnel with experience in international negotiations, foreign language proficiency and access to centers of knowledge. In these respects, capacities and practices of ASEAN countries differ widely. While ASEAN founding members have been able to develop a competent diplomatic and ministerial staff, often with degrees from foreign or leading national universities, the situation is – despite improvements over time – quite different in the new mainland member countries of Myanmar, Laos and Cambodia.

[45] On the concept of "arguing," see Risse (2000).

After joining ASEAN, these countries hardly had the capacity to send well-trained, English-speaking staff to the rapidly increasing number of ASEAN meetings.

This variation is particularly evident with regard to the staffing of key missions such as in New York and Geneva, the locations of many international organizations. Sally has documented how much ASEAN member countries' trade delegations based in Geneva varied (Sally 2004). These differences persist, albeit in somewhat less marked form than previously. While Indonesia has a delegation of twenty-three diplomats based in its Geneva mission to the UN, WTO and other international organizations, Singapore and Cambodia have only seven, Laos six and Brunei Darussalam four. Yet the delegations of ASEAN's small member countries also perform other diplomatic functions such as representing their country in Switzerland, Italy and other countries.[46] The number of WTO negotiators also varies; with about ten, Indonesia again has the largest staff pool. Smaller and economically less advanced countries such as Cambodia and Myanmar have only one or two negotiators.[47] Figures for New York also show variation: somewhat surprisingly, the Philippines has the largest delegation (twenty-four), followed by Indonesia (twenty-three), whereas Laos eight and Singapore and Cambodia (seven) have the smallest delegations. Compared with Western countries, ASEAN missions tend to be markedly smaller and, in particular, to be professionally less diversified (see Table 3.1).

[46] Authors' interview, 14 December 2012.

[47] Authors' interviews, 14 December 2012.

Table 3.1 *Diplomatic and expert staff of Permanent Missions at the United Nations, New York and Geneva, 2012*

Country	Diplomatic and expert staff, UN Mission, New York	Diplomatic and expert staff, UN Mission, Geneva
Brunei Darussalam	10	4
Cambodia	7	7
Indonesia	23	23
Laos	8	6
Malaysia	12	8
Myanmar	8	11
Philippines	24	13
Singapore	8	7
Thailand	12	13
Vietnam	18	11
	For comparison	
European Union	31	32
Germany	74	37
Italy	24	14
India	30	30
USA	172	54

Source: Compiled from the Blue Book, "Permanent Missions to the United Nations No. 303," dated April 2013 (last update 21 February 2014) and "Missions permanentes auprès des Nations Unies à Genève," No. 112 (2014).

All of these missions, even the larger ones, are short of expert staff. This holds particularly true for highly technical matters such as trade, disarmament and environmental negotiations. If the need arises, ASEAN missions tend to reinforce their delegations with government experts from the respective line ministries. In negotiations under the auspices of the World Health Organization (WHO), the Thai government, for instance, would strengthen the country's mission with experts from the Health Ministry. If agriculture was negotiated in the WTO, officials from the Ministry of Agriculture would join the delegation. If trade facilitation was on the agenda, the Customs Department would second expert officials. And if other trade-related issues were at stake, the Ministry of Commerce would dispatch officers. The majority of Thai WTO negotiators have a professional background in law, economics and business administration, but in our interviews we did not find evidence that either Thailand or other ASEAN countries would also integrate corporate lawyers, academics, civil society representatives or other private consultants in their negotiation teams, unlike the USA, Germany[48] and other economically advanced countries.[49] Also, the Indonesian mission would mainly rely on government expertise available in the capital.[50] Larger countries, however, differ in the extent to which they rely on government expert staff. While in the Thai case, the majority of WTO negotiators have been seconded to Geneva from the Department of Trade Negotiation for four years, the Indonesian delegation seems to rely more on diplomats from the Ministry of Foreign Affairs.[51] With the partial exception of Singapore, interaction of the missions with think tank researchers, university scholars, business organizations and, in particular, civil society, is rare,

[48] Authors' conversation with a German diplomat, 11 December 2012.

[49] Authors' interviews, 14 December 2012; *Jakarta Post*, 6 September 2003.

[50] Authors' interviews, 14 December 2012. [51] *Ibid.*

underdeveloped and, in many cases, possibly due to persisting distrust towards non-governmental expert staff, not actively sought.[52]

The situation is quite similar in climate change negotiations. The Thai negotiating team, for instance, comprises twenty members. Economically more advanced countries such as Japan have more than seventy negotiators. Thai negotiators tend to compensate for this disadvantage by relying on friends from the G77, according to a high-ranking government source.[53] This does not rule out ASEAN cooperation, as all ASEAN countries are also G77 members, but it does reveal the limited degree of ASEAN regional identity that the source referred to the G77 instead of ASEAN.

Some foreign ministries, such as that of Indonesia, have built up a planning staff that provides policy inputs to the ministry or have formed advisory teams. In Indonesia, the Ministry of Foreign Affairs is supported by a Policy Analysis and Development Agency that writes policy papers for the minister and other relevant government agencies. One subdivision of the agency, the Centre for Policy Analysis and Development on International Organizations, has a watchful eye on global fora and advises negotiators and high-ranking ministerial officials.[54] Apart from this intra-ministerial think tank, retired senior diplomats form an advisory body offering

[52] Authors' interviews, 30 and 31 July and 14 December 2012.

[53] *Bangkok Post*, 30 June 2010.

[54] Information available at: http://web.archive.org/web/20100521220309/http://www.deplu.go.id/Pages/Orgz.aspx?IDP=11&IDP2=63&l=en (accessed 4 November 2014); authors' interviews, 10 April 2014.

expertise to the Ministry of Foreign Affairs.[55] "Indonesia," argued former ambassador to Australia Sabam Siagian, a member of the body, "has increased its leverage in international forums and we are looking to use our experience and knowledge to enhance the ministry's diplomatic capacity."[56] Earlier in the last years of the Suharto era, the Indonesia Council of World Affairs (ICWA) was founded, an independent organization serving as a platform to discuss foreign policy issues, inform the public on international affairs and provide expertise to the government. In an attempt to reach out to a broader section of foreign policy stakeholders, Foreign Minister Hassan Wirajuda organized the Foreign Policy Breakfast, a forum in which academia, media representatives, politicians, religious leaders and civil society representatives were invited to the Foreign Ministry to discuss contemporary events (Nabbs-Keller 2013).[57] Under Hassan the meeting took place on a regular basis, at least once a month,[58] but the frequency of the meetings seemed to have declined (*ibid.* 72). At the same time, Indonesia also began to set up advisory boards in other policy fields. In the field of trade policy, in 2002, President Megawati Sukarnoputri set up a forum composed of economists, businessmen and NGO representatives to study the issues of the upcoming WTO Ministerial in Cancun, Mexico.[59] Another example is a panel set up during the global financial crisis of

[55] *Jakarta Post*, 7 April 2010.

[56] However, observers such as University of Indonesia international relations scholar Hariyadi Wirawan believed that the real contribution to shaping foreign policy is limited: *ibid.*

[57] *Jakarta Post*, 15 September 2011. [58] Authors' interviews, 10 April 2014.

[59] *Jakarta Post*, 25 March 2003 and 24 September 2004.

the late 2000s advising the President and officials in advance of the G20 Summit meetings that was established to reform global financial policies.[60] A third case is the National Council on Climate Change (DNPI), which was set up in 2008 with the objective of strengthening Indonesia's position in climate change negotiations.[61] Yet creating such bodies is not a panacea for knowledge generation if there is only a limited scholarly basis as a publication of the DNPI deplores, citing the fact that Indonesia has only 138 climate-related experts in universities, research centers and public agencies.[62] In the Philippines in 1998 the Department of Agriculture organized a Task Force on Agreement on Agriculture (Re)negotiations (TF-WAR) as a multi-sectoral consultative body, including selected civil society organizations, to prepare WTO negotiations on Agriculture (Madriaga-Quinsaat 2013: 986). However, at least in Indonesia, these advisory bodies often seem to be composed mainly of experts who do not fundamentally oppose government policies. Moreover, as much as providing the government with expertise, these forums were also founded for "explaining basic foreign policy orientation to the public in general."[63] In other words, rather than "arguing" about the issues at stake and providing professional advice and expertise, they perform

[60] *Antara*: "Indonesia to Propose Global Expenditure Support Fund in G20 Summit," available at: www.ssig.gov.my/blog/2008/11/11/indonesia-to-propose-global-expenditure-support-fund-in-g20-summit/ (accessed 15 November 2014).

[61] *Jakarta Post*, 4 September 2010. [62] *Jakarta Post*, 29 September 2013.

[63] *Jakarta Post*, 15 September 2011. Megawati had formed her advisory team also with the aim of "boosting people's awareness and understanding of the benefits of market liberalization." See *Jakarta Post*, 25 March 2003.

transmission belt and legitimating functions for the government in its quest for support and public reassurance.[64]

Virtually all ASEAN governments get academic support from the Institutes of International and Strategic Studies (ISIS). ASEAN founding members began to set up these think tanks in the 1970s, providing them with expertise with particular regard to regional security and economic issues. These think tanks joined forces in 1988 to become ASEAN-ISIS, a network recognized by ASEAN as entities associated with the grouping (ASEAN Charter, Annex 2) (Kraft 2000; Stone 2000; Simon 2002; Morrison 2006). Since then ASEAN-ISIS scholars have had regular access both to their national governments and to ministerial and senior officials meetings of ASEAN, to the ASEAN Secretariat and occasionally also to the Leaders (Hernandez 2007). However, the competence and performance of these institutes vary markedly. ASEAN-5 institutes have developed remarkably well, particularly in countries such as the Philippines and Indonesia where they benefited from democratization and a more open atmosphere for academic discourse. In these countries and also in Thailand (prior to the 2014 coup), ISIS emancipated itself from government control and managed to increase their academic autonomy. Especially in Indonesia democratization provided a fertile ground for the rise of new think tanks and also for university-based scholars to participate in the foreign policy discourse. Far from the monopoly of government access that the Centre for

[64] This at least is the impression we gained from insights into the foreign ministry's "breakfast meetings." See *Jakarta Post*, 20 August 2005.

Strategic and International Studies (CSIS) enjoyed during the Suharto era,[65] advisory services became more competitive and allowed the government to draw from a wider spectrum of scholarly inputs, including think tanks such as the Habibie Center, the Indonesian Institute of Science (LIPI), SMERU Research Institute and an increasing number of universities (Guggenheim 2012: 146).[66]

This is less the case in the region's authoritarian or semi-authoritarian political systems, where they remained closely affiliated with governments. In Vietnam, Myanmar, Laos and Cambodia especially, all countries that joined ASEAN in the 1990s, ASEAN-ISIS are government appendices. Singapore has developed probably the most extensive academic infrastructure supporting the government, with the Institute of Southeast Asian Studies (ISEAS), the Rajaratnam School of International Studies (RSIS) at Nanyang Technological University (NTU) and the Singapore Institute of International Affairs (SIIA) spearheading the phalanx of influential think tanks. All of them, including university-based institutes such as the Lee Kuan Yew School of Governance and RSIS, are headed by prominent ex-diplomats, ensuring that academic output has a strong policy orientation and that researchers are in close contact with government officials. The Singaporean think tanks, as well as those in Indonesia, the Philippines, Thailand and Malaysia, are productive, highly visible in public debates through opinion pieces in the media, well embedded in global academic networks and in constant

[65] Jusuf Wanandi, *Jakarta Post*, 16 September 2011.

[66] *Jakarta Post*, 15 September 2011.

exchange with their peers in East Asia, North America and Europe. While they are thus familiar with novel trends in their respective disciplines, their links to universities with their greater orientation towards theory-guided basic research, is less well developed. In the more reclusive new member countries, they are much less integrated into global and regional epistemic communities and therefore have usually not reached the same academic standards as their counterparts in the original ASEAN-5. More than providing technocratic expertise to their governments, they often chiefly perform legitimizing functions for government policies.

While at least in some ASEAN countries knowledge generation and management capacities are improving, a comparison with countries at a similar stage of economic development reveals major shortcomings. This holds particularly true for Indonesia, which – despite the changes described above – is still reeling from the centralistic and bureaucratic legacies of the New Order period that curtailed academic freedom and suppressed critical thinking (Guggenheim 2012: 147). If the share of research on a country carried out by domestic researchers is taken as a benchmark, Indonesia and the Philippines noticeably trail other countries inside and outside the region. By contrast, Brazilian scholars publish more than four times as much on their country as those of Indonesia do (*ibid.* 144). A similar picture emerges if research intensity, that is, the number of international publications per 1 million people, is measured. Again, Indonesia, the Philippines and Vietnam are far behind other countries, although Singapore appears here on top of the ranking, whereas Malaysia and Thailand occupy rankings in the middle (*ibid.*

145). More-recent UNESCO research also reveals that, except for Singapore, ASEAN countries' government expenditure on Research and Development (R & D) is miniscule compared with other newly emerging economies (*ibid.* 162). At the same time, very much in line with the executive dominance highlighted in the previous section, government R & D expenditure relative to the country's total R & D expenditure is very high in the ASEAN region, with the sole exception of Malaysia (*ibid.* 163).

Quality media also play a vital role in defining a country's position for international negotiations. They are a forum for debate in which the pros and cons of certain policy options can be discussed. To fulfill such functions, the media need to operate under conditions of at least a modicum of political freedom that does not a priori rule out policy alternatives for ideological reasons. Vibrant quality media both vernacular as well as English language can be found in particular in Thailand (prior to 2014) and Indonesia, to a lesser extent in Singapore, Malaysia and the Philippines. In the new member countries, the media hardly perform any such forum functions. Hence, there are markedly fewer channels for feedback that would help the government to sound out and determine its negotiating positions in international organizations.

Hardly less important is a vociferous, knowledgeable and well-connected sector of NGOs. NGOs have often acquired a lot of know-how in areas where government presence is limited, such as in the social consequences of trade liberalization, or in issues like labor migration, sustainability and environmental protection, human rights, and women's and children's rights, to name some very obviously contested policy fields. Despite lingering suspicions about NGOs in Indonesia and to a lesser extent the Philippines, Thailand and Malaysia, governments have established channels for regular consultation and interaction. Such interactions can provide not only expertise that officials may not have, but also defines the win sets government negotiators may expect in international fora. During its ASEAN chairmanship in 2011, the Indonesian government, for instance, hired a consultant with an NGO background as a liaison person for civil society.[67] Ignoring civil society views could become particularly costly at the stage of policy implementation when NGOs and social movements frustrated with international agreements may organize public protests and demonstrations. WTO deals and (bilateral) free trade agreements often give rise to such campaigns. Yet even though in the countries named above state–society interactions have multiplied and improved markedly, there is still a tendency to limit their role to transmission belts in "socializing" government policies and decisions to the wider public rather than including them in the preparation of negotiation positions or even in the negotiation teams. This suggests that there is still a quite strong top-down dimension in public–private discourses.

Business groups are in many countries a prime source of information for government negotiators. Their expertise may be particularly valuable in trade negotiations and in fora concerned with international finance. When they have their own research facilities, they may provide detailed data on the putative effects of policy choices on the economy

[67] Email information ASEANcats@googlegroups.com, 5 November 2010.

as a whole or on individual economic sectors. They may help develop negotiation strategies, gauge the trade-offs inherent in package solutions, or even act as advisors of the negotiators behind the scenes.

Comparatively close links between the government and the business sector do indeed exist in the ASEAN-5. Exchanges are here much closer and more frequent than between governments and civil society representatives. The national Chambers of Commerce and Industries and other business and professional associations are usually lobbying the government and also comprise a useful source in the recruitment of economic ministers. Yet, as Sally showed in the case of WTO negotiations after the Uruguay Round in the second half of the 1990s and under the auspices of the Doha Round (since 2001), bottom-up flow of information is limited and the influence of economic interest groups on government policies is rather modest (Sally 2004). In Indonesia, for instance, they are primarily vehicles for rent-seeking activities of their board members who instrumentalize business associations for providing them access to government contracts (Hicks 2012: 6). Revealing is also the remark of former Indonesian WTO-chief negotiator in Geneva, Gusmardi Bustami: referring to the ever increasing significance of services in trade, he admitted in an interview with the *Jakarta Post* that "[t]he service sector has been somewhat neglected. We know it exists, but we do not know how big its contribution is to our economy. [. . .] Frankly speaking Indonesia has no figures on the sector."[68]

[68] See *Jakarta Post*, 24 September 2004.

Even more than in the case of civil society organizations, ASEAN governments tend to use business associations as transmission belts with the task of explaining the business sector government policies. A major reason for this practice is the still-strongly corporatist pattern of interest representation in many ASEAN countries highlighted in the previous section (Rüland 2012a). Moreover, most business associations, including the Chamber of Commerce and Industries, have only weak research capacities and are thus hardly able to convey to government negotiators more than very general concerns of their membership. Owing to their proximity to the government, business representatives are less prone to criticize or oppose government policies and decisions than civil society organizations (Yoshimatsu 2007; von Lübke 2012). More often than not business influence on trade agreements negotiated by the government is thus of an *ex post* nature. Economic interest groups only start mobilizing their members and building anti-government coalitions with trade unions and NGOs when something has gone utterly awry. A good example is the protest wave in Indonesian business circles after the ASEAN–China Free Trade Area (ACFTA) went into effect in January 2010, which raised fears of a flooding of the Indonesian market with cheap Chinese-manufactured goods.[69] By contrast, business influence on the negotiation of the modalities of the ACFTA was very limited.[70]

[69] See, inter alia, *Jakarta Globe*, 9 February 2010; 9 June 2010; *DetikNews*, 9 February 2010; 4 May 2010.

[70] On the limited participation of civil society organizations and business groups on bilateral trade negotiations, see also Chandra (2005).

Regional negotiation capacities

Successful negotiation in international fora is not only strongly dependent on national knowledge generation, but also on regional capacities of fact finding and data collection, identifying and tapping existing sources of expertise, exchange of information, developing policy alternatives and consolidating diverging national preferences into a binding common position. In an intergovernmental organization such as ASEAN, one would expect the preparatory steps in the process of developing a common negotiation position to fall into the domain of the grouping's Secretariat. Other important bodies involved in defining the agenda to be pursued and the strategies employed to achieve agreed goals in the negotiation process are the regional decision-making bodies such as the Summit, the ASEAN Council and ministerial meetings and, as "sherpas" evaluating and preparing the political dimensions of the envisaged common position, the Committee of Permanent Representatives (CPR). Finally, a diplomatic infrastructure is needed at the venue of the negotiations. ASEAN countries have therefore established ASEAN Committees in major capitals. Crucial for negotiations in the UN and the WTO are the ASEAN New York and Geneva Committees. In the subsequent paragraphs we scrutinize the extent to which this institutional infrastructure helps ASEAN to develop common negotiation positions.

The ASEAN Secretariat has never been an actor in the preparation of common negotiation positions of ASEAN. Even though the position of the Secretary General has been strengthened over time, the Secretariat has few formal powers. The Secretariat has thus basically remained a service provider for ASEAN decision-making bodies with virtually no scope for autonomous action.[71] At best, the Secretary General is able to influence the decision-making processes at the leaders' or ministerial levels informally, depending on his or her personality, acceptance and role perception and the expertise he or she has to offer on the issue at stake. He or she may also influence decision-making by briefing the leaders and ministers, framing the issues, portraying the context in which decision-makers operate, and appraising the effectiveness of previous policies.

The Secretariat installed in the mid-1970s was hardly able to perform these functions systematically and effectively. Initially, Secretariat staff was way below 100 and consisted mainly of career diplomats. However, at the time, owing to its limited authority, a posting in the Secretariat was not regarded as an advancement of a diplomat's career. The latter's generalist orientation and the low prestige a post in the Secretariat bore, contributed to the Secretariat acquiring the reputation of a unit characterized by inertia and a lack of professionalism. How weak the Secretariat actually was is well illustrated by President Suharto's decision unceremoniously to replace Indonesian ASEAN Secretary General Hartono Dharsono in February 1978 after the latter had dared to criticize his government (Anwar 1994: 113). As a keen observer and one-time Secretariat official caustically remarked: "The job [of the Secretary General of the ASEAN Secretariat, as the post was initially designated] was literally to serve as a channel

[71] Authors' interviews, 30 and 31 July 2012.

of information, in other words, running errands as a senior postman to deliver messages between capitals."[72]

By the early 1990s, ASEAN governments began to realize that a stronger Secretariat was a requisite for a more cohesive process of regional cooperation. At the Singapore Summit in 1992, ASEAN elevated the Secretary General to ministerial status and, in an attempt to upgrade competence, allowed the Secretariat to hire professional staff by open recruitment based on merit (Haas 1997: 335). Today, the Secretariat employs a staff of about 270, many of them professionals, and seventy-nine recruited in an open process from all member countries.[73] The ASEAN Charter further strengthened the position of the Secretary General, who can now speak on behalf of ASEAN, provide good offices, conciliation and mediation in intra-regional disputes and monitor compliance with decisions resulting from the dispute settlement mechanism.[74] The increased significance the Charter attaches to the Secretariat is also highlighted by the addition of two more Deputy Secretary Generals (Article 11, 6). Yet, compared to the European Commission, which has a staff of more than 23,600 (albeit that this includes a huge number of interpreters), this is still a miniscule technocratic support base, though larger than that of other non-Western regional organizations.[75] This was even admitted by the late Indonesian

[72] *The Nation*, 21 May 2012.

[73] *Ibid.* See also ASEAN Deputy Secretary General, Bagas Hapsoro, *Jakarta Post*, 23 January 2010.

[74] *Jakarta Post*, 23 January 2010; ASEAN Charter, Article 23(2) and Article 27(1).

[75] Mercosur, for instance, has a secretariat staff of 160 officials.

Foreign Minister Ali Alatas – during his time in office an ardent adherent of the ASEAN Way and its underlying sovereignty norms. Alatas, who served for Indonesia on the Eminent Persons Group in drafting a blueprint for the ASEAN Charter, stated in an interview with the *Jakarta Post*:

> Then, we should also establish a new body, called the ASEAN Institution, because we found that the secretariat lacks the capacity for thorough research and analysis and so on. They are taken up too much by day-to-day tasks.[76]

Moreover, after the Asian financial crisis of 1997/98, and amid growing clamor to transform ASEAN into a more people-oriented organization, leading Secretariat officials markedly intensified their interaction with non-governmental stakeholders. More frequently than before, high-ranking ASEAN officials attended the annual meetings of regional NGO-networks such as the (now defunct) ASEAN People's Assembly (APA), the Solidarity for Asian People's Advocacy (SAPA) and the ASEAN Civil Society Conference (ACSC)/ASEAN People's Forum (APF) (Igarashi 2011). Yet NGO critics frequently complain that these interactions are confined to the opening ceremonies and keynote addresses rather than representing a full-fledged dialogue.[77] More regular interaction is still restricted to a highly non-representative and largely irrelevant group of fifty-eight civil society organizations recognized by ASEAN (Collins 2008; Rüland 2012a; Gerard 2013). However, the expertise many of the independent regional NGO networks mentioned above have to offer for negotiations in global forums is

[76] *Jakarta Post*, 17 January 2007. [77] Authors' interviews, 26 March 2012.

largely ignored. There is also no evidence that the ASEAN University Network (AUN), established in 1995 with the objective of "promoting collaborative study, research and educational programs in the priority areas identified by ASEAN" and serving as "a policy-oriented body," has been systematically tapped by the ASEAN Secretariat and other ASEAN decision-making bodies.[78]

An intensification of interactions can also be noted with think tanks and, in particular, with ASEAN-ISIS. The expertise the Secretariat can draw from these think tanks is substantial, even though, following ASEAN enlargement, diversity and disagreements among ASEAN-ISIS likewise increased markedly.[79] But, despite a modicum of emancipation of ASEAN-ISIS in the ASEAN-5 countries from too much proximity to governments, many observers still complain that ASEAN-ISIS are in general closer to government positions than to civil society (Kraft 2000; Stone 2000; Morrison 2006; Freistein 2008). Yet apart from ASEAN-ISIS new think tanks emerged that increasingly provided backstopping services to the ASEAN Secretariat. One of them is the Economic Research Institute for ASEAN and East Asia (ERIA), established in 2008 on Japanese initiative and strongly supported by Japanese funding. However, ERIA mainly provides expertise in the domain of regional economic integration. Among the many publications of ERIA, there

[78] An article in the *Jakarta Post* discussed the opportunities such a university network, which currently consists of thirty member universities, would create: *Jakarta Post*, 17 November 2011.

[79] Authors' interviews, 19 February 2010 and 25 August 2010.

is only one that discusses ASEAN's role as a negotiator in international forums (Tay 2013). More relevant for international negotiation is a project launched in March 2010 by the National University of Singapore's Centre for International Law (CIL) that established an online searchable database of ASEAN and International Law documents. Along with over 320 ASEAN and International Law documents accessible through the database it also contains over 120 significant global treaties and legal documents.[80]

The Secretariat, leaders and economic ministers also cooperate with regional business networks such as the ASEAN Business Advisory Council (ABAC) and the ASEAN Chamber of Commerce and Industries (ASEAN-CCI). Both groups, however, share many traits of national business groups. ABAC consists of representatives handpicked by the leaders, whereas ASEAN-CCI has been bogged down by highly particularistic nationalist policies for a long time.[81] Overall, rather than being forceful representatives of regional businesses, both organizations are much more transmission belts supporting ASEAN governments in conveying their regional policies to the business sector (Yoshimatsu 2007; Rüland 2012a). The conclusion is thus that even though the Secretariat has tangibly improved its interaction with stakeholders there are still two major flaws: first, there is a tendency of the Secretariat to interact with stakeholders such as economic interest groups

80 "NUS Research Centre Pioneers the Region's First Online Searchable Database of ASEAN Documents," National University of Singapore press release, 18 March 2010.

81 Authors' interviews, 1 March 2010 and 23 March 2010.

that are believed to be sympathetic to ASEAN executive bodies; and second, owing to the limited staff and resources, there is a lack of absorptive capacity of the Secretariat regarding non-governmental inputs. Former Secretary General Surin Pitsuwan's strategy to develop a "Networked Secretariat" with the objective of tapping "into the vast pool of intellectuals and local wisdom in member countries" has so far improved absorption capacity only to a limited extent.[82] Much more than that, it also primarily serves as a transmission belt, as Surin himself explained: "The ASEAN Secretariat would cooperate with various entities (business or otherwise) with a large clientele base that already have their regular gatherings and activities in disseminating the idea of ASEAN, its vision and mission and its noble objectives so as to raise the awareness of the people of ASEAN about a new chapter in our regional organization."[83]

Finally, with the enactment of the ASEAN Charter, the funding of the ASEAN Secretariat through the annual contributions also improved from US$1 million per member to US$1,576,300 in 2012 (see Table 3.2), translating into US$0.026 per capita for operating costs. In comparison, the European Union had a budget of well over 147.2 billion euros

[82] *The Nation*, 21 May 2012.

[83] "Getting ASEAN Ready to Realise its Vision With the ASEAN Business Community," speech by Dr. Surin Pitsuwan, Secretary General of ASEAN, at the Launch of the ASEAN Business Club (ABC), 28 October 2011, available at: www.asean.org/news/item/speech-by-dr-surin-pitsuwan-secretary-general-of-asean-at-the-launch-of-the-asean-business-club-abc (accessed 20 January 2014).

Table 3.2 *Operational budget of the ASEAN Secretariat*

Budget year	Operational budget (US$)	Percentage increase from previous budget year	Percentage of utilization of the allocated budget
June 2003–May 2004	7,320,000	+ 1	104 (overspending by 4)[1]
June 2004–May 2005	7,680,000	+ 5	101 (overspending)
June 2005–May 2006	7,990,000	+ 4	103 (overspending)
June 2006–May 2007	8,490,000	+ 6	104 (overspending)
June 2007–May 2008	9,680,000	+ 14	99 (underspending)[2]
June–December 2008[3]	7,830,000		84 (underspending by 16)
January–December 2009[4]	14,350,000		75 (underspending)
January–December 2010	14,330,000	standstill budget[5]	82 (underspending)
January–December 2011	14,360,000	standstill budget	100%
January–December 2012	15,763,000	+10	

[1] Overspending was caused mostly by higher numbers of ASEAN meetings than projected. ASEAN Secretariat staff are expected to attend and serve on every ASEAN meeting everywhere.

[2] Underspending was caused mostly by unfilled staff vacancies, which has been a recurring problem in recent years.

[3] In the past, the budget or financial year of the ASEAN Secretariat ran from June to May of the following year. In 2008, there was a decision to change the duration of the budget or financial year to the calendar year, to parallel the Chairmanship of ASEAN, which runs from January to December. Hence the need to have the seven months of bridging budget from June to December 2008.

[4] A major staff build-up in response to increased workload and new functions of the Secretary General of ASEAN and the ASEAN Secretariat following the entry into force of the ASEAN Charter on 15 December 2008.

[5] ASEAN member states decided to go for a standstill budget in the wake of serious underspending.

Source: ASEAN Secretariat; updated email information, provided by a former high-ranking ASEAN official, 10 September 2012.

(or 295 euros per person) for the same year.[84] The Secretariat's budget thus certainly does not allow for the marked expansion of professional staff that would enable it to perform the functions mentioned at the beginning of this subsection much more effectively.

In recent years especially, the Secretariat has tried to compensate its resource constraints through external funding such as from the ASEAN Project for Regional Integration Support (APRIS) I and II programs supported by the EU or German assistance to upgrade the Secretariat's absorptive capacity (Jetschke and Portela 2012). Yet it is unlikely that these projects will solve the Secretariat's capacity problems, as they primarily seek to improve the Secretariat's ability to disseminate information to the public and to mobilize societal support for ASEAN policies.[85] Moreover, the external support is not without drawbacks as it confronts the Secretariat with charges that as a core institution of ASEAN it is open to external influences that may compromise the association's independence and capability of pursuing its interests in international forums.

Given the weakness of the Secretariat, summits, the ASEAN Council, Ministerial Meetings and the Committee of Permanent Representatives are thus the key bodies in coordinating and finding common ground for forthcoming negotiations in global forums. While the Secretary General presents assessments of the situation, defines points of departure for

[84] *The Nation*, 21 May 2012.

[85] See "Capacity Building for the ASEAN Secretariat," available at: https://www.giz.de/en/worldwide/16385.html (accessed 22 July 2012).

negotiations and clarifies where ASEAN stands on any given issue,[86] working out the details of an agenda pursued in global forums and determining the common preferences, positions and goals is a highly political process. Since the enactment of the ASEAN Charter the preparation of this process has been the responsibility of the Committee of Permanent Representatives (previously the Senior Officials Meetings) that jealously guards these prerogatives against the Secretariat. Decisions for common positions are then made either by the ministers responsible for the negotiation or the leaders. In an attempt to strengthen its influence in G20 Summits, in October 2009 ASEAN established a G20 Contact Group consisting of the ASEAN Chair, the ASEAN Secretary General, and Indonesia, the only G20 member from Southeast Asia. The association also agreed that prior to G20 Summits the finance ministers would meet in order to formulate the grouping's collective views, which at the Summit would be represented by the ASEAN Chair and the Secretary General.[87]

Yet it is very difficult to assess the extent to which these preparatory meetings have decisively improved intra-ASEAN policy coordination. The chairman statements of ASEAN Summits and the documents of ministerial meetings suggest that there are only intermittent consultations prior to UN, WTO or climate change negotiations, if any. If our information is correct, the G20 Contact Group has met only once.[88] Moreover, the declarations that summits and

[86] Authors' interviews, 12 March 2010.

[87] *Antara*, 24 October 2009 and *Jakarta Post*, 25 October 2009.

[88] Email communications, 9 January 2013 and 14 January 2014.

ministerial meetings have occasionally passed still leave member countries much leeway to pursue their national interests. In fact, such declarations are often little more than the lowest common denominator, devoid of (binding) obligations and precision.[89]

At major venues of international organizations such as New York and Geneva, ASEAN has set up consultative and coordinative mechanisms in the form of the ASEAN New York Committee and the ASEAN Geneva Committee. Members are ASEAN ambassadors accredited to these international organizations and the chair is the ambassador of the country holding the ASEAN presidency. While the ASEAN Geneva Committee was established in 1973 in order better to coordinate ASEAN policies in the GATT (Jorgensen-Dahl 1977: 45; Meepiarn 2009: 165), the ASEAN New York Committee was set up in the 1980s during the Cambodian occupation by Vietnam. Their coordination performance varies according to the issues at stake and the presidency. In New York, ASEAN ambassadors normally convene once a month or every six weeks like in 2012 under the Cambodian presidency.[90] Under the Indonesian presidency in 2011 it met more frequently, whereas under Vietnamese chairmanship in 2010 it reportedly met only every four to five months.[91] The intensity of activities under these chairs is similar in the ASEAN Geneva Committee,

89 This view is corroborated by authors' interviews conducted on 30 and 31 July 2012.

90 Authors' interviews, 30 July 2012. EU head of mission meetings take place once a week: see *Der Spiegel*, 26 August 2013, p. 65.

91 Authors' interviews, 30 July 2012.

which at the time of research met monthly.[92] Preparatory meetings at an expert level take place more often, as do informal and rather casual meetings to exchange information.[93]

In the ASEAN Geneva Committee, UN affairs and WTO issues are separated. The larger ASEAN countries such as Indonesia, Thailand and Malaysia have thus posted two ambassadors in Geneva, one accredited to the UN, the other to the WTO. Comparing the frequency of meetings, we may conclude that there seems to be a decline in activity in the ASEAN Geneva Committee that, as Sally reports, met on a weekly basis in the 1990s (Sally 2004: 4). It is thus hardly surprising that overall, in the UN General Assembly but also in Geneva-based UN bodies, national perspectives prevail and ASEAN rarely acts in unison, even though there is a tendency for joint statements to increase in frequency over the last three to four years in UN bodies and the WTO (see also in Chapter 5).[94]

Occasionally ASEAN seeks to improve its coordination performance at the UN through holding Informal ASEAN Ministerial Meetings at the sidelines of the UNGA. Yet a careful reading of the chairman statements and press releases shows that much of the time given over to these meetings is occupied by regional affairs. Coordination of policies in the UN is limited to general issues of ASEAN-UN relations and the coordination of campaigns for leadership positions in the UN system.

[92] Authors' interviews, 14 December 2012.

[93] Authors' interviews, 30 and 31 July 2012.

[94] Authors' interviews, 30 July 2012.

Thus, unsurprisingly, mechanisms to overcome the divide in expertise among ASEAN delegation in New York and Geneva do not exist. One minor exception was the ASEAN-organized training of the government staff of the accession countries in the 1990s, which included English language courses and familiarizing officials with ASEAN procedures in order to enable them to participate meaningfully in the association's gatherings, chair ministerial meetings and represent their country and ASEAN in global forums. While this has helped to narrow the capacity divide between old and new members, it was not enough completely to eliminate capacity asymmetries. Also supportive of the smaller countries is the practice of ASEAN to provide member countries in the UN and the WTO the opportunity to send their staff to committees of their choice. They would then report to the other members and share the know-how and information acquired there.[95] Yet small ASEAN countries, often grappling with the complexities of the policy matters, do not trust fellow members enough to leave the formulation of bargaining positions to them and to support them. Better-staffed missions on the other hand provide expertise to the smaller and less developed ASEAN members only in cases where it is obvious that they share their positions. Overall, therefore, joint positions can only be developed where common interests have been identified. By contrast, in highly political and sensitive matters ASEAN members tend to bowl alone, a tendency for which we will provide more evidence in the next chapter. In the majority of cases and, for that matter, the politically

[95] Authors' interviews, 30 and 31 July 2012.

significant ones, we must therefore expect that ASEAN will act more frequently as a caucus than a quasi-bloc.

Summing up, with reference to our theoretical proposition, we can state that ASEAN's national and regional negotiation capacities are indeed affected by cognitive factors on three major counts. First, historically entrenched state-centrism accounts for the fact that the generation of expertise for international negotiations relies mainly on governmental resources and the state bureaucracy, while largely bypassing societal know-how. Second, the strong quest for national autonomy and mutual distrust explain why there is very little generation and provision of knowledge at the regional level and why the Secretariat is neither financed nor staffed adequately to act as an effective catalyst of knowledge for negotiating ASEAN member governments. And, third and finally, for much the same reason, negotiations in global forums are not prepared with the primary objective of increasing the association's cohesion by working out common standpoints and positions.

Chapter 4

ASEAN as a negotiator in global fora: stages of negotiation

In Chapter 3 we explored the *internal* dimension of ASEAN's collective action capacities in global fora. Our analysis revealed that, as predicted in the theoretical section, member countries' historical experiences have given rise to institutional arrangements that are not very conducive for building common knowledge-based negotiation positions in international fora. In this chapter we change the perspective and examine the *external* dimension. That is, ASEAN's practices as a negotiator in global fora. In this regard, we investigate how cohesively ASEAN operates in international organizations such as the UN and the WTO. Commensurate with the theoretical concept outlined in Chapter 2, we try to establish the type of cohesion that characterizes ASEAN activities in global fora and ask how ASEAN or individual ASEAN member countries act at different stages of negotiation processes. To what extent are they initiators and agenda-setters, to what extent does ASEAN or its member countries act as norm entrepreneurs, how do they act in voting and how do they comply with decisions?

With the findings of Chapter 3 as a starting point, we expect ASEAN mainly to be operating as a caucus in international forums. Member countries share an essentially skeptical outlook on the external world, distrust still lingers among them despite nearly five decades of cooperation, some regional identity has developed but is still clearly secondary to national identity, power sensitivity still strongly guides the behavior of member states and epistemic capacities are mediocre and distributed inequitably among the membership. As a result, we anticipate that ASEAN member states will frequently defect from collective action: in fact, whenever it suits their national interest.

4.1 Phase 1 identifying problems, defining issues and agenda-setting

While ASEAN as a regional organization has been a frequent agenda-setter in the Asia-Pacific region, this is less obvious for its global activities. In global fora its record as initiator, innovator and agenda-setter has been rather ambiguous. Certainly, there have been cases in the past in which ASEAN, acting as a quasi-bloc, did play a crucial role as an agenda-setter, with substantial influence on UN policies. The high point in this regard was the conflict in Cambodia. After the Vietnamese invasion of Cambodia in December 1978, ASEAN sponsored the annual UN resolutions condemning the Vietnamese aggression and mobilized support for them, while later, in the second half of the 1980s, it became a key actor in the search for peaceful conflict resolution (Narine 2002; Haacke 2003).

However, in other major international issues such as UN reform, climate change or disarmament, ASEAN has played a less visible collective role as problem identifier, initiator, innovator or agenda-setter.[1] Member countries have

[1] For ASEAN's weak agenda-setting performance in the climate change negotiations, see an opinion piece by Zelda D. T. Soriano, Gia Ibay and

discussed these issues at the regional level in summits and ministerial meetings, but the respective Chairman Statements hardly transcended the lowest common denominator and did not pave the way for noteworthy ASEAN initiatives in global fora. Barely concealing his impatience with ASEAN's slowly evolving role as an agenda-setter in the global arena, Indonesian Foreign Minister Marty M. Natalegawa admonished fellow members that "we must actually be shaping and molding developments. [. . .] We must have an extra-ASEAN, an extra-Southeast Asian vision."[2]

UN reform is an especially good example, as the issue has been on ASEAN's agenda since the mid-1970s. ASEAN member countries basically agree that in the light of the existing power asymmetries the United Nations needs urgent institutional reforms. They have come out with such statements time and again since the 1990s. ASEAN addressed the issue of UN reform at its tenth Summit in Vientiane (2004), at the twelfth Summit in Cebu (2007) and at the nineteenth Summit held in Bali in November 2011.[3]

That ideas of member countries on the specifics of UN reform diverge, preventing ASEAN from acting collectively as a bloc or quasi-bloc, is indicated by the very general terms in which the issue was treated. The most substantive of the three statements was the Bali document of 2011, identifying five key issues of reform: categories of membership,

Riza Bernabe, three prominent Southeast Asian NGO activists, *Jakarta Post*, 29 October 2010.

[2] *Bangkok Post*, 15 July 2013.

[3] Chairman Statement, 19th ASEAN Summit, 17 November 2011, para. 163.

the veto held by the five permanent members of the Security Council, regional representation, the size of an enlarged Security Council and its working methods, and the Security Council-General Assembly relationship.[4] Yet the document was devoid of concrete proposals of how these issues should be tackled. The other two statements were even vaguer and hardly went beyond affirming ASEAN's general commitment to a comprehensive UN reform, the need for a stronger role of ASEAN and the enhancement of the voice and role of developing countries within the UN system. The more frequent foreign ministers' endorsements of UN reform also did not go beyond these general statements.[5]

If we leave the regional level, and take a closer look at individual ASEAN member countries' statements on UN reform in the UN General Assembly, we may find occasional cases of agenda-setting, but of a kind that rarely rises above declaratory politics. When, in the mid-1990s, with the formation of an "Open-ended Working Group on the Question of Equitable Representation on and Increase in the Membership of the Security Council and Other Matters Related to the Security Council" the UN-reform debate gained momentum, Malaysia was one of the front-runners in favor of an enlargement of the number of permanent members of the Security Council and the abolition of the current five permanent

[4] *Ibid.*

[5] Foreign ministers commented on UN reform at the 33rd AMM in Bangkok (2000), the 35th AMM in Bandar Seri Begawan (2002), the 37th AMM in Jakarta (2004), the 38th AMM in Vientiane (2005), the 39th AMM in Kuala Lumpur (2006), the 40th AMM in Manila (2007) and the 44th AMM in Bali (2011).

members' veto power. Malaysian Prime Minister Mahathir Mohamad in particular incessantly demanded that the Security Council should be made more representative, transparent and democratic and also that the General Assembly, as the highest deliberative body in the world, should be accorded a greater role.[6] For Mahathir, democratizing the UN was thus equivalent to a shift of power from the Security Council to the General Assembly.[7] The General Assembly, added his Foreign Minister Syed Hamid Albar, must become the UN's main decision-maker.[8] More recently, Indonesian officials have repeatedly and vocally aired similar views.

While ASEAN members by and large share this broad position,[9] current reform debates brought to the fore the differences among ASEAN countries, preventing the grouping from spearheading common moves towards UN reform. While Indonesia articulated demands for becoming a permanent Security Council member,[10] thereby reclaiming for herself emerging power status, Singapore as the founder of the Forum of Small States (FOSS) and a member of the now-defunct Small Five Group (S5) in the UN (with Costa Rica, Jordan, Liechtenstein and Switzerland as the other members), became an ardent advocate of small countries' interests (see also section 5.3 on coalition-building). Although Singapore agreed with other ASEAN members that the Security Council

[6] *New Straits Times*, 29 September 1996.

[7] *New Straits Times*, 19 September 1996.

[8] *New Straits Times*, 6 January 1996. [9] *The Nation*, 20 June 2005.

[10] Indonesian UN permanent representative Marty M. Natalegawa, *Jakarta Post*, 26 November 2008. In this press interview, Marty, without naming Singapore, took a clear position against the island state's ideas on UN reform.

must be enlarged, it maintained that the enlargement should provide a stronger voice not to the great and middle powers, but to small states. More than most other ASEAN states, and ASEAN as a whole, Singapore also propagated reforms that would increase the UN's and, in particular, the Security Council's effectiveness.[11] UN reform must therefore target the Security Council's working methods and the flow of communication between the Security Council and the General Assembly.[12]

But not only do ASEAN member countries obviously have different priorities, unlike the African Group in the UN and the Organization of Islamic Cooperation (OIC),[13] they also

[11] Statement by Ambassador Vanu Gopala Menon, Permanent Representative of Singapore to the United Nations, at the Plenary Debate on the Report of the Security Council and the Question of Equitable Representation on and Increase in the Membership of the Security Council, 19 November 2008, available at: www.mfa.gov.sg/content/mfa/overseasmission/newyork/archive/plenary/2008/200811/press_200811_01.html (accessed 18 December 2012).

[12] Statement by Ambassador Vanu Gopala Menon, Permanent Representative of Singapore to the United Nations, at the Plenary Debate on the Report of the Security Council and the Question of Equitable Representation on and Increase in the Membership of the Security Council, 13 November 2009, available at: www.mfa.gov.sg/content/mfa/overseasmission/newyork/archive/plenary/2009/200911/press_200911_02.html (accessed 18 December 2012).

[13] Statement by Ambassador Vanu Gopala Menon at the General Assembly Second Meeting of the Open-ended Working Group on the Question of Equitable Representation on and Increase in the Membership of the Security Council and other Matters Related to the Security Council, 10 April 2008, available at: www.mfa.gov.sg/content/mfa/overseasmission/newyork/archive/plenary/2008/200804/press_200804.html (accessed 18 December 2012).

joined different groupings in the reform debate. Submitting a draft resolution on improving the Council's Working Methods in April 2011, Singapore[14] spoke for S5,[15] while Indonesia and Malaysia supported proposals of the OIC and Vietnam supported the Non-Alignment Movement's (NAM) suggestions.[16]

Yet this does not mean that ASEAN members failed to show initiative in the UN. Most of their advances, however, were in the area of "low politics," such as a Singaporean proposal for worldwide measures to improve sanitation,[17] a Philippine initiative for inter-religious dialogue[18] and the

[14] Statement by Ambassador Albert Chua, Permanent Representative of Singapore to the United Nations, at the Informal Plenary Meeting on the Intergovernmental Negotiations on the Question of Equitable Representation on and Increase in the Membership of the Security Council and other Matters Related to the Council, 2 May 2012, available at: www.mfa.gov.sg/content/mfa/overseasmission/newyork/nyemb_statements/plenary/2012/201205/press_20120502.html (accessed 3 February 2014).

[15] The S5 was dissolved in 2012 and replaced by the Accountability, Coherence and Transparence (ACT) grouping. Singapore, however, did not join the ACT, which at the time of writing had twenty members. Available at: www.eda.admin.ch/eda/en/home/topics/intorg/un/missny/wormet.html (accessed 9 February 2014) and www.whatsinblue.org/2013/12/extraordinary-election-to-the-security-council.php (accessed 3 February 2014).

[16] Statement by HE Ambassador Hoang Chi Trung, Deputy Permanent Representative on Agenda Item 9: Report of the Security Council of the United Nations and Item 111: Question of Equitable Representation on and Increase in the Membership of the Security Council, 18 November 2008, available at: www.vietnam-un.org/en/vnun.php?id=105&cid=25 (accessed 18 December 2012).

[17] See United Nations General Assembly, A/RES/67/291.

[18] See United Nations General Assembly, A/RES/65/138, A/RES/66/226 and A/RES/67/104.

speech of Indonesian President Yudhoyono in which he proposed a resolution to ban blasphemy and to promote dialogue between different faiths, civilizations and cultures,[19] an intervention triggered by the release of a US-made internet film ridiculing the Prophet Mohammed that created outrage and caused riots across the Islamic world.[20]

Although as a collective entity ASEAN did not excel as an agenda-setter in crucial global issues in the UN, this should not obscure the fact that its member countries have been active players in the General Assembly. Table 4.1 records the frequency of speeches made by members of ASEAN delegations in New York in the plenary of the 65th to the 67th UN General Assemblies. The figures show that joint statements are quite rare, but obscure the fact that they are markedly higher if we also take into account joint statements issued in the UNGA's six committees and other UN bodies in New York and Geneva. According to a Geneva-based diplomat, under Indonesia's activist Chairmanship in 2011, more than forty-one joint statements were tabled in UN bodies.[21]

A similar picture emerges if we take a closer look at the number of resolutions sponsored or co-sponsored by ASEAN members in the UNGA. While ASEAN members have been active in sponsoring resolutions especially in the 66th and 67th UNGA, only one to four have been sponsored jointly by the

[19] Speech by HE Dr. Susilo Bambang Yudhoyono, President of the Republic of Indonesia at the General Debate of the 67th Session of the United Nations General Assembly, New York, 25 September 2012.

[20] *Jakarta Post*, 26 September 2012.

[21] Authors' interviews, 14 December 2012.

Table 4.1 *Statements of ASEAN Delegations in the United Nations General Assembly, 65th, 66th and 67th UNGA*

UNGA country	*65th UNGA*	*66th UNGA*	*67th UNGA*	*Total statements by ASEAN countries*
ASEAN Joint Statements	3[1]	1[2]	4[3]	8
Brunei Darussalam	–	–	0 + 1	1
Cambodia	–	–	0 + 3	3
Indonesia	7	12 + 1	9	29
Laos	1	2	2	4
Malaysia	2	8	8	18
Myanmar	2	2	1	5
Philippines	7	4	3	14
Singapore	3	5	10	18
Thailand	–	3	4	7
Vietnam	4 – 3	7	4	18
Total individual country statements	**29**	**44**	**45**	**117**

Source: Compiled from meeting records A/65/PV.1–A/65/PV.118; A/66/PV.1–A/66/PV.131; A/67/PV.1–A/67/PV.99.

[1] Introduced by Vietnam.

[2] Introduced by Indonesia.

[3] One Joint Resolution introduced by Brunei Darussalam, three by Cambodia.

grouping (see also Table 4.2).[22] Mercosur members have sponsored nearly the same number of resolutions in the three years under scrutiny, eighty-two compared with the eighty-four of

[22] *Ibid.*

Table 4.2 *Resolutions sponsored or co-sponsored by ASEAN countries*

Country	*65th UNGA*	*66th UNGA*	*67th UNGA*	*Total*
ASEAN Joint Resolutions	–	1	–	1
Brunei Darussalam	–	4	3	7
Cambodia	2	–	2	4
Indonesia	4	8	5	17
Laos	–	–	1	1
Malaysia	–	4	4	8
Myanmar	–	1	2	3
Philippines	1	7	6	14
Singapore	–	3	2	5
Thailand	4	9	4	17
Vietnam	–	6	2	8
Total individual country statements	11	42	31	84

Source: Compiled from meeting records A/65/PV.1–A/65/PV.118; A/66/PV.1–A/66/PV.131; A/67/PV.1–A/67/PV.99.

ASEAN, while with 136 SAARC has sponsored markedly more resolutions in the same time period.[23]

Moreover, some members have frequently participated in UNGA plenary debates, such as Indonesia, followed by Malaysia, Singapore and Vietnam. An analysis of ASEAN missions' websites further suggests that others, such as Malaysia, have also been remarkably active in the UNGA's six committees. Yet, given the low number of joint statements in the UNGA plenary, and corroborated by a content analysis

[23] For the research on the speeches and resolutions sponsored in the UNGA, we are indebted to Lukas Maximilian Müller.

of ASEAN members' contributions to the UNGA plenary (see also section 5.2 on framing), it must be concluded that the overwhelming majority of interventions are made in a national capacity.

In absolute terms, ASEAN's performance is better than that of Mercosur, the members of which made twenty-eight interventions in the 65th and 66th UNGA respectively, and thirty-five in the 67th UNGA (see Table 4.1). Mercosur also made only three joint statements in the UNGA plenary during these three years, although the organization has only half the membership of ASEAN, a structural property that the theoretical literature claims would make it easier to speak with one voice. ASEAN's performance is also better than that of SAARC, which made no joint statement and whose members made between twenty-five and twenty-nine interventions per annum over the respective time frame.

In the WTO, ASEAN or individual ASEAN countries have also occasionally acted as agenda-setters. One example is Singapore's membership in the "Friends of the New Round," an informal group working towards a new trade liberalization round in the late 1990s. Together with Australia, New Zealand and Hong Kong, Singapore managed to propose and pass a Declaration at the end of the Geneva Ministerial Conference in 1998 that called for an early new trade liberalization round (Liang 2005: 128). Yet this initiative was not supported by other ASEAN countries, most notably Malaysia and Indonesia, which demanded that before any new round is inaugurated the Uruguay Round agreements must be fully implemented (Kwa 2003).

The Malaysian, Indonesian and concerted ASEAN moves during the post-Uruguay Round ministerials seeking to thwart plans of economically advanced Western nations to include "extraneous issues" in the WTO agenda are another example.[24] Such contentious issues included links between labor and environmental standards on the one hand, and trade on the other. In the end, ASEAN and other developing countries succeeded in transferring labor rights to what they regarded as the appropriate forum, that is, the ILO.[25] An additional case is ASEAN member countries' vocal support of developing countries' opposition to OECD plans for a Multilateral Agreement on Investment (MAI) and other so-called Singapore themes,[26] such as government procurement. While Indonesia, Malaysia, the Philippines and Thailand played a salient role in orchestrating the opposition against the inclusion of new WTO rules on government procurement, ASEAN failed to take a united stance as Singapore, together with the USA, the EU and various economically advanced countries, had joined a plurilateral agreement on government procurement that took effect in January 1996.[27] These latter countries argued that there is no level playing field in government procurement owing to bribery and corruption in developing countries, while the former

[24] *Straits Times*, 21 June 1996. [25] *Straits Times*, 26 June 1996.

[26] Four issues proposed by developed countries (i.e., trade facilitation, competition policy, procurement and investment) have become known as Singapore themes owing to the fact that they have been first proposed at the WTO's ministerial meeting in Singapore in December 1996. See also *Philippine Star*, 14 September 2003.

[27] *Straits Times*, 11 December 1996.

feared that new procurement rules would infringe on their sovereignty.[28] In yet another example of agenda-setting, Singapore has been credited with playing an advanced role in liberalizing financial services;[29] again, however, without support from other ASEAN countries. And at the height of the Asian financial crisis Malaysia emerged as a vocal advocate for a thorough reform of the international financial system,[30] foreshadowing similar calls on the part of developed countries such as Germany after the outbreak of the global financial crisis in 2008.

More-recent examples of agenda-setting include Indonesian President Yudhoyono's proposal at the Washington G20 meeting in 2008 to set up a Global Expenditure Support Fund with the objective of securing budgetary stability for developing countries in order to ensure their continued growth. Indonesia also played a central role in the G20's decision at the 2009 London Summit to shift funds from the IMF and World Bank to regional development banks, particularly the Asian Development Bank (Dobson 2011: 15).

Summarizing these admittedly eclectic examples, we find much evidence that ASEAN does not tend to act as a bloc or quasi-bloc in the process of agenda-setting in global forums. In those cases where it did, the majority of the more prominent examples date back to the 1980s and 1990s. Moreover, individual countries have advanced themes in global fora much more frequently than ASEAN as a group, though often not in consonance with fellow members.

[28] *Straits Times*, 27 April 1996. [29] *Straits Times*, 1 November 1997.
[30] *Straits Times*, 2 December 1997.

Collectively, ASEAN is thus to a considerable degree a more reactive player than an agenda-setter. Moreover, based on our still limited empirical evidence and pending further research, we conclude that in the 1980s and 1990s ASEAN was more successful in influencing decisions in global fora when it had assumed agenda-setting functions than in the more recent past. One possible explanation for this puzzling insight is that prior to the Asian financial crisis ASEAN was widely regarded as an ascendant organization. After the Asian financial crisis and with the grouping's dismal policy implementation record becoming more widely known (Jones and Smith 2007), its prestige suffered, and with it its authority as an international negotiator. At least for the first stage of negotiation processes, we therefore conclude that virtually all criteria for a caucus apply and that, hence, ASEAN's cohesion resembles more a caucus than a bloc or quasi-bloc.

4.2 Phase 2 setting principles, norms, rules and procedures of negotiation and international cooperation

Norm entrepreneurship

This section explores the extent to which ASEAN operates as a norm entrepreneur in global forums. Norm entrepreneurs are agents actively promoting norms that they believe guide appropriate behavior. Several questions emerge regarding ASEAN's norm entrepreneurship: does the grouping seek to impose its own normative order on the international fora in which it participates? Or is its norm entrepreneurship of a defensive nature, seeking to protect the region against competing external norm entrepreneurs by actively rejecting or reconstructing the norms they propagate (Acharya 2004; Acharya 2009)? Or are ASEAN and ASEAN member countries mere norm takers, willingly appropriating norms others promote? And, finally, is ASEAN a normative status quo actor or a reformist or even revisionist norm entrepreneur in global fora?

Contrary to fora in the Asia-Pacific region, ASEAN's ability to set principles, norms and rules of negotiation and cooperation is limited in global organizations. In the Asia-Pacific, ASEAN has been remarkably successful in exporting its cooperation norms. The ASEAN Way has become the underpinning normative platform for talks in the ASEAN Regional Forum (ARF), the Asia-Pacific Economic Cooperation (APEC), the East Asian Summit (EAS) and the Shanghai Cooperation Organization (SCO) (Stubbs 2008; Nair 2010). Even more remarkable is that ASEAN was also able to leave a strong imprint on the cooperation culture in interregional dialogues, such as the Asia–Europe Meeting (ASEM), where it faces counterparts like the EU with a strong normative agenda of their own (Rüland 2010). Yet the Asia–Europe Cooperation Framework (AECF) largely reflects the ASEAN Way (University of Helsinki 2006) and, despite subsequent European normative (counter-)offensives, still determines the mode of interaction between Asians and Europeans.

While ASEAN has been remarkably successful in exporting key norms of its cooperation culture, including the bracketing of contentious issues, consensus orientation, creating a comfortable atmosphere in meetings, the search for harmony, institutional minimalism and a preference for "soft law" to its "Near Abroad," it has been less successful in doing so in major global fora. Even where ASEAN member countries chair meetings, negotiations may take the form of the highly contentious bargaining processes the ASEAN Way expressly seeks to avoid.

Beyond the procedural aspects, ASEAN's normative positioning in international negotiations is largely conservative and status quo-oriented. In consonance with the association's repository of cooperation norms, sovereignty and state-centeredness strongly determine ASEAN's agency in global fora. Member statements in the UNGA thus almost habitually include strong references to the Westphalian sovereignty norms laid down in the UN Charter.

A telling example of ASEAN's conservative normative stance is the democratization of international negotiations. While on a global scale scholars, legislators and civil society representatives deplore the growing distance between arcane circles of decision-makers in global fora and the people affected by their decisions, and hence call for the broadening of international negotiations by including people's representatives, ASEAN as a collective entity is not known to have come up with statements supporting the empowerment of non-state actors. To what extent ASEAN should involve civil society representatives in regional governance is highly controversial even at the regional level. ASEAN has so far hardly been able credibly to implement the ASEAN Charter's call for a people-oriented regional organization. The guidelines for the registration of civil society organizations as entities associated with ASEAN, which the Committee of

Permanent Representatives revised in December 2012, retain the essentially state corporatist pattern of relationships with civil society that ASEAN has transferred from domestic politics to the regional level.[31] Interfaces between ASEAN leaders and civil society representatives have taken place, but in most cases lacked communicative substance and repeatedly ended in acrimony. At the time of writing it is too soon adequately to assess whether the more recently installed meetings between the Committee of Permanent Representatives (CPR) and civil society representatives will markedly improve communicative channels between officialdom and people's representatives.[32] Thus far, however, it has not decisively changed the verdict of many observers that the normative divide beneath the ASEAN Charter's declaratory surface is particularly evident in this domain (Rüland 2012a).

Commensurate with their Westphalian normative outlook, ASEAN governments can therefore, as argued above, easily agree on the democratization of the currently prevailing executive multilateralism. "The sovereignty of states must be preserved if there is to be a democratic spirit in international relations," argued Indonesian Foreign Minister Hassan Wirajuda in his address to the 63rd UN General Assembly.[33] Such a sovereignty-based concept of democratization entails demands for greater equality of the members of international organizations through reforming membership

[31] See www.asean.org/asean/entities-associated-with-asean (accessed 15 April 2013).

[32] Email information provided by Yuyun Wahyuningrum, 1 November 2013.

[33] The transcript of the speech has been reprinted in the *Jakarta Post*, 28 September 2008.

rules, abolishing the procedural privileges of Great Powers and rich countries and creating greater transparency of decision-making through opening mini-lateral informal fora such as the Green Room meetings in the WTO. In line with these objectives Indonesian government representatives often vocally question the Security Council's legitimacy. They highlight the need to make it more representative, responsive, accountable, effective and credible[34] and criticize its "biased composition."[35] They aired similar calls for the democratization of other international institutions such as the G8 and the International Monetary Fund (IMF).[36] In their eyes, the latter are elitist, exclusivist and protectionist,[37] lacking any commitment "to fight towards a better and fairer world order and the betterment of the less economically advanced countries."[38] This asymmetric power structure in international organizations is, in the view of Indonesian

[34] *Jakarta Post*, 17 October 2006 and 27 November 2006.

[35] See Annual Press Statement of the Foreign Minister of the Republic of Indonesia, Dr. R. M. Marty M. Natalegawa, 7 January 2011, available at: http://indonesia.gr/speech-of-the-minister-of-foreign-affairsannual-press-statement-of-the-foreign-minister-of-the-republic-of-indonesia-dr-r-m-marty-m-natalegawa/ (accessed 17 January 2011); *Jakarta Post*, 5 April 2005. See also an opinion piece contributed to the *Jakarta Post* by S. Hary Suwahyo and Evan Oktavianus, both officials at the Indonesian Ministry of Finance: *Jakarta Post*, 18 November 2010.

[36] See, for instance, the statement of Indonesia's Foreign Minister N. Hassan Wirajuda at the 63rd session of the UN General Assembly in New York, 27 September 2008, reprinted in the *Jakarta Post*, 28 September 2008.

[37] *Kompas*, 15 August 2009, p. 10; *Detik* and *Suara Pembaruan*, 15 November 2011.

[38] *Detik*, 15 November 2011.

and other Southeast Asian foreign policy stakeholders, the main reason for the unfair global distribution of resources and wealth. If G8 countries air concern over these issues, Indonesians dismiss it as hypocrisy.[39]

Interestingly, however, while spearheading ASEAN governments in advocating a more people-oriented ASEAN, Indonesian calls for the democratization of the UN included neither proposals for the parliamentarization of the world organization nor ideas for the creation of a civil society chamber.[40] Indonesian activities in this respect did not go beyond endorsing a resolution promoting closer cooperation between the UNGA and the Inter-Parliamentary Union (IPU) and vague suggestions to intensify cooperation between the UNGA on the one hand, and regional and national parliaments and civil society on the other.[41] In other words, even Indonesia effectively promotes a type of democratization which, in the end, would strengthen government over governance.[42] While more recently Foreign Minister Marty M. Natalegawa, in a contribution to the *Jakarta Post*, spoke of the "democratization of governance" of global institutions,[43] it remained unclear whether he used the more participatory term "governance" deliberately. Overall, ASEAN member countries are not known for being ardent advocates of a more inclusive, stakeholder-oriented negotiation and decision-making process in global fora, as a carefully worded

[39] *Ibid.* [40] For such proposals, see, inter alia, Czempiel (1994).

[41] See United Nations General Assembly, A/RES/66/261.

[42] On the distinction between "government" and "governance," see the classical treatment of Rosenau (1992).

[43] *Jakarta Post*, 26 January 2010.

comment of former Singaporean diplomat Barry Desker on NGO participation in the WTO suggests (Desker 2009: 17).[44] This distinguishes ASEAN from other Southern regional organizations such as Mercosur, the Andean Community and the African Union, the parliamentary bodies of which have all passed resolutions calling for the establishment of a United Nations Parliamentary Assembly (UNPA).[45]

At a more general level, ASEAN member countries share an avowed aversion to norms with behind-the-border effects that – except in the case of Singapore – also translates into protectionist positions of varying degrees in the field of global and regional trade. Even though ASEAN adheres to the increasing legalization trend in international relations as embodied in the WTO's dispute settlement mechanism or rulings of the International Court of Justice on territorial disputes, the association is not a driver of the accelerating legalization, contractualization and constitutionalization of international fora that, in particular, liberal institutionalists diagnose (Zangl and Zürn 2004). With the adoption of the ASEAN Charter it purports to have become more amenable to "hard law," with which it complies in global economic

[44] This view is confirmed by authors' interviews with ASEAN diplomats based in New York and Geneva, 30–31 July 2012.

[45] Campaign for a United Nations Parliamentary Assembly, "Lawmakers of Regional Community Mercosur Support Creation of a UN Parliamentary Assembly," available at: http://web.archive.org/web/20120114144126/http://en.unpacampaign.org/news/594.php (accessed 13 November 2012). The European Parliament has supported the creation of a UNPA since 1994. See "European Parliament Calls on EU Council to Promote Parliamentary Participation in the UN," http://en.unpacampaign.org/news/490.php (accessed 23 January 2013).

organizations such as the WTO and the IMF, but still struggles to accept at the regional level and in other issue areas such as that of climate change.[46]

By the same token, ASEAN member countries also have reservations about other progressive international norms. A case in point is the United Nation's Responsibility to Protect (R2P) norm (Acharya 2012: 11). Although ASEAN governments reluctantly consented to the norm at the 2005 UN World Summit (Tan 2012: 162), compliance with it is inconsistent, contradictory and ambiguous. Vietnam, for instance, while initially displaying serious reservations, gradually endorsed elements of R2P, at least as long as they did not jeopardize national sovereignty. Such elements are pillars one and two named in the UN Report "Implementing the Responsibility to Protect" that focused on "The protection responsibilities of the state" and "International assistance and capacity building" (UNGA 2009). Khong attributed this attitudinal change to an attempt to build an image of a responsible member of the international community (Khong 2014: 141). Yet Vietnam's reluctance fully to embrace R2P was also a result of the limited knowledge its diplomats had about domestic conditions of African and Middle Eastern countries that were frequently targeted by R2P measures (*ibid.* 170).

In a 2011 draft resolution supported by the S5 group, Singapore harshly criticized the overstepping of UN mandates such as in the case of Libya, which it believed had greatly damaged R2P, a fact to which it attributed the current

[46] *Jakarta Globe*, 13 April 2010.

impasse over Syria. R2P is thus not the order of the day, but "Responsibility while Protecting," a Brazilian initiative to enhance the legitimacy of humanitarian interventions. Quite boldly, and hence uncompromisingly rejected by the P5, the S5 resolution also proposed that the Security Council's permanent members refrain from using their veto right in R2P votes.[47]

With ASEAN's intervention in Myanmar in the aftermath of Cyclone Nargis some observers predicted a shift in ASEAN's lackluster attitude towards R2P (Bellamy and Beeson 2010). Following the tsunami disaster in Aceh, Indonesia also began to exhibit a more open attitude towards the human security concept underlying R2P, although Indonesian authorities had initially demanded that foreign relief organizations leave the country early. In other cases, however, such as in the 1999 East Timor crisis and in the Papua conflict, the country has categorically defied what it regards as foreign interference.[48]

Indonesia's attitude towards the R2P norm and human security is thus particularly puzzling. While at an intra-regional level it has advocated for a dilution of the non-interference norm in the negotiations on the ASEAN Charter, at the global level, and when the country itself is the target of critique for norm violations, it strongly rejects any internationalization of internal conflicts. Thailand, which

[47] Statement by Ambassador Albert Chua, Permanent Representative of Singapore to the United Nations, at the Informal Interactive Dialogue on the Responsibility to Protect (R2P), 5 September 2012.

[48] *The Nation*, 28 May 2012.

at certain times has similarly called for a relaxation of ASEAN's non-interference norm,[49] has also thus far adamantly rejected third-party mediation in the Muslim insurgency in the country's south. While in the aftermath of the Libya conflict the UN General Assembly recognized the National Transitional Council as the new government, ASEAN was divided on the vote: Brunei, Malaysia, the Philippines, Singapore, Thailand and Vietnam voted in favor, Indonesia abstained and Cambodia, Laos and Myanmar were absent and did not participate in the vote (Desker and Ng 2011).[50] Finally, further highlighting the hesitant and ambiguous approach of ASEAN member countries towards sovereignty-transcending norms in global fora is the non-ratification of the Rome Statute of the International Criminal Court. So far only Cambodia and the Philippines have ratified the Statute, making Asia the world region with the lowest number of ratifications.[51]

The still strongly sovereignty-based attitude of ASEAN member countries in global fora was aptly expressed in a *Jakarta Post* interview with former Indonesian Permanent Representative to the UN, Ambassador Hassan Kleib. When asked what Indonesia's priorities in the UN Security Council were after being elected as a non-permanent member for the 2007–2008 period, he answered

[49] See, for instance, the then Thai Foreign Minister Surin Pitsuwan's overtures at the ASEAN Ministerial Meeting in Manila in November 1998 to replace "non-interference" by "flexible engagement." Rüland (2000: 441).

[50] See also www.un.org/News/Press/docs/2011/ga11137.doc.htm (accessed 2 March 2014).

[51] *Jakarta Post*, 15 November 2011.

> securing our national interest. This means that any adoption of a resolution in the Council shall not in any way undermine our interests, including the very basic principle of maintaining our sovereignty and territorial integrity.[52]

Within limits, therefore, ASEAN may well be considered to be an international organization seeking to create greater procedural and, eventually, material justice in international negotiations by trying to change principles, norms and rules guiding the composition of and the interaction within global forums. Ironically, though, member states have a tendency to weaken their normative impact on global forums by relinquishing regionally accepted norms and institutional channels and seeking mediation by referring regional disputes to global institutions that operate on the basis of a different set of norms and rules to ASEAN. Cases in point are the conflicts related to maritime zones between Malaysia and Singapore over Pedra Blanca island, between Malaysia and Indonesia over the islands of Sipadan and Ligitan in the Celebes Sea and, more recently, the Thai–Cambodian conflict over territory surrounding Preah Vihear temple. Claimants did not use the regional institutional framework, such as the ASEAN High Council, but preferred to refer the disputes to the International Court of Justice in The Hague or – as in the case of Cambodia – ask the UN to intervene to establish a buffer zone in the disputed area.[53] During the Asian financial crisis, seriously affected countries such as Thailand and Indonesia also opted for solutions outside the region by

[52] *Jakarta Post*, 27 November 2006.

[53] *Jakarta Post*, 11 February 2011; 16 February 2011; 19 June 2011.

seeking IMF rescue packages that they negotiated individually (Rüland 2000). While one may argue that such behavior strengthens global norms and rules, one must also note that it displays a low level of trust in the association's own institutions and its set of underlying norms and rules. It thus also limits the chance to be emulated by others and actively to promote regional norms in global fora. Far from acting as a cohesive bloc or quasi bloc-type norm entrepreneur, ASEAN's normative cohesion in global fora has – unlike in the Asia-Pacific region – thus far not transcended the comparatively low cohesion of a caucus. Its behavior in global forums therefore reflects the normative divisions among member states that have become apparent in the contradictory set of norms that eventually found their way into the ASEAN Charter.

Negotiation style and procedural aspects of negotiation

In terms of negotiation style, ASEAN has – unlike India (Narlikar 2006) – rarely been an obstructive negotiator. In the literature on international negotiation obstructive behavior is usually described using the concept of "distributive bargaining." Distributive bargaining denotes "value-claiming behavior" (Walton and McKersie 1965; Odell 2002: 40) in which, as aptly described by former WTO Director General Pascal Lamy, "each negotiator is trying to give as little as possible and take as much as possible."[54] Negotiators start

[54] *Straits Times*, 30 December 2010.

with high opening demands, seek to avoid concessions, conceal information about their true priorities and criticize the positions of their opponents. Often they operate with threats in an attempt to weaken the other's resolve (Conceição-Heldt 2006: 158), try to manipulate the other's beliefs about alternative options and seek to curtail the other's alternatives in favor of one's own (Odell 2002: 41).

Even though ASEAN member countries are vociferous critics of the power distribution in the majority of international organizations, and often find themselves closely aligned with the interests of developing countries, their negotiation behavior is rarely intransigent. Even in organizations where decision-making is by consensus ASEAN is not known to hold the majority of states hostage through a veto. While the negotiation behavior of ASEAN member countries differs markedly (ranging from a more assertive behavior, such as in the case of Malaysia in the Mahathir era, to a more accommodating behavior, as in the case of Indonesia, Thailand and Singapore), individually and collectively, ASEAN and its members have acquired the reputation of a reasonable, moderate, constructive and largely pragmatic actor.[55] If ASEAN member countries engage in distributive bargaining, it is usually in the initial stages of the bargaining process. In the later stages, when options for solutions appear, member states are closer to what studies on international negotiations call "integrative bargaining." Integrative bargaining stands for "value-creating behavior" (Odell 2002: 40). It is a less competitive process that involves actions aimed at increasing

[55] *Jakarta Post*, 27 November 2006.

the benefits, facilitating the mutual attainment of negotiating goals (Odell 2002: 42; Conceição-Heldt 2006: 148) and creating new and possibly more just and transparent institutional arrangements for the solution of common problems.

This is also precisely the self-image ASEAN member states seek to project: the image of good global citizens (see also section 5.2 on framing) that do not forego compromises as long as these are not unilaterally imposed upon them and as long as they entail a modicum of short- and long-term gains. Following Malaysian Prime Minister Datuk Seri Najib Razak's maiden speech at the 65th United Nations General Assembly in 2010 in which he introduced the concept of a Global Movement of Moderates (GMM),[56] the twentieth ASEAN Summit in Phnom Penh, Cambodia, endorsed ideological and behavioral moderation as a regional concept.[57] Indonesia also has cultivated the image of a bridge-builder in international fora; a bridge-builder between Asia and Europe, between "developed nations, developing nations and least-developed countries (LDCs)"[58] and also between the Muslim and the non-Muslim world (Nguitragool 2012: 740),[59] an image that it also seeks to create for ASEAN as a regional grouping.

However, on closer scrutiny it becomes evident that this pragmatism often stands in the way of acting as a bloc or quasi-bloc. Pragmatism is closely geared to ASEAN member

[56] For details, see the GMM website, available at: www.gmomf.org/index.php?_m=content&cid=779 (accessed 13 January 2014).

[57] *New Straits Times*, 4 April 2012. [58] *Jakarta Post*, 3 January 2012.

[59] See, inter alia, *Media Indonesia*, 16 December 2008; *Jakarta Globe*, 6 June 2010; *Jakarta Post*, 5 March 2009; 26 January 2010; 1 November 2010.

states' national interests. This, in effect, means that they may support decisions fellow members dislike or even reject, if they are lured into compromising by sufficient material or ideational side payments. A case in point is the behavior of the Malaysian and Indonesian governments, which in the second half of the 1990s vehemently opposed the inauguration of a new trade liberalization round. But, in the end, as NGOs allege, they were lured into giving their consent to the new Doha Round by putative side payments from the USA and other industrialized countries (Kwa 2003: 33; Desker 2011: 33). Given pragmatism's potential for defection from collective action, the relatively low level of coordination and knowledge sharing and the prevailing power sensitivity, this means – as predicted at the end of Chapter 3 – that in the second phase of negotiations ASEAN countries also act more as a caucus than as a bloc or quasi-bloc.

4.3 Phase 3 concluding the negotiations: voting and compliance

Voting

Negotiations usually end with a decision. Such a decision may be made by consensus or by majority vote. A consensus may need a unanimity in a formal vote, but may also be attained if nobody objects to the results achieved in a negotiation. A majority vote may require a qualified majority or only a simple majority. As we have outlined in the theory section of Chapter 2, the mode of decision-making may have a bearing on negotiation style and actor cohesion. The subsequent paragraphs therefore seek to explore ASEAN's voting and decision-making behavior in global fora.

Empirical evidence about ASEAN's voting behavior in global fora is still largely unexplored.[60] However, based on a ten-year analysis of votes on resolutions in the United Nations General Assembly, we are able to offer at least some tentative conclusions. Voting in the UN follows the one state, one vote principle and is based on majority rule. A resolution is thus adopted if a simple majority of the member countries supports it.

In order to get a preliminary insight into the voting behavior of ASEAN countries in the UN General Assembly, we analyzed the votes taken on resolutions in the ten-year period between the beginning of the 57th United Nations General Assembly (October 2002) and the end of the 66th General Assembly (September 2012).[61] In this period, 731 votes were held in the General Assembly. At first sight, empirical evidence seems to depict ASEAN as a reasonably cohesive grouping. In 501 cases – or more than two-thirds of all votes (68.53 percent) – it voted jointly; that is, all ten members supported the respective resolution. In 230 decisions (31.46 percent), its vote was split; that is, at least one member abstained, voted against the resolution or was absent (see Table 4.4). This score indicates that ASEAN was somewhat less cohesive than Mercosur, which had a joint voting score

[60] For a very recent exception, see Ferdinand (2013) and (in a response to Ferdinand) Burmester and Jankowski (2013).

[61] For their research assistance in compiling the UN General Assembly votes, we thank Jan-Simon Dörflinger and Felix Idelberger.

of nearly 76 percent, whereas it was more cohesive than SAARC with a score of only about 56 percent of joint votes.

Cohesion appears to be even greater if we take a closer look at the non-unanimous votes. Here we find that in 147 out of 230 non-unanimous votes only one member did not vote in agreement with fellow ASEAN members. This means that only in eighty-three (or slightly more than 11 percent) of the votes did more than one ASEAN member vote against their peers. Moreover, all of these deviations were the result of abstentions or absence in the voting. The number of votes in which only one member defected from the majority owing to abstention or absence is particularly high in the 64th and 66th UNGA when ASEAN unity appeared to be markedly lower than in the other UNGAs (see Table 4.3).

Absences are an interesting case in ASEAN's voting behavior. They are relatively frequent, although other regional organizations such as SAARC also have high rates of absences from voting. While for countries like Cambodia, Laos and Myanmar, which have very limited diplomatic capacities, absences from voting may be attributed to shortages in diplomatic personnel, this explanation is less plausible for Vietnam, a country with a larger mission in New York. In contrast, Brunei, with the smallest representation of all ASEAN member countries in New York, missed no votes in the period in question. The same holds true for Singapore. New York-based diplomats deny that there is political intention behind absences,[62] but the fact that ASEAN's four new

[62] Email information by a New York-based ASEAN diplomat, 19 September 2013.

Table 4.3 *ASEAN voting behavior in the United Nations General Assembly, 2002/2003–2011/2012*

United Nations General Assembly	*ASEAN joint voting (unanimous vote by all ten ASEAN members)*	*ASEAN split voting (including absences)*
57th UNGA 2002/2003	50 (70.4%)	21 (29.6%)
58th UNGA 2003/2004	55 (72.4%)	21 (27.6%)
59th UNGA 2004/2005	48 (67.6%)	23 (32.4%)
60th UNGA 2005/2006	52 (69.3%)	23 (30.7%)
61st UNGA 2006/2007	60 (68.9%)	27 (31.1%)
62nd UNGA 2007/2008	59 (76.6%)	18 (23.4%)
63rd UNGA 2008/2009	52 (71.2%)	21 (28.8%)
64th UNGA 2009/2010	36 (52.4%)	33 (47.6%)
65th UNGA 2010/2011	53 (79.3%)	14 (20.7%)
66th UNGA 2011/2012	36 (55.4%)	29 (44.6%)
Total	**501 (68.53%)**	**230 (31.5%)**

Source: Based on Anton Strezhnev and Erik Voeten, "United Nations General Assembly Voting Data" (2013), UNF:5: NpHV5DXWPNWMWOrLGTjQYA== Erik Voeten [Distributor] V5 [Version], http://hdl.handle.net/1902.1/12379.

members are particularly frequently absent, and that absences have a pattern (individual countries forego their vote every year on the same resolutions, including themes such as human rights,[63] Palestine, the law of the sea, the arms trade, or in the individual instance of the important R2P resolution on Libya in 2011), gives rise to the assumption that they may be a form of abstention, albeit one which masks disagreements

[63] In the 67th UNGA the Philippines was even absent in the vote on a resolution on the human rights situation in Myanmar.

Table 4.4 *ASEAN split votes in the United Nations General Assembly with one member defecting through abstention or absence*

UN General Assembly	*Number of votes with one member defecting from ASEAN majority*
57th UNGA	9
58th UNGA	11
59th UNGA	13
60th UNGA	10
61st UNGA	8
62nd UNGA	5
63rd UNGA	7
64th UNGA	22
65th UNGA	5
66th UNGA	17
Total	107

Source: Compiled from www.un.org/depts/dhl/resguide/r57.htm to www.un.org/depts/dhl/resguide/r66.htm.

and, if nobody else defects, suggests unanimous voting behavior.

An interesting picture emerged when we examined the defections (including absences) by country. Table 4.5 shows that three different clusters of countries can be identified based on the frequency of defections from ASEAN unity in UNGA votes. A first cluster, consisting of Brunei, Malaysia and Indonesia, may be characterized as promoters of ASEAN unity. They exhibit the lowest number of defections from ASEAN unity in UNGA voting. This is quite an interesting finding that raises the question of whether Indonesia is indeed playing the leading role in ASEAN that it often claims for itself.

Table 4.5 *ASEAN, split voting, defections from ASEAN majority, by member country*

Member country	*Number of defections, 57th–66th UNGA (including absence from voting)*
Brunei	19
Cambodia	66
Indonesia	31
Laos	78
Malaysia	28
Myanmar	77
Philippines	43
Singapore	43
Thailand	51
Vietnam	72

Source: Compiled from www.un.org/depts/dhl/resguide/r57.htm to www.un.org/depts/dhl/resguide/r66.htm. See also Anton Strezhnev and Erik Voeten, "United Nations General Assembly Voting Data" (2013), UNF:5: NpHV5DXWPNWMWOrLGTjQYA== Erik Voeten [Distributor] V5 [Version], http://hdl.handle.net/1902.1/12379.

Defecting less frequently than most other ASEAN member countries could mean that Indonesia indeed seeks to play a key role in shaping ASEAN consensus in the UN. But it could also mean that Indonesia's low defection rate is the result of a compromise-based regional policy that takes seriously the doctrine that ASEAN is the cornerstone of Indonesia's foreign policy. New York-based diplomats offered a third explanation: for them it was the shared Islamic identity of the three countries, which often voted with other OIC and NAM members.[64]

[64] Authors' interviews, 30 July 2012.

A second group of countries, consisting of Singapore, the Philippines and Thailand, forms the middle ground with markedly higher defection rates than the first cluster of states. The Philippines and Thailand occasionally deviate from ASEAN's predominantly Islamic countries in votes on Palestine and Israel owing to their close relationship with the USA, although Thailand has in recent years shifted closer to the Islamic countries, in an obvious attempt to shield itself from external critique against its handling of the Islamic rebellion in its south.[65] Finally, a third cluster consists of the mainland Southeast Asian accession states. Cambodia, Vietnam, Myanmar and Laos are the countries that most frequently defect from ASEAN unity in UNGA votes. If it can be shown that this pattern of voting behavior also prevails in other international organizations, it will raise questions regarding the integration of the new members in the association.

It should be noted here that recent studies on ASEAN's voting behavior in the UNGA have applied more sophisticated measurements of voting cohesion. They indicate a high cohesion of ASEAN in UN votes, even higher than that of the EU (Ferdinand 2013: 8). Yet these indices do not take into account absences from voting. Moreover, as Burmester and Jankowski argue, they overstate agreement given the fact that many resolutions in the UNGA are not contentious as they constitute the lowest common denominator of a large membership or address "low politics" issues (Burmester and Jankowski 2013: 4). In fact, ASEAN's voting cohesion alone is neither a necessary nor a sufficient condition for arguing that

[65] *Ibid.*

it exhibits a coherent identity on the global stage. As argued in this study, many more factors must be taken into account before arriving at such a conclusion.

Following Haas and Rowe's categorization of the votes according to policy fields, we distinguished votes on (a) *economic issues*, including development, social affairs and technology; (b) *human rights*, including refugee issues; (c) *military and diplomatic affairs*; and (d) *other issues* (Haas and Rowe 1973: 10–12). Here our analysis reveals that ASEAN acted quite coherently in military and diplomatic affairs, with a defection rate of only 23.2 percent for the ten-year period. Many of the military and diplomatic issues, in which ASEAN exhibited considerable coherence, revolved around disarmament and non-proliferation, issues on which at a regional level ASEAN had usually taken a firm stance, as the long-term objectives of creating a Zone of Peace, Freedom and Neutrality (ZOPFAN) and the 1995 signing of a Treaty on a Southeast Asian Nuclear Weapons Free Zone (SEANWFZ) suggest (see Table 4.6).

While ASEAN coherence in the military and diplomatic field does not come as a surprise, the same is also true for its lack of cohesion in the field of human rights. Split voting was particularly pronounced when resolutions on the human rights situations in North Korea, Iran, Syria, Belarus, the Democratic Republic of Congo, Sudan, the Caucasus region and ASEAN fellow member Myanmar were voted upon. In these cases, the voting behavior reflected the normative divisions within ASEAN, which – as we have seen in Chapter 3 – have become obvious in the aftermath of the Bali Concord II and in the ASEAN Charter writing process

Table 4.6 *ASEAN voting behavior in the United Nations General Assembly, by issue area*

	ASEAN joint voting					*ASEAN split voting*				
UNGA	*Military and diplomatic*	*Human rights*	*Economic*	*Other issues*	*Total*	*Military and diplomatic*	*Human rights*	*Economic*	*Other issues*	*Total*
57th UNGA	40	28	2	1	71	13	8	–	–	21
58th UNGA	39	33	4	–	76	9	11	1	–	21
59th UNGA	39	30	2	–	71	12	11	–	–	23
60th UNGA	42	29	3	1	75	9	13	–	1	23
61st UNGA	50	32	2	3	87	13	13	–	1	27
62nd UNGA	38	31	5	3	77	3	13	2	–	18
63rd UNGA	44	26	3	–	73	10	10	1	–	21
64th UNGA	32	29	5	3	69	8	21	2	2	33
65th UNGA	38	26	2	1	67	6	8	–	–	14
66th UNGA	30	26	3	6	65	8	13	3	5	29
67th UNGA	43	25	4	1	73	11	9	1	–	21
Total	435	315	35	19	804	102	130	10	9	251

Source: www.un.org/depts/dhl/resguide/r57.htm to www.un.org/depts/dhl/resguide/r66.htm.

(Rüland 2014). While ASEAN member countries still very much attached to the non-interference norm and struggling with human rights violations at home such as Vietnam, Laos and Myanmar displayed a tendency to vote "no" in country-specific human rights resolutions, those with greater sympathies with liberal human rights norms, such as the Philippines, Thailand and Indonesia, either supported the resolutions or abstained.

Yet it is obviously not only the positioning of ASEAN countries towards human rights norms that had a bearing on voting decisions but also specific foreign policy affinities. Vietnam, for instance, did not vote against communist North Korea, whereas Indonesia abstained in the case of Iran, a country with which it has relatively close relations on an Islamic platform. Also, with regard to Myanmar, although ASEAN governments maintained solidarity with its fellow member in resolutions where Myanmar's human rights violations came to a vote,[66] the voting behavior could hardly conceal the normative disagreements among ASEAN members. Yet this solidarity crumbled. In the 61st UNGA three members abstained and seven rejected the resolution. Five years later, in the 66th UNGA, the number of ASEAN countries rejecting the resolution had decreased to five. Five other members abstained, thereby exhibiting a thinly veiled displeasure with Myanmar's poor democracy and human rights record. Yet the minimum agreement of a caucus-type behavior can be detected in the fact that no country actively supported the resolution (see also Case Study 2 in Chapter 6).

[66] United Nations General Assembly, A/RES/66/230.

ASEAN's behavior in decision-making is different in the WTO. Scattered evidence suggests that in the aftermath of the Uruguay Round some ASEAN countries, such as Malaysia and Indonesia, acted – at least temporarily – in the way that we predicted in our theoretical section: if decision-making is by consensus, weaker countries would exploit their veto power in order to extract concessions from the countries leading the majority. However, as NGO accounts of the pre-Doha Round negotiations suggest, neither Malaysia nor Indonesia has sustained obstructive behavior and at a certain point they succumbed to offers of side payments by the USA and other developed countries (Kwa 2003: 33; Desker 2011: 33). While this may be rational for negotiating governments, it appears as unprincipled and opportunistic in the eyes of those who – like many NGOs – criticize trade liberalization as a process that works to the detriment of developing countries and the poorer segments of the latter's societies. Disagreements and caucus-type behavior has – as argued below – increased even further in the post-Uruguay Round era and during the thus far inconclusive Doha Round.

Compliance

Like ASEAN negotiation behavior in global fora in general, its compliance record is also ambiguous. If we take compliance with WTO rules as a rough indicator, we find that, like most other non-Western regional organizations, ASEAN member countries are more often complainants than defendants in the WTO's dispute settlement mechanism. Moreover, the cases where ASEAN members appear as

Table 4.7 *Major non-Western regional organizations and WTO dispute settlement*

Regional organization	*Complainant*	*Defendant*
ASEAN	28	15
Mercosur	43	36
SAARC	26	22
Andean Community	12	12
SADC	–	4
ECOWAS	–	–

Source: www.wto.org/english/tratop_e/dispu_e/dispu_status_e.htm.

defendants are markedly fewer than in the case of Mercosur and SAARC (see Table 4.7). This seems to suggest that ASEAN member countries are more compliant with WTO rules than the members of other regional organizations. Without deeper scrutiny, however, this finding could also mean that ASEAN settles trade disputes without litigation in bilateral negotiations. That the Philippines, Thailand and Indonesia are most frequently involved as defendants is hardly surprising (see Table 4.8) as they are also the most protectionist members of the original ASEAN-5 (Ravenhill 2008).

Our examination of ASEAN's involvement in WTO dispute settlement brought to the fore another interesting insight: among the six non-Western regional organizations compared here, ASEAN members display the greatest number of trade disputes (three) among themselves. However, while ASEAN provides for institutional arrangements to solve such disputes intramurally, member states take them to the WTO dispute settlement mechanisms, thus indicating the same low level of trust in regional institutions that we have already

Table 4.8 *ASEAN members in the WTO dispute settlement mechanism*

Country	*Complainant*	*Defendant*
Indonesia	6	4
Malaysia	1	1
Philippines	5	6
Singapore	1	–
Thailand	13	4
Vietnam	2	–
Total	28	15

Source: www.wto.org/english/tratop_e/dispu_e/dispu_status_e.htm.

encountered with regard to territorial disputes.[67] Levels of compliance have also been comparatively low in environmental issues where the positions of member countries lie far apart.[68]

The degree of compliance with negotiated rules is also closely related to domestic politics. The greater the number of domestic veto players, the greater the likelihood that implementation of international treaties and agreements is flawed. As the number of veto players tends to be greater in democracies, paradoxically – despite their rhetorical commitment to the rule of law and good governance – the compliance record of democracies is not necessarily better than for authoritarian regimes. After all, in democracies – and Indonesia is an excellent example – political decision-makers

[67] See Chapter 4. [68] *Jakarta Globe*, 13 April 2010.

and stakeholders also share the essentially skeptical world view outlined in Chapter 3. Parliaments in particular may emerge as powerful veto players if international agreements must be ratified by them. In the case of regional agreements, the Indonesian legislature is a good example, refusing to ratify the Defense Agreement with Singapore (Rüland 2009) and for more than a decade the ASEAN Haze Pollution Agreement (Nguitragool 2011a; Nguitragool 2011b). However, the opposition against international agreements is also the result of the non-integration of interest groups and NGOs in the negotiation process. Both economic interest groups and NGOs for different reasons have repeatedly become vocal veto players, when ASEAN governments have consented to trade liberalization agreements. The vociferous domestic protest concomitant with WTO trade liberalization ministerials and appearing in the aftermath of the conclusion of free trade agreements such as those under the auspices of APEC and ACFTA are cases in point. Because governments had virtually insulated themselves from any societal influence during the negotiation process, opposition surged once the agreements entered the implementation stage. If this opposition does not subside and seriously challenges the legitimacy of the government, as has repeatedly been the case for Indonesia, the government tends to resort to the imposition of non-tariff trade barriers.[69] This assures that the government formally complies with the agreements, but in reality acts against their spirit.

[69] *Jakarta Post*, 2 January 2010; 5 March 2010; 21 December 2012; *Kabar Bisnis*, 18 May 2011.

4.3 PHASE 3 VOTING AND COMPLIANCE

We may sum up this chapter by concluding that at the final stage of the negotiation process – in terms of voting and compliance – ASEAN does not act as a bloc or quasi-bloc. It is, however, closer to a quasi-bloc in UN voting, but only when less significant issues are being voted upon. In the WTO the behavior of member countries in decision-making differs markedly, depending to a great extent on their national interests, which in turn are shaped by the strength of domestic veto players such as the legislature, nongovernmental organizations and business associations. Overall, in this stage of negotiations as well, ASEAN's collective behavior is closer to a caucus than to a quasi-bloc.

Chapter 5

ASEAN as an actor in global fora: negotiation strategies

While in Chapter 4 we examined ASEAN behavior and cohesion at various stages of international negotiations, in the next sections we explore which strategies ASEAN as a collective actor and ASEAN member countries individually employ to increase their bargaining power in global fora. Following our analytical framework devised in Chapter 2, we discuss strategies such as leadership, framing, coalition-building, forum shopping and image-building – that is, the formation of "soft power" – and try to determine the degree of cohesion ASEAN develops in applying these strategies.

5.1 Competing for executive and leadership positions

Earlier, in our theoretical part, we argued that formal leadership positions, even if of a merely symbolic nature at first glance, may entail significant powers. They may allow the incumbent to influence the agenda of a negotiation process, the way issues are framed and communicated and impact on the outcome of negotiations. Moreover, leadership in international organizations may gratify the country or – if acting collectively – the regional organization from which the incumbent originates with a high level of visibility and may give substance to actors' often self-styled image of a "multilateral utility." Leadership positions may signify internationally recognized "soft power" resources of a country and a country's acknowledged competence as a broker and mediator. They also express technical competence in the light of increasingly complex policy issues. Reiterated appointment of representatives of a country tends to affirm these putative capacities and social resources. Finally, ASEAN members' strong penchant for international leadership positions is also a reflection of the high significance Southeast Asian cultures attach to leadership (Solidum 1974: 85; Rüland 2014).[1]

A key arena in which ASEAN member countries sought to exert influence through occupying leadership positions was the United Nations, in particular, the General Assembly and, within limits, the Security Council. All ASEAN member states are members of the United Nations and as a regional organization ASEAN has enjoyed observer status in the United Nations General Assembly since 2006, following the adoption of a resolution sponsored by the Philippines.[2] ASEAN also holds regular meetings with the UN, although the latter have little more than declaratory character.[3] However, no ASEAN member state is a permanent member of the UN Security Council.

[1] For the great importance Southeast Asian elites attach to leadership, see also Jayakumar (2011: 15–16).

[2] *Philippine Daily Inquirer*, 26 October 2006 and 5 December 2006.

[3] Most of them end with very general declarations for synergizing ASEAN and UN agendas and of mutual support for a multilateral global order. See press release, Informal ASEAN Ministerial Meeting, New York, 24 September 2011, received from ASEANcats@googlegroups.com (accessed 2 March 2014).

Since 2004, the Indonesian government has repeatedly aired its intention to become a permanent member, resuming overtures in this direction originating from the Suharto era.[4] In a speech held at the 59th UN General Assembly then Indonesian Foreign Minister Hassan Wirajuda justified Indonesian aspirations with the country's successful democratization, which set a good precedent not only for Muslim nations but also for Western countries, its leadership role among developing countries and its contributions to international peace.[5] The *Jakarta Post* quoted Hassan as saying that

> A developing world striving not only for social and economic progress but also for democratization must have a voice on the Security Council. Moderate Islam must have a voice on the Council. Indonesia would be that voice.[6]

However, Indonesia's overtures found little resonance in other ASEAN capitals. At the time, the majority of ASEAN member countries voiced strong support for Japan, another Asian contender for a permanent seat.[7] Nevertheless, the 2004 Vientiane Summit expressly endorsed "Indonesia's intention to seek permanent membership in the United Nations Security Council."[8] However, since then, high-level ASEAN meetings have never repeated this endorsement, suggesting

[4] *Jakarta Post*, 8 April 2004; 28 September 2004; 26 March 2005; 16 October 2006; 26 November 2008; 8 April 2010; 20 November 2010; 28 December 2010; 8 January 2011 and 20 November 2011; see also *Tempo Interaktif*, 25 December 2005.

[5] *Jakarta Post*, 28 September 2004. [6] *Ibid.* [7] *The Nation*, 24 April 2005.

[8] Chairman's Statement, 10th ASEAN Summit, Vientiane, 29 November 2004, para. 24.

that the 2004 endorsement was a face-saving act for Indonesia and that fellow members did not feel comfortable with the Indonesian bid.[9]

Many ASEAN governments also had problems with accepting the normative framing of Indonesia's ambitions. In fact, ASEAN's non-Muslim member states and countries with more autocratic orders found especially little common ground with it. They regard Indonesia's rationale for a permanent membership in a reformed UN Security Council as an expression of the country's resurgent nationalism and regional leadership ambitions rather than a position representing the association's common interests. More than the Indonesian aspirations for a permanent Security Council seat per se, it is thus the normative framing of Jakarta's ambitions that is undermining ASEAN cohesion, which in this crucial issue is thus rather fragile and at best of a caucus type.

While it is highly unlikely that any ASEAN member will get a permanent seat on the Security Council in the foreseeable future, ASEAN countries regularly compete for non-permanent seats. Their applications are usually carefully prepared at the regional level based on a consensual decision concerning which member country should run. In New York, ASEAN expects its permanent representatives to the UN to promote the ASEAN candidate by "non-stop courtesy calls"

[9] It may be worth a footnote to add that also the USA, despite markedly improving bilateral relationships with Indonesia under the Obama administration, did not support Indonesian aspirations and disclosed that it would back India's campaign for a permanent seat. See *Jakarta Post*, 10 November 2010.

to their peers.[10] Yet it is perplexing that in the political autobiography of former Singaporean Foreign Minister Jayakumar much is said about the enormous burden to be shouldered by a country vying for a non-permanent seat in the UN Security Council (UNSC),[11] but nothing about ASEAN solidarity and cooperation to achieve this objective.

If Jayakumar's silence on ASEAN cooperation in gaining a non-permanent seat in the UNSC is indeed an indication of lukewarm solidarity it may provide at least one reason why the success of ASEAN candidacies is mixed. However, two major structural impediments working against ASEAN campaigns must also be taken into account: first, ASEAN countries must mobilize support in the UN's Asia-Pacific regional group that is accorded only two non-permanent seats. This is one less than the Africa Group that has an almost equal number of member countries but no permanent member in the Security Council.[12] Second, in the Asia-Pacific Group ASEAN countries persistently compete with international political heavyweights such as Japan, India and South Korea. Thus, compared to other Southern regional organizations, ASEAN has less

[10] *The Nation*, 10 September 1998.

[11] Jayakumar mentioned that, as Foreign Minister, during his annual two-week UNGA stint he had as many as thirty bilateral meetings and another two dozen at the Commonwealth Heads of Government Meeting (Jayakumar 2011: 67–68).

[12] Asia also has to make reservations for an Arab seat every two years. This is related to an informal agreement of one seat for an Arab country. As the Asia-Pacific and the Africa group provide this seat on an alternate basis, this seat is known as the "Arab Swing Seat." Center for UN Reform, available at: www.whatsinblue.org/2013/12/extraordinary-election-to-the-security-council.php (accessed 3 February 2014).

Table 5.1 *Non-permanent memberships in the UN Security Council, by members of selected regional organizations*

Regional organization	*Number of memberships*
ASEAN (1967)	9
Mercosur (1991)	7
ECOWAS (1975)	19
SADC (1980)	10
Andean Community (1969)	12
SAARC (1985)	7

Source: Authors' compilations.

frequently garnered a non-permanent seat on the UN Security Council (see Table 5.1). Yet, despite this heavy competition, all ASEAN founding members have been elected as a non-permanent member of the Security Council at least once. From the new members, only Vietnam held a non-permanent seat (see Table 5.2). Thailand and Cambodia launched their candidacy for the 2011–2012 and 2013–2014 period respectively, but failed to get elected.[13]

Yet, it is interesting to note – much in line with the cognitive disposition of the region's foreign policy elites discussed in Chapter 3 – what motivates ASEAN member countries to run for a non-permanent seat in the UNSC. In the case of Singapore, former Singaporean Foreign Minister Jayakumar reports that, advised by New Zealand – a close partner of the country – Singapore eventually decided to run in 2001–2002. The rationale for this decision was that only

[13] *Cambodia Daily*, 21 October 2012.

Table 5.2 *UN Security Council memberships, since 1967*

Country	*Year*
Indonesia	1973/1974
	1995/1996
	2007/2008
Philippines	1980/1981
	2004/2005
Thailand	1985/1986
Malaysia	1989/1990
	1999/2000
Singapore	2001/2002
Vietnam	2008/2009

Source: Authors' compilations; https://www.un.org/en/sc/members/elected.shtml; *Jakarta Post*, 28 December 2010.

from within the UNSC can one really understand the body's inner workings and the interplay among the P5 (Jayakumar 2011: 65). It would also help better to understand other UN bodies and would entail the opportunity to expand the country's diplomatic network. Internally, Jayakumar pointed out that all other ASEAN-6 members except for Brunei had already served at least once in the UNSC. This placed Singapore at a distinct disadvantage, particularly against "Malaysia and Indonesia, the immediate neighbors with which relations were not always smooth, and with whom Singapore would most likely be involved in any serious dispute or conflict situation," who had had the experience of serving in the Security Council (*ibid.* 67). Jayakumar went on to argue that Singapore should not come into a position where it "would be simply outmaneuvered because of a lack of

Table 5.3 *Presidencies of UN General Assembly, by members of selected regional organizations*

Regional organization	*Number of presidencies*
ASEAN (1967)	2
Mercosur (1991)	2
ECOWAS (1975)	2
SADC (1980)	2
Andean Community (1969)	2
SAARC (1985)	1

Source: Authors' compilations.

understanding and familiarity with the UNSC system" (*ibid.*). The lesson from these statements is clear: ASEAN members did not in the first place join the UNSC in order to strengthen ASEAN as a collective body but rather to strengthen their national interests. It is thus hardly surprising that at no point in the discussion of Singapore's activities in the UN did Jayakumar mention ASEAN as a collective actor.

Throughout the years, ASEAN member countries occupied top positions in major bodies of the United Nations. With two General Assembly presidencies ASEAN was largely on a par with other major non-Western regional organizations. Only SAARC had a lower number of presidencies (see Table 5.3).

Additionally, ASEAN's average share of presidencies in the UN Security Council equals those of Mercosur, ECOWAS and the Andean Community and was slightly better than that of SAARC (see Table 5.4).

One of ASEAN's greatest collective successes was the election of Malaysian diplomat Razali Ismail as President of the 51st General Assembly of the United Nations in 1996. After

Table 5.4 *Presidencies of UN Security Council, by members of selected regional organizations*

Regional organization	*Number of presidencies*
ASEAN (1967)	19
Mercosur (1991)	7
ECOWAS (1975)	32
SADC (1980)	13
Andean Community (1969)	19
SAARC (1985)	10

Source: Authors' compilations.

former Indonesian Foreign Minister Adam Malik was UNGA President in 1971, Razali became only the second UNGA President from a Southeast Asian country. While Malik was elected when ASEAN still consisted of its five founding members, Razali was supported by an ASEAN-7, thus necessitating more intra-ASEAN coordination than in Malik's time.

Razali's election was facilitated by the fact that he was not only the common candidate of ASEAN, but also faced no challenge from other Asian countries. Malaysian then Foreign Minister Abdullah Badawi informed his ASEAN colleagues of his government's nomination of Razali for the post during the fifth ASEAN Summit and received a positive response.[14] All ASEAN members subsequently supported the Malaysian candidacy, as did many developing countries.[15] Apart from ASEAN's united stance, Razali also benefited from Malaysia's high-profile role in the UN as an avid advocate of the Global

[14] *New Straits Times*, 20 December 1996.

[15] *Straits Times*, 21 December 1996.

South during much of the Mahathir era (1981–2003). However, the candidate's own distinguished career in the UN and other international organizations was also a great asset for the ASEAN campaign. Razali was a veteran diplomat in the UN, having served as Malaysia's Permanent Representative to the world organization since 1988. In 1989 he was the Chairman of the Group of 77, in 1991 Vice-President of the UN's Economic and Social Council (ECOSOC) and in 1993 he became Chairman of the Commission on Sustainable Development.[16] The election of Razali as President of the UN General Assembly suggests that quasi-bloc unity, gaining strong support from the developing world without provoking opposition from major Western countries and a highly competent personality is the formula of success in ASEAN's bid for international executive posts.

Unfortunately, however, ASEAN failed to apply this formula in subsequent campaigns for top positions. While Supachai Panichpakdi's candidacy for the post of WTO Director General had strong backing from ASEAN and many developing countries, the candidacy met with stiff opposition from the USA and other industrialized countries. Yet the support he received was strong enough to engineer a compromise solution in which he shared the term of office with his main opponent, former Prime Minister of New Zealand, Mike Moore. Some years later, former Thai Foreign Minister Surakiart Sathirathai's race for UN Secretary General

[16] Razali Ismail (Malaysia). Elected President of the 51st session of the General Assembly, available at: www.un.org/en/ga/president/bios/bio51.shtml (accessed 3 December 2012).

and Indonesian Deputy Senior Minister for Public Welfare Indroyono Susilo's candidacy for Director of the UN Food and Agriculture Organization (FAO) lacked virtually all the key ingredients for a successful campaign. Although ASEAN governments formally endorsed their bid, they could hardly count on an active promotion of their candidacies by fellow ASEAN members and thus had to rely exclusively on the campaign team of their home countries. With only lukewarm ASEAN support, they also faced great difficulties in mobilizing noteworthy support in other world regions. Even worse, however, was the fact that throughout their campaigns both had to contend with strong doubts about their competence to perform successfully if elected.

The Thai government announced its intention to field Supachai Panichpakdi as a candidate for the post of the WTO Director General at the ASEAN Ministerial Meeting in Manila in July 1998.[17] At the meeting, Supachai was obviously the only ASEAN candidate,[18] but after announcement of the Thai candidacy other ASEAN members also seemed to show interest in fielding their own candidates.[19] Writing personally to his ASEAN counterparts, then Thai Prime Minister Chuan Leeekpai sought to rally ASEAN support for Supachai.[20] At an ASEAN foreign ministers' meeting at the margins of the UN General Assembly in September 1998, ASEAN member states eventually agreed to unite behind Supachai's bid.[21] Coordinated by the Foreign Ministry,[22] the Thai government

[17] *The Nation*, 13 August 1998. [18] *The Nation*, 11 August 1998.
[19] *The Nation*, 7 August 1998. [20] *Straits Times*, 29 August 1998.
[21] *The Nation*, 7 August 1998. [22] *The Nation*, 25 August 1998.

created a task force to take the lead in drumming up international support for Supachai.[23] It subsequently announced the Thai candidacy at all relevant international gatherings, both regional and global.[24] This included lobbying at the 1998 NAM Summit in South Africa and in the UN General Assembly in New York.[25] Supachai became part of the Thai delegation to the 53rd session of the UN General Assembly,[26] providing him with opportunities for informal lobbying in support of his candidacy, public speaking and calling on senior US officials in Washington.[27] Yet, ASEAN soon realized that Supachai's path to the WTO's top post would be difficult, as other candidates including Mike Moore (New Zealand), Roy MacLaren (Canada) and Hassan Abouyoub (Morocco) joined the race. Even after the last two withdrew their candidacies in early 1999 for lack of support, the contest was deadlocked for months.[28] The main opposition to Supachai came from the US government, which raised doubts about Supachai's commitment to trade liberalization, and the powerful US labor union the American Federation of Labor and Congress of Industrial Organizations (AFL–CIO), which criticized Thailand for the country's alleged dismal record on labor rights.[29] Opponents of the Thai candidacy also played up the fact that Supachai represented the country that triggered the Asian financial crisis. How could somebody with a questionable domestic performance, they asked, successfully

[23] *Straits Times*, 29 August 1998. [24] *The Nation*, 10 September 1998.
[25] *Straits Times*, 29 August 1998. [26] *The Nation*, 10 September 1998.
[27] *The Nation*, 10 September 1998. [28] *Straits Times*, 18 June 1999.
[29] *The Nation*, 25 August 1999.

run a much more complex international organization such as the WTO?

In February 1999 Supachai's prospects for victory dimmed further with the change of the chairmanship in the WTO General Council. The outgoing chairman, Ambassador Celso Laffer of Brazil, whose country had sympathized with Supachai's bid, was replaced by Tanzanian Ambassador Ali Mchumo, who under US pressure gradually tilted to the Moore camp.[30] Supachai's campaign faced an additional setback when, during the March 1999 foreign ministers' meeting of the Asia-Europe Meeting (ASEM) in Berlin, Europeans retreated from a common stance in favor of Supachai.[31] After the meeting, only the United Kingdom, Sweden and the Netherlands continued to back Supachai.[32]

This turn of events took the Thais and their ASEAN backers by surprise, as before both the USA and the EU had promised that the successor of Italian WTO Director General Renato Ruggiero should for the first time come from a developing country.[33] However, despite the increasingly acrimonious and divisive battle, and US pressure on ASEAN, the association retained its quasi-bloc unity and continued to support Supachai. In mid-April 1999, the Chairman of the ASEAN Geneva Committee, Ambassador Hamidon Ali of Malaysia,[34] urged the WTO General Council to seek a consensus in favor of Supachai on the ground that he (still) commanded the support of 65 percent of the member

[30] *The Nation*, 1 April 1999. [31] *Ibid.*

[32] *Straits Times*, 24 April 1999 and *The Nation*, 25 August 1999.

[33] *The Nation*, 31 October 1997. [34] *The Nation*, 15 April 1999.

countries.[35] This claim was made based on a January 1999 survey conducted by two intermediaries, ambassadors William Rossier of Switzerland and Celso Laffer of Brazil, which saw Supachai as the front-runner in the race.[36] At the same time, the Philippine ambassador to the WTO asked Mchumo to name the countries that support Supachai and those that supported his opponent Mike Moore.[37] The Philippine demand was supported by Australia, Malaysia, Egypt, India, Mexico and Slovakia.[38] Even Singapore, with its reputation as a close ally of the USA, did not defect from ASEAN unity. ASEAN and the Supachai camp also fended off a sudden move of Mchumo who, allegedly under US influence, declared that a majority of WTO members support Moore[39] and therefore urged WTO members to make a consensual decision in favor of Moore.

Finally, in June 1999, a compromise solution broke the eight-month stalemate. In an unprecedented decision, WTO members decided to divide the six-year term of the WTO Director General between the two contenders. Moore would head the WTO from 1999 to 2002, Supachai from 2002 to 2005.[40]

[35] *The Nation*, 17 April 1999 and 25 August 1999.

[36] *The Nation*, 25 August 1999. [37] *The Nation*, 15 April 1999. [38] *Ibid.*

[39] *Asia Times*, 7 May 1999.

[40] In late December 2012, the Indonesian Government nominated Mari Pangestu, former Trade Minister and Minister for Tourism and Creative Economy, as a candidate for the position of WTO Director General to succeed Pascal Lamy, whose term was due to end in August 2013. The General Council of the WTO considered nominations from several countries in early 2013 and the selection process went through various rounds. In late April 2013, Brazilian diplomat Roberto Carvalho de Azevêdo was elected to succeed Pascal Lamy and assumed office on 1 September 2013.

The Thai press and ASEAN celebrated Supachai's proclamation as a "victory for ASEAN,"[41] highlighting the association's "relevancy, efficacy and resilience," as Thai Foreign Minister Surin Pitsuwan proudly stated.[42] Supachai thus became the first Asian to head the WTO.[43] The case has impressively shown what group solidarity and regional cohesion may achieve.

ASEAN was much less united when, after ending his term as WTO Director General, the Thai government nominated Supachai to run for the post of the Secretary General of the United Nations Conference on Trade and Development (UNCTAD) in 2005.[44] While Supachai's candidacy for the WTO post received support from ASEAN governments right from the beginning,[45] his candidacy for UNCTAD was opposed in particular by the Philippines and Cambodia. Both countries fielded their own candidates – namely former ASEAN Secretary General Rodolfo C. Severino, Jr. and Cambodian Vice Commerce Minister Sok Siphana – for the position. Yet Supachai's appointment eventually sailed through in May 2005, as it had the blessing of UN Secretary General Kofi Annan and the US government.

Disagreement among ASEAN member countries also prevailed as the Thai government's nomination of Supachai for the UNCTAD position coincided with Bangkok's decision to support then Deputy Prime Minister and former Foreign Minister Surakiart Sathirathai's candidacy for the position of

[41] *Straits Times*, 18 June 1999. [42] *Ibid.* [43] *Straits Times*, 29 August 1998.
[44] With an exception of Laos, all ASEAN countries are member of the G77.
[45] *The Nation*, 13 August 1998.

UN Secretary General. Fellow ASEAN members and members of the G77 criticized that holding two top positions of UN agencies at the same time is normally only possible for major donor countries or large developed countries.[46]

The Thai government had nominated Surakiart for the UN top post because the chances of election, based on an informal agreement of UN Security Council members to give due regard to "regional rotation," in principle were good.[47] In accordance with this convention, the successor of outgoing Secretary General Kofi Annan would have to come from Asia.

However, Surakiart's candidacy was doomed right from the start. The Thai government quite obviously nominated Surakiart without prior consultation with its ASEAN partners. Thailand reportedly proposed Surakiart's candidacy to fellow ASEAN members for the first time at the grouping's foreign ministers retreat in Ha Long Bay, Vietnam, in March 2004. At the time, other ASEAN countries were also contemplating fielding a candidate. Indonesia's former Foreign Minister Ali Alatas and Malaysia's former Deputy Prime Minister and Chairman of the UN Human Rights Commission Musa Hitam were both named as potential candidates.[48] The names of Singaporean candidates were

[46] *Matichon Daily*, 4 April 2005.

[47] *Ibid.* and "Secretary General Watch: Choosing Kofi Annan's Successor," available at: www.unwatch.org/site/c.bdKKISNqEmG/b.1867287/k.F23A/SecretaryGeneral_Watch_Choosing_Kofi_Annans_Successor.htm (accessed 22 March 2012).

[48] "ASEAN's UN Secretary General Candidate," Center for Strategic and International Studies, features, 16 March 2004, available at: http://csis.or.id/post/aseans-un-secretary-general-candidate (accessed 6

also floated, among them former Prime Minister Goh Chok Tong and former Foreign Minister S. Jayakumar as well as Ambassadors Kishore Mahbubani, Tommy Koh and Chan Heng Chee (Jayakumar 2011: 73).[49]

However, despite this cacophony, which, in effect, weakened Surakiart's candidacy right from the start, there was agreement among ASEAN foreign ministers that ASEAN should support only one candidate. Nevertheless, in the following months only Malaysia officially expressed its support for Surakiart.[50] Finally, after a lot of behind the scenes wheeling and dealing and after other ASEAN countries pulled out of the nomination race,[51] the association's foreign ministers eventually endorsed Surakiart in September 2004 on the sidelines of the UN General Assembly.[52]

When, in 2005, despite a landslide election victory, the Thai government of Prime Minister Thaksin Shinawatra came under increasing fire by an opposition alliance of royalist and urban-based liberal forces led by the opposition Democrat Party, Surakiart's candidacy became entangled in domestic political turbulences. It seemed that Thaksin had supported Surakiart's candidacy primarily in order to field a government candidate for a top position in a major international organization in response to the 2002–2005 leadership of the WTO by Supachai Panichpakdi, a member of the opposition Democrat Party (Chachavalpongpun 2010: 144).

November 2014) and *The Nation*, 8 March 2004 and *Jakarta Post*, 16 March 2004.

[49] *Straits Times*, 2 October 2004 and *The Nation*, 6 September 2004.

[50] *The Nation*, 6 August 2004 and 21 August 2004.

[51] *The Nation*, 30 September 2004. [52] *The Nation*, 16 October 2004.

Domestic criticism of Surakiart, a long-time loyal supporter of Thaksin, intensified as he fared poorly in straw polls in the UN Security Council. Former Thai Ambassador to the UN, Asda Jayanama, for instance, urged the government to withdraw Surakiart's bid and permit ASEAN to field more prospective candidates[53] such as former Singaporean Prime Minister Goh Chok Tong or former Thai Foreign Minister Surin Pitsuwan.[54] Asda publicly dismissed Surakiart as a "third-rate politician"[55] who simply lacked the qualifications for the job.[56] Kasit Piromya, until 2005 Thai Ambassador in Washington, after falling out with Thaksin, also asked the government to withdraw Surakiart's candidacy.[57] In a telex to the Thai government leaked to the media months later, Kasit stated that the USA would not support Surakiart, as US Secretary of State Condoleezza Rice and her predecessor Colin Powell were "unresponsive" to Thailand's campaign.[58] It also did not help Surakiart's domestic standing when reports surfaced that he had allegedly tried to derail Supachai Panichpakdi's appointment as head of UNCTAD, out of fear that Supachai's appointment would hurt his own chances of becoming the next UN Secretary General.[59] Meanwhile, the Thai press derided the government's campaign for Surakiart as a "soap opera *par excellence*."[60]

As Surakiart's candidacy was controversial at the domestic level and hardly aroused enthusiasm at the regional

[53] *The Nation*, 26 July 2006. [54] *Ibid.* [55] *The Nation*, 17 February 2006.
[56] *The Nation*, 7 March 2006. [57] *Ibid.*
[58] *The Nation*, 23 December 2005. [59] *The Nation*, 22 December 2005.
[60] *The Nation*, 27 April 2005.

level, he primarily relied in his campaign on a small task force that the Thai government had created for him (Chachavalpongpun 2010: 149).[61] With its assistance, he traversed the world in search of support.[62] According to Pavin, Surakiart made more than fifty trips abroad in the first year of his campaign (Chachavalpongpun 2010: 146). The organizations Surakiart was lobbying included the Asian Cooperation Dialogue[63] – an obscure twenty-eight member forum formed by Thaksin in 2002 – the meeting of representatives of the fourteen-member Leaders' Network in Support of UN Reform (for details, see below), the Non-Aligned Movement,[64] the African Union, ASEAN Dialogue partners and all regional groups at the United Nations in New York in July 2006.[65]

Most significantly, however, the Thai government concentrated its efforts on Washington. In early May 2005 Surakiart met US Secretary of State Condoleezza Rice, who reportedly remained tight-lipped about her government's position.[66] Allegedly, Washington feared that owing to the close relations between Thailand and Beijing Surakiart's election would strengthen China's position in the world organization.[67] China itself, which initially appeared to support the

[61] *The Nation*, 7 March 2006. [62] *The Nation*, 17 February 2006.
[63] *The Nation*, 29 September 2004. [64] *The Nation*, 30 May 2006.
[65] "ASEAN Candidate for United Nations Secretary General," press release, available at: www.asean.org/communities/asean-political-security-community/item/press-release-asean-candidate-for-united-nations-secretary-general-2 (accessed 22 March 2012).
[66] *The Nation*, 8 May 2005.
[67] *The Nation*, 16 October 2004 and 8 May 2005.

Thai candidate, remained non-committal[68] after it transpired that Surakiart had asked a Taiwanese diplomat to mobilize support for his candidacy among the twenty-five or so UN members still entertaining diplomatic relations with the island republic considered by Beijing as a renegade province.[69]

In the face of the many reservations against the candidate, ASEAN's support for him hardly transcended the declaratory level. The association's 2004 Vientiane Summit,[70] for instance, endorsed the candidacy of Surakiart, reaffirmed by the following Summit held in Kuala Lumpur in November 2005. ASEAN foreign ministers also gave support to Surakiart, as expressed in the Chairman's Statements of the 38th AMM held in Vientiane in July 2005 and the 39th AMM held in Kuala Lumpur in July 2006. The latter document, after a hearing with foreign ministers, explicitly designated him as ASEAN candidate. Only at this stage were concerns that another ASEAN member might field a candidate allayed. Overtures by US President George W. Bush and the EU Commissioner for External Relations Benita Ferrero-Waldner, who tried to persuade Goh and Jayakumar respectively to run for the post, had contributed to these uncertainties (Jayakumar 2011: 74). At the Kuala Lumpur meeting ASEAN announced the organization of a coordinated campaign for Surakiart, arranging meetings for him with ASEAN Dialogue partners and

[68] *The Nation*, 24 January 2005; 27 April 2005 and 8 May 2005.

[69] *The Nation*, 22 December 2005.

[70] "ASEAN Candidate for United Nations Secretary General," press release. available at: www.asean.org/communities/asean-political-security-community/item/press-release-asean-candidate-for-united-nations-secretary-general-2 (accessed 12 May 2012).

members of the ASEAN Regional Forum (ARF). ASEAN Committees in major capitals and ASEAN embassies worldwide also received instructions to support the campaign.[71]

However, despite these pronouncements, ASEAN support remained lukewarm. Reluctant Malaysian support in the NAM and the OIC[72] and a statement of the Philippines during the NAM Summit[73] did not equal the determined bid with which ASEAN had lent its support to the earlier Razali and Supachai candidacies. ASEAN governments acutely realized that Surakiart's campaign did not have the support of the P5.[74] Similarly damaging to the Thai campaign was the fact that Thailand's standing in the UN had suffered during the Thaksin era. Thailand came into the focus of the UN Human Rights Commissioner over Thaksin's controversial drug war that caused nearly 3,000 deaths in 2004.[75] Thaksin government's refusal to grant permission to the UN special rapporteur on extrajudicial and summary executions to visit the country and complete an investigation into the Tak Bai massacre in southern Thailand, where Thai security forces had killed eighty-seven unarmed Muslim demonstrators, also cast Thailand in a bad light.[76]

In the end, after three straw polls in which he never came out better than third, and as the candidate with the highest "discourage" votes, Surakiart ended a poor fourth in the fourth and final straw poll of the Security Council. In this poll South Korean front-runner Ban Ki-moon received the highest number of affirmative votes and no "discourage"

[71] *Ibid.* [72] *The Nation*, 30 September 2004.
[73] *The Nation*, 16 September 2006. [74] *The Nation*, 16 October 2004.
[75] *The Nation*, 8 May 2005. [76] *Ibid.*

vote from any P5 members. With this endorsement of the Security Council, the General Assembly eventually elected Ban Ki-moon as Kofi Annan's successor.[77] In ASEAN circles, however, the sentiment prevailed that Surakiart's candidacy had been more detrimental than helpful for the association as an actor in global forums, because it nourished doubts over ASEAN's ability to present a highly qualified candidate. Moreover, observers feared future candidacies promoted by ASEAN would be a priori greeted with skepticism. As one veteran Western diplomatic observer pointed out, the Surakiart candidacy suggests that, with the exception of Singapore, ASEAN member countries tend to promote candidacies for patronage reasons, proposing well-connected persons as a reward for previous services delivered to their government.[78] Another consequence of the campaign was intensifying tensions between Thailand and Singapore. It was testimony to the low trust between ASEAN members that Thailand persistently feared that Singapore would field a candidate to upset Surakiart. In retaliation, the Thais dragged their feet on the extension of an agreement governing Singapore's use of Thai facilities for military training (Jayakumar 2011: 75).

Finally, in 2011, Indonesia sought to install Indroyono Susilo as Director General of the UN's Food and Agriculture Organization (FAO). At the time Indroyono was the deputy senior minister to Coordinating Public Welfare Minister

[77] "Secretary General Watch: Choosing Kofi Annan's Successor," 19 October 2006, available at: www.unwatch.org/site/c.bdKKISNqEmG/b.1867287/k.F23A/SecretaryGeneral_Watch_Choosing_Kofi_Annans_Successor.htm (accessed 22 March 2012).

[78] Authors' interviews, 22 March 2012.

Agung Laksono.[79] Indonesia first announced Indroyono's candidacy in June 2010.[80] It received the support of ASEAN's ministers of agriculture and forestry, who endorsed his candidacy at their 32nd meeting in Phnom Penh in October 2010.[81] Yet, in the election, Indroyono fared poorly, gaining only twelve out of 180 votes.[82] Apart from ASEAN, Indonesia had also lobbied NAM countries, its African members in particular, but these nevertheless failed to support Indroyono.[83]

What went wrong? Based on press reports, it seems that the campaign Indonesia and ASEAN had orchestrated in support of Indroyono was a typical case of too little and too late, as other countries such as Brazil had started the campaign for their candidates long before.[84] But, again, perhaps even more significant was the comparative competence deficit of the ASEAN candidate, as Indroyono – by training a geologist[85] – was not known to have acquired much expertise in agriculture.[86] This contrasted sharply with the winning candidate, former Brazilian Food Security Minister José Graziano da Silva, who was the architect of Brazil's successful "Zero Hunger" program, and who had been the FAO's Assistant Director General for Latin America and the Caribbean since 2006.[87] To a lesser extent, the same can be said of narrowly defeated Spanish candidate Miguel Angel Moratinos, a former Foreign Minister, who had doubled Spanish development aid

[79] *Jakarta Post*, 24 October 2010. [80] *Jakarta Post*, 18 April 2011.

[81] *Jakarta Post*, 24 October 2010. [82] *Jakarta Post*, 27 June 2011. [83] *Ibid.*

[84] *Ibid.* [85] *Jakarta Post*, 19 March 2011.

[86] Indroyono had acquired some expertise in marine and fisheries research and natural resources management. See *Jakarta Post*, 4 September 2010.

[87] *Jakarta Post*, 28 June 2011.

between 2004 and 2010 and could converse fluently in at least three foreign languages.[88] While Moratinos had tirelessly toured more than ninety countries in an effort to drum up support for his candidacy, Indonesian lobbying efforts seemed to be lukewarm and more of an ad hoc nature. Indroyono, for instance, was reported to have traveled to the FAO headquarters in Rome to present himself as late as April 2011.[89] In sum, ASEAN's competitors fielded political and professional heavyweights, whereas ASEAN prided itself in nominating a "dark horse."[90] Again, given these birth defects of the candidacy, ASEAN at best acted as a caucus, thus failing to show the collective strength that would have garnered the international support needed to lift Indroyono into office.

In the WTO ASEAN's representation in leadership positions was better compared to other major non-Western regional organizations. To a considerable extent, this can be attributed to the fact that ASEAN countries better coordinate with and mutually support each other in their bid for WTO leadership positions.[91] ASEAN's overall declining cohesion in the WTO, of which Sally speaks (Sally 2004), thus does not extend to the candidacy for leadership positions, where ASEAN still acts as a quasi-bloc.

ASEAN trade diplomats chaired the WTO General Council twice and, in former Thai Deputy Prime Minister Supachai Panichpakdi, a member of an ASEAN country also

[88] *Ibid.* [89] *Jakarta Post*, 14 April 2011.

[90] A euphemistic description used by the *Jakarta Post*, 28 May 2011.

[91] Authors' interviews, 14 December 2012.

held the position of the WTO Director General. Mercosur was the only other non-Western regional organization that also held two WTO General Council chairmanships. SADC had one, while ECOWAS, the Andean Community and SAARC had thus far held none.

Taking a closer look at leadership positions in the WTO Council's numerous subsidiary bodies, ASEAN also fares comparatively well. In the period between 1995 and 2010, ASEAN was able to fill fifty-four chairman positions, compared to forty-four for Mercosur, thirty-five for SADC, thirty-three for SAARC, nineteen for the Andean Community and fifteen for ECOWAS. Translated into a leadership quotient, ASEAN occupies the second highest position behind Mercosur among the six regional organizations (see Table 5.5). With sixteen leadership positions each, the

Table 5.5 *WTO leadership positions and leadership quotient, six major regional organizations, 1995–2010*

Regional organization	*Leadership positions, in absolute numbers*	*Leadership quotient*[1]
ASEAN	54	0.40
Mercosur	44	0.69
SADC	35	0.16
SAARC	33	0.29
Andean Community	19	0.25
ECOWAS	15	0.08

[1] Number of leadership positions divided through group membership and years.

Source: Compiled from www.wto.org/english/thewto_e/secre_e/current_chairs_e.htm.

Table 5.6 *ASEAN members occupying leadership positions in the WTO*

Country	*Number of leadership positions*
Philippines	16
Singapore	16
Thailand	14
Malaysia	7
Indonesia	1
Total	54

Source: Compiled from www.wto.org/english/thewto_e/secre_e/current_chairs_e.htm.

Philippines and Singapore followed by Thailand with fourteen, were the most successful ASEAN countries in gaining WTO leadership positions. Quite striking, however, is the fact that Indonesia, ASEAN's self-proclaimed leader, has occupied only one leadership position since 1995 (see Table 5.6).

While ASEAN attempts to place Southeast Asians in the top executive positions of international organizations produced ambiguous results, individual countries were quite successful in translating their "soft power" into leadership positions. Tiny Singapore, for instance, in recognition of the competence of its negotiators, has often been requested by fellow WTO members to act as Chair in committees and working groups during the Uruguay Round and the thus far inconclusive Doha Round. While Singapore – like in the UN – had been approached by other members to assume chairing functions, fellow ASEAN countries had to lobby for them

(Jayakumar 2011: 72, 73, 77).[92] Singapore, therefore, also had fewer problems than ASEAN fellow members in getting access to the WTO's Green Room negotiations,[93] informal mini-lateral closed-door meetings with the objective of breaking negotiation deadlocks.

Former Singaporean Minister for Trade and Industry B. G. Yeo acquired the reputation of an honest broker, chairing several of the highly sensitive agricultural sessions at WTO Ministerial Conferences. In October 2001 he convened an informal "mini-ministerial" meeting in Singapore, in the process brokering a compromise declaration on agriculture that eventually allowed the Doha Round to be launched. Yeo was also one of the crucial players in the ill-fated 2003 Cancun Ministerial. The Mexican chair of the ministerial, Luis Ernesto Derbez, invited Yeo to join his team of mediators tasked with reconciling the incongruent positions of key actors in the highly contested field of agriculture (Sally 2004: 26; Odell 2005: 439). Yeo's role in the WTO is thus a good example of entrepreneurial leadership. Moreover, corroborating the international trust in the city state, WTO members mandated Singapore's permanent representative in Geneva, Ambassador Kesavapany, to chair the WTO's General Council (Sally 2004: 26).

Given the variegated access to WTO leadership positions and the concomitant influence ASEAN member countries are able to wield, it is thus hardly surprising that their appraisal of WTO decision-making processes also

[92] Authors' interviews, 21 March 2012.

[93] Authors' interview, 21 March 2012.

varied considerably. While Green Room negotiations have often been harshly criticized by developing countries including those from Southeast Asia (Kwa 2003; Wilkinson 2007) owing to their seeming lack of transparency and inclusiveness, former Singaporean trade negotiator Margaret Liang gave them a more positive rating (Liang 2005: 132). For her, "considerable progress has been made with respect to informal consultations and the Green Room process in recent years. Greater care has been taken to ensure that these informal meetings are balanced, representative and accountable" (*ibid.*). She concludes that "there is no need for a major overhaul of the decision-making process in the WTO" (*ibid.*).

The lesson of the Singaporean example is clear and confirms what we have already stated in the case of Razali's election as President of the UN General Assembly: expertise, high qualification of negotiating delegations, consistency, reliability and credibility pay. This is precisely what former Singaporean Foreign Minister Jayakumar sought to convey when he praised the high standards of information among Singaporean negotiators and the country's practice of "send[ing] diplomats of high caliber to serve in our New York and Geneva missions" (Jayakumar 2011: 62). However, despite being keenly aware of the criteria for influence in international forums, Singapore could not avoid the erosion of its capital of trust, particularly among developing countries, during the Doha Round. This loss of trust was the result of an intensifying polarization along North–South lines, in which Singapore embarked on an aggressive bilateral free trade policy with developed countries, subsequently adopting the negotiation positions of the latter, including the Singapore themes (Sally and Sen 2005: 102).

Outside the UN system, Indonesia made great efforts during the 1980s to assume the presidency of the Non-Alignment Movement (NAM). While Indonesia's first candidacy in 1987 was defeated, the country succeeded in 1991 and subsequently took over the NAM presidency for the 1992–1995 period (Perwita 2007: 15). However, ASEAN played only a minor role in Indonesia's campaign for the NAM chairmanship. Malaysia, for instance, had its own designs on a leadership role in NAM and hence at best paid lip service in support of Indonesia's ambitions for the organization's presidency. Therefore, Indonesia relied more on the Organization of Islamic Cooperation (OIC) as a support base for its candidacy than it did on ASEAN, though even here it faced Malaysian competition as a leading post-colonial voice and respected advocate of the Global South (*ibid.* 48).

More specifically, Indonesia used its influence in the NAM and the OIC to avert UN resolutions against its 1976 annexation of the former Portuguese colony East Timor. Especially after the Dili massacre in November 1991, when Indonesian security forces had gunned down hundreds of unarmed protesters, the severe human rights violations committed by the Indonesian occupation forces in the territory came into the international limelight (Schwarz 1994). Western governments and transnational human rights advocacy groups subsequently markedly stepped up their pressure on Jakarta to end its repressive policies in the province.

In its capacity as NAM Chair, Indonesia also sought informal access to G7/8 meetings, claiming to represent the interests of developing countries (Smith 2000: 522). Prior to the formation of the G20 in 2008, the G8 had been the world's most powerful financial coordinating body, which over time had extended its agenda into a rapidly increasing number of policy issues (Roloff 2001; Rüland 2012b). However, at the 1993 G7 Summit in Tokyo, Indonesian President Suharto was only granted a pre-summit meeting with US President Clinton and the Japanese host, Prime Minister Miyazawa (Hook et al. 2005: 421). This was different and less accommodating treatment from that later reserved for the emerging powers of China, India, Brazil, South Africa and Mexico under the G8+5 formula (Manz 2007).[94] Thus, unsurprisingly, Indonesia greeted the formation of the G20 as an opportunity for itself and ASEAN to increase their global influence and as an act of democratizing international organizations.[95]

More recently, in an attempt to mobilize support for its global mediation activities, such as in the Iran nuclear dispute, the Iraq and the Arab-Israeli conflicts, Indonesia likewise turned to NAM and the OIC. It also prided itself on being the host as well as an "honest broker," mediating the acrimonious negotiation that resulted in the historical Bali package at the end of the WTO 9th Ministerial Conference in 2013.[96] These activities serve to give credence to Jakarta's self-styled role of an international "bridge-builder," though these activities are more part of a nationalist political agenda

[94] But also the G8+5 formula was at the time often criticized by emerging powers as discriminatory and not reflecting their growing global economic influence.

[95] *Detik News*, 15 November 2011. [96] *Jakarta Globe*, 9 December 2013.

than one of strengthening ASEAN. Indonesia's foreign policy may thus be more precisely characterized as one in search of international stature, attaching legitimacy to its aspirations for regional and global leadership roles and strengthening the domestic legitimacy of the government through a high-profile foreign policy. A secondary effect of such a policy is – at least in the view of Indonesian foreign policy stakeholders, but not those of fellow-ASEAN members – that it also positively reflects on ASEAN as a regional organization. When Indonesia's global activities succeed and ASEAN has supported them, the reasoning goes, Indonesia's international prestige will rise and ASEAN will also appear to be a valuable "multilateral utility" (Rüland 2014).

More recent successes for ASEAN are Malaysia's presidency in the Organization of Islamic Cooperation (OIC) in 2005 and, with the global financial crisis and increasing pressure on the leading industrial nations to place international financial organizations on a broader footing, Indonesia's membership in the newly formed G20. Although contrary to government rhetoric, Indonesia's role is limited in the G20; the country has co-chaired two working groups, one of them on the World Bank and international financial institutions (IFIs), and one on anti-corruption measures (Dobson 2011: 11). Indonesia's successful push for the representation of the ASEAN Chair and the ASEAN Secretary General as observers of the G20 Summits had a dual effect. It added substance to Indonesian claims to act as a responsible leader of ASEAN while at the same time strengthening the grouping's cohesion.

Yet, despite forming the Contact Group to strengthen ASEAN unity in the G20 (see Chapter 3) and lobbying for observer status for the ASEAN Chairman, Indonesia's membership in the forum is not without problems for ASEAN cohesion. Frustration over the ASEAN Charter, that many Indonesian observers regard as a diluted version of the considerably more progressive blueprint drafted by the Eminent Persons Group, and a perceived lack of deference to the country's regional leadership aspirations by fellow ASEAN members fueled a domestic debate that climaxed in demands for a "post-ASEAN foreign policy."[97] The latter called for the downgrading of ASEAN as the centerpiece of Indonesian foreign policy and the revitalization of the country's longstanding "free and active" (*bebas dan aktif*) doctrine. "Indonesia must not neglect ASEAN," writes Rizal Sukma, the main advocate for a post-ASEAN policy, "but our national interests oblige us to start thinking beyond it."[98] Sukma and other contributors to this debate thus urged the Indonesian government to strengthen bilateral relations with the BRICS states, other multilateral forums in the Asia-Pacific region and relations with forums of developing countries such as NAM and Islamic organizations such as the OIC and D8[99] at the expense of ASEAN.[100] Sukma's 2010 proposal that Jakarta spearhead the formation of an Asia-Pacific Caucus of G20

[97] See Rizal Sukma, *Jakarta Post*, 30 June 2009.

[98] See Sukma, *Jakarta Post*, 22 December 2009.

[99] The Developing Eight (D8) was formed in 1996 on the initiative of then Turkish Prime Minister Necmettin Erbakan and is a forum of eight major Islamic countries including Turkey, Iran, Pakistan, Bangladesh, Malaysia, Indonesia, Egypt and Nigeria. See Muhibat (2006).

[100] See, for instance, readers' comments on an article on ASEAN's global role in the *Jakarta Post* (26 April 2011).

comprising Indonesia, China, Japan, South Korea, the USA, Russia, India and Australia is in line with an "ASEAN-Plus" thinking.[101]

Overall, therefore, ASEAN's balance in securing leadership positions remains a mixed bag. There are cases where ASEAN has indeed acted as a quasi-bloc, but also many others where it has behaved only as a caucus. Given its limitations as an agenda-setter and opinion leader, ASEAN also exerts formal leadership more frequently than entrepreneurial leadership. Ironically, the successful election campaign for Razali Ismail as president of the UN General Assembly did not have a long-term deepening effect on ASEAN cohesion in the quest for leadership positions in international forums. Instead, it seemed to have sparked national aspirations and, by coincidence, intra-ASEAN competition for such positions. A Thai press report, for instance, critically noted that the country had "very few qualified people working in UN-related or other international organizations. In fact, most of them are working in administrative posts without any influential role in shaping policies of the day."[102] The Asian financial crisis and the dependence of the crisis-stricken countries on Western-dominated international organizations may have exacerbated such notions. Thai governments subsequently scrambled for leadership positions in global forums. The nomination process, however, was poorly coordinated, acting on the maxim that the early bird catches the worm. In other words, member governments proposed candidates unilaterally without early

[101] *Jakarta Post*, 26 March 2010. [102] *The Nation*, 7 August 1998.

and effective coordination. Other members may have had objections to these candidates, but the norms of the ASEAN Way, in which open contestation is frowned upon, do not allow for the embarrassment of the early proponent by persuading him to withdraw the envisaged candidate. Even though, as we have seen above, there have been cases of open competition between ASEAN members for leadership positions, normally the candidacy announced first eventually gets a reluctant endorsement and subsequently receives insufficient support from the association in the campaign.

That the competition for and occupation of leadership positions in international forums is less a collective regional objective than a national endeavor is also corroborated by the reaction of governments and the media. The latter usually highlight the blessings and benefits that the respective nation, not ASEAN, receive as a result of a successful election campaign. Successes are then celebrated in a self-congratulatory way; as reflecting the dignity, prestige, international image and achievements of the candidate's country or, to be more precise, its government. The Thai press, for instance, highlighted Supachai's candidacy for the post of WTO Director General as epitomizing

> the new confidence, if not the assertiveness, of Thailand, after it was badly bruised by the economic tsunami of July 1997. Through painful reforms on all fronts, the country has slowly emerged as a flag bearer of developing countries that want to do the right thing.[103]

[103] *The Nation*, 6 January 1999.

Nearly one-and-a-half decades later, not much has changed. Approvingly commenting on the candidacy of former Indonesian Trade Minister Mari Elka Pangestu, the *Jakarta Post* wrote: "It is something we all can be proud of. Indonesians taking top positions in global organizations is a testament to the progress we have made as a nation."[104] ASEAN, even if markedly contributing to the successful campaign, rarely appears in these eulogies. Surin's earlier cited praise for ASEAN following Supachai's proclamation as WTO Director General is an exception.[105] The nationalist media echo to such successes is a clear indicator that in searching for international leadership positions ASEAN is still far from consistently thinking and acting as a quasi-bloc. In many cases it behaves like a caucus. Yet it should also be noted that the ASEAN Way in most cases, but not always, was able to prevent a situation in which an ASEAN candidate would be challenged by another ASEAN candidate. One such exception was the race between the Philippines and Indonesia,[106] and subsequently between Vietnam and Indonesia, for membership of the Human Rights Council.[107] However, it may be noted that ASEAN does not stand alone in this respect. Other regional organizations such as Mercosur also faced such embarrassment, for example, when in 2005 Brazil nominated Luiz Felipe Seixas Correa as candidate for the post of WTO Director General and

[104] *Jakarta Post*, 25 February 2013. [105] *Straits Times*, 24 July 1999.
[106] *Jakarta Post*, 13 May 2011. [107] Authors' interviews, 30 July 2012.

fellow-member Uruguay challenged him by nominating its own candidate.[108]

5.2 Framing

As noted in the theoretical chapter, framing signifies a communicative strategy for attaching meaning to political phenomena. In international negotiations the strategic use of communicative frames can change the way the issue at stake is perceived and discussed. Skillful framing may ultimately enable negotiators to alter the preferences and priorities of other negotiating parties. In order to identify frames that ASEAN member countries use in international forums when speaking for the region or for themselves, we conducted a thorough content analysis of their contributions to debates in plenary sessions of the 65th, 66th and 67th United Nations General Assembly (UNGA). We also analyzed the speeches of ASEAN representatives in the UNGA's First Committee on Disarmament and International Security and those of Singaporean, Vietnamese and Indonesian diplomats, which have been documented on the websites of the respective missions in New York.[109]

Our analysis brought to the fore several general patterns of framing and frames applied by individual countries. One of these framing strategies, practiced by virtually

[108] *Washington Post*, 27 January 2005 and Danny Reinhard, "Brasiliens Rolle in Südamerika: Detached Power or Regional Dominator?", term paper, Department of Political Science, University of Freiburg, 2013, p. 11.

[109] For details on the selection of these countries and the content analysis, see the methodological section in Chapter 2.

all ASEAN members, is the celebration of national achievements related to the theme under discussion in the UNGA. Singaporean diplomats, for instance, showcased the city state's sanitary and health policies,[110] Thai representatives the country's disaster preparedness[111] and members of the Indonesian mission to the UN focused on Indonesia's successful democratic transition and improved human rights record.[112] Many more examples could be named: highlighting national achievements as best practices is a rhetorical figure ASEAN diplomats apply in virtually every speech in the UNGA. National success stories are shared with the international community, with the tacit intention of elevating the country in question to the status of a model to be emulated by others. At the same time, such showcasing enables ASEAN diplomats to portray their country as one that through the fulfillment of its international obligations behaves responsibly and acts as a good and reliable partner of the UN.

The purpose behind this framing pattern is obvious. It is part of a deliberate strategy of image-building and "soft power" generation (see also section 5.5 on "soft power") with the objective of presenting the country in question as a good global citizen. The country should be viewed by the international community as a dynamic achiever and problem solver, as an actor seriously concerned with the progress of humanity. This framing strategy is also closely aligned with the desire

[110] See UNGA, A/RES/67/291. [111] See UNGA, A/RES/67/84.

[112] Statement by Andy Rachminato, Minister Councellor, Permanent Mission of the Republic of Indonesia to the United Nations at the 67th Session of the Third Committee on Agenda Item 28: Advancement of Women.

of ASEAN countries for international recognition (Katsumata 2009), a trait we have already discussed in Chapter 3.

Interestingly, UNGA speeches of ASEAN diplomats highlight regional achievements much less frequently than national performances and usually only after showcasing the former.[113] This means that regional "soft power" building is clearly relegated to a secondary priority; ASEAN member states consider national interest and the national image much more important than portraying regional cohesion.

Coinciding with these priorities is the fact that ASEAN member countries – as shown above – quite rarely launch joint statements in the UNGA's plenary sessions. But while acting individually may be a deliberate strategy to increase ASEAN's impact on decision-making by repeating shared arguments and negotiation positions, there is little evidence that ASEAN member countries actually do so. Remarkably, when ASEAN diplomats speak in UNGA plenary sessions, they rarely refer to each other's speeches and positions. Only when one country has spoken for the entire region will other ASEAN members occasionally refer to this statement.[114] Sometimes, such as in the case of the Law of the

[113] Examples include an Indonesian speech on Global Counter-terrorism (A/RES/66/282), a Thai speech on disaster relief assistance (A/RES/66/117) and a Philippine speech on the Report of the International Atomic Energy Agency and nuclear safety (A/RES/66/7).

[114] For instance, Thailand in the joint statement made for ASEAN by Cambodia on the participation of volunteers ("White Helmets") in the activities of the United Nations in the field of humanitarian relief, rehabilitation and technical cooperation for development. See UNGA A/RES/67/84.

Sea, the interests ASEAN member countries expressed in the UNGA plenaries can even be contradictory. While Singapore with a relatively small Exclusive Economic Zone (EEZ) highlights free navigation and the safety of communication infrastructure through the need to protect underwater sea cables, Vietnam directs attention to conflicting claims in the South China Sea and Indonesia is concerned with marine biodiversity "in areas of the seabed, the ocean floor and the subsoil beyond the limits of national jurisdiction."[115] Much more often than referring to ASEAN or fellow members, ASEAN diplomats make references to positions taken up by NAM, G77, China[116] and, less frequently, OIC. ASEAN member countries' debating behavior thus ignores the fact that coordinated references to the arguments of fellow members would make ASEAN more visible as a regional entity, would heighten the grouping's international weight and reputation and therefore would make it a more sought after partner in international coalition-building.

ASEAN members' close alignment with NAM and the G77, organizations widely perceived as broad coalitions of developing countries lobbying for a more equitable international order and greater global distributive justice, cannot be separated from the dominating discourse along the dichotomies of North–South (developed-developing) and East–West, which have structured negotiations in many international forums. The use of Third-Worldist rhetoric is a

[115] See UNGA, A/RES/65/37 A.

[116] For the increasing convergence of UNGA votes between ASEAN and China, see Ferdinand (2013).

result of ASEAN's frame of thought, namely attitudes towards the existing international order that have been critical for most of the time. Yet members' discontent with the international order varied. More vocal criticism has come primarily from member states that are also activist members of NAM and the G77.[117] NAM founding member Indonesia and, under the premiership of Mahathir Mohamad (1981–2003), Malaysia, have especially often articulated their dissatisfaction with the global institutional order in Third Worldist language. The Philippines and Thailand, both joining NAM late in 1993, were more circumspect in their criticism. Sharing many positions of the economically advanced countries in international forums, Singapore usually refrained from using blunt Third-Worldist rhetoric, although as a member of NAM and the G77 it positioned itself in the camp of developing countries in the East (Desker 2001; Liang 2005: 126).

The use of the Third-Worldist rhetoric by ASEAN members fluctuated as a result of many factors. During much of the Cold War period, the communist threat emanating from Indochina and domestic insurgencies were a pivotal factor in why ASEAN's founding members avoided more radical criticism of the West and the established international order. Their economies were heavily dependent on access to Western markets, Western investment, Western technology and, with the exception of Singapore, Western development aid. In the security domain especially, ASEAN often sided

[117] Since the early 1990s, all ASEAN members are members of NAM and the G77, but especially Indonesia and Malaysia regard the two organizations as major amplifiers and lobby groups for their foreign policies.

with the West. In other policy areas, it took more autonomous positions, such as in its support for a New International Economic Order (NIEO) in the mid-1970s (Thambipillai and Saravanamuttu 1985). Yet, even then, neither ASEAN as a group nor individual member countries spearheaded this movement.

In a similar vein, even though ASEAN has taken neutralist rhetorical positions since the late 1960s, it has never promoted this position in a vociferous way. It could hardly do so, as ASEAN's neutralism only served thinly to gloss over major differences in foreign policy outlooks. While it elevated the establishment of a Zone of Peace, Freedom and Neutrality (ZOPFAN) to a key objective of its regional security agenda, the formula could not conceal markedly differing neutrality concepts. Indonesia and Malaysia sought to establish a region free from Great Power involvement, but Singapore and Thailand retain Great Power presence in the region, albeit a presence in which Great Powers would balance each other. The Singaporean and the Philippine governments regarded US military bases in the region – which ZOPFAN and TAC sought to end – as vital for their security (Hänggi 1992; Narine 2002; Narine 2008; Haacke 2003).

After the end of the Cold War, anti-Western sentiments among ASEAN members intensified and increasingly crept into their rhetoric and the framing of issues. Alienating ASEAN member states was the normative offensive of the West under the auspices of a New World Order, propagated by US President George W. Bush in 1991. The New World Order, never elaborated upon in detail, triumphantly promoted a liberal universalism based on norms such as democracy, market economy, human rights, good governance, rule of law, development orientation and disarmament. By the early 1990s, authoritarian governments irrespective of their pro-Western orientation thus came under increasing pressure, facing Western sanctions if they failed to initiate major political reforms. The majority of Southeast Asian countries, attributing their unprecedented economic growth to an illiberal strong state, countered the Western normative advances with the culturally relativist concept of Asian values (Mahbubani 1993; Mahbubani 1995). Their growing confidence, inspired by economic success and growing international reputation as "regional security manager[s]" (Haacke 2003) went hand in hand with a display of increasingly vocal Occidentalist attitudes (Buruma and Margalit 2005) that in particular targeted the EU and what, in the eyes of Southeast Asians, was its self-righteous and self-styled role of a "normative" or even "transformative power" (Manners 2002; Börzel and Risse 2009).[118]

Subsequently, these aversions also spurred tendencies to question the legitimacy of international institutions insofar as they were suspected of being normative strongholds of the West. Western attempts to give liberal ideas greater prominence in international institutions were thereby regarded as a thinly veiled neo-imperialist ploy to consolidate political dominance in the wake of newly rising powers and the economic challenges from erstwhile developing countries. Ironically, many ASEAN leaders challenged Western liberal

[118] For examples, see Mahbubani (1993; 1995; 1998; 2008).

norms such as prioritizing individualist notions of human rights over collectivist rights concepts, and pluralist democracy, although they continuously pushed for greater economic liberalism in sectors where they suspected industrialized countries of protecting their markets. And they were indeed successful in sidelining human rights, the environment and labor standards as "trade-related" issues in the General Agreement on Tariffs and Trade (GATT) and the World Trade Organization (WTO).

Although ASEAN member countries may have shared a certain degree of anti-Western sentiment in the 1990s, they never did so to the same extent. Occidentalist views[119] resonated more in the region's authoritarian and semi-authoritarian regimes than in the polities positioning themselves closer to liberal democracy. With the Asian financial crisis Asian values ceased to cement East Asian identities and to serve as an ideological rallying point against the Western Other. While the Asian financial crisis undermined Asian values as the region's normative foundation, it had an additional effect. It reinforced the discontent with the Western-dominated international order, which was seen as undemocratic, discriminating against developing countries and hence utterly unfair. International financial institutions (IFIs) came especially to be regarded as actors whose policies had caused and exacerbated the crisis. Much in accordance with the skeptical world view discussed in detail in Chapter 3, conspiracy theories flourished, giving rise to the

[119] On Occidentalism, see Buruma and Margalit (2005).

belief that in an attempt to subdue economic competitors Western countries and the IFIs they controlled waged an economic war against Asia's previously booming economies (Ba 2009: 204).

Despite the fluctuations in emphasis over time, economic prosperity has arguably been a prioritized frame that ASEAN countries have used since the organization's inception.[120] It transmits an age-honored and widespread norm in the region, bestowing legitimacy on rulers at the international level. Often couched in anti-Western and Third-Worldist language, the perception that the existing international order is unjust and imbalanced continues to shape the frames of communication ASEAN chooses in international forums such as the UN. Much of this rhetoric converges on strong appeals for the achievement of the Millennium Development Goals (MDGs) in 2015.[121] Together with their counterparts in the ASEAN Plus Three (APT) grouping, that is, China, Japan and South Korea, ASEAN member countries tabled a draft resolution for "sustained, inclusive and equitable economic growth for poverty eradication and achievement of the Millennium Development Goals (MDGs)."[122] Speaking

[120] See Bangkok Declaration.

[121] The MDGs include: (1) eradicating extreme poverty and hunger; (2) achieving universal primary education; (3) promoting gender equality and empowering women; (4) reducing child mortality rates; (5) improving maternal health; (6) combating HIV/AIDS, malaria and other diseases; (7) ensuring environmental sustainability; (8) developing a global partnership for development.

[122] See United Nations General Assembly, A/65(L.12).

on behalf of the draft initiators, the Vietnamese mission chief propagated a development agenda that was to benefit everyone equally.[123] In line with the goal of global partnership for development, equitable economic growth may be spurred by an open economy and regional cooperation, the factors behind Southeast Asia's economic success story and also those that made many East Asian economies the "key drivers" in the recovery from the global economic crisis in the second half of the 2000s.[124] Although ASEAN delegates did not directly employ the conventional Third-Worldist rhetoric as they had during the 1980s and 1990s, the message conveyed is shared by the critics of the post-war world order, namely China, G77, NAM and the OIC. Using the MDGs as a frame, the need for open markets and equitable economic growth to alleviate poverty and other socio-economic problems becomes more salient. In fact, ASEAN delegates to the UN General Assembly have persistently reiterated the MDG theme between 2010 and 2012.[125] Besides, the prosperity discourse also addresses domestic audiences. As shown in Chapter 3, prosperity of the population as a major source of political legitimacy can be traced back as far as the region's

[123] UN Webcast, 52nd plenary meeting – General Assembly, 23 November 2010, available at: www.unmultimedia.org/tv/webcast/2010/11/general-assembly-52nd-plenary-meeting-original-language.html (accessed 23 March 2014).

[124] *Ibid.*

[125] Statement by the Indonesian delegate to the United Nations General Assembly 66th Session, Official Records of the 15th Meeting held at Headquarters, New York, 19 October 2011 (A/C.2/66/SR.15).

pre-colonial empires and kingdoms. In the more recent past, authoritarian or semi-authoritarian regimes have especially stressed the restriction of individual civil and political liberties as an inevitable trade-off for economic growth perceived as a collective public good. Yet it must be noted that the rhetorical emphasis on inclusive and equitable economic growth has diverted attention from domestic problems such as corruption, human rights violations, lack of transparency, legal laxness and inequitable distribution of wealth, power and knowledge, which in many countries continue to be endemic.

Although trade protectionism in several ASEAN countries has rendered ASEAN's calls for an open and equitable trading system a rhetoric, selectively framing economic objectives in liberal terms to some extent reflects the dominance of the laissez-faire ideology that contributed to the Asian economic miracle and upon which ASEAN members' political self-confidence prior to the Asian financial crisis thrived. Open markets for developing countries, irrespective of dogged resistance from the domestic losers of free trade, also resonate well with the promotion of South–South Cooperation and seemingly liberal norms in ASEAN's official statements, such as democracy, human rights (especially that of women and children), legalized ASEAN integration, and the democratic reforms of international institutions. These normative frames serve ASEAN members' objectives of eliminating export subsidies in the developed countries, and improving transparency, equity and equality as well as increasing the voice and participation of developing countries in the international trade regime. They likewise support demands for a greater role in UN decision-making in the area of peace and security.[126]

ASEAN's developmentalist frames, however, have their limits. While strongly sympathizing with developing countries and advocating their interests as Indonesian Foreign Minister Marty M. Natalegawa did in his annual foreign policy address in 2011,[127] statements by individual member countries – including Indonesia – also made clear that they no longer wanted to be seen as on a par with these countries. In a session on MDGs and the New Partnership for Africa's Development (NePAD), Indonesian UN diplomat Hassan Kleib, speaking for ASEAN, used language that resembled the paternalistic attitude of donor countries more than that of a developing country. He criticized African countries for not doing enough to implement the MDGs, even though ASEAN's record in this arena is also mixed.[128] This may have to do with the fact that, in reality, ASEAN member countries do not want to be seen as developing countries, but rather – as mentioned in Chapter 3 – as countries successfully closing the gap to (Western) industrialized countries (Katsumata 2009; Thompson 2012: 668).

[126] Speech delivered by a Thai delegate to the 66th Session of the United Nations General Assembly, UNGA Official Records (A/C.2/66/SR.8 and A/66/PV.79).

[127] Annual Press Statement of the Foreign Minister of the Republic of Indonesia, Dr. R. M. Marty M. Natalegawa, 7 January 2011, available at: http://web.archive.org/web/20130511050015/http://www.deplu.go.id/Pages/SpeechTranscriptionDisplay.aspx?Name1=Pidato&Name2=Menteri&IDP=698&l=en (accessed 6 November 2014).

[128] UNGA A/RES/66/4.

While ASEAN members use the MDGs as a communicative frame in calling for international cooperation and a fairer international trading system, they couch their demands for a more equitable global institutional order in a democracy frame. As already noted earlier in this chapter, ASEAN argued for inclusiveness and transparency, the "revitalization" of the UN General Assembly in the areas of peace and security, more balanced relations between the Security Council and General Assembly,[129] and the full implementation of Resolution 64/301 on "The Revitalization of the Work of the General Assembly" adopted on 13 September 2010.[130] Although the resolution cannot strike down the mandate of the Security Council in maintaining international peace and security under Article 24 of the UN Charter, the revitalization of the General Assembly would allow ASEAN and other countries to exert more influence in global decision-making.[131]

Peace rhetoric is another prolific element in speeches of ASEAN diplomats in the UNGA. In fact, "peace" and "peaceful" are among the most frequently uttered words in

129 Speech delivered by the Vietnamese delegate to and on behalf of ASEAN at the 65th Session of the UNGA, Official Records A/65/PV.56, 6 December 2010.

130 *Ibid.*

131 Statement by HE Ambassador Hussein Haniff, Permanent Representative of Malaysia to the United Nations, at the Meeting of the Ad-Hoc Working Group on the Revitalization of the General Assembly, New York, 1 June 2012, www.un.int/malaysia/Recent%20Statement/66th GA.htm; statement by HE Ambassador Le Hoai Trung, Permanent Representative of Vietnam to the United Nations, on Revitalization of the General Assembly, New York, 1 December 2011, www.vietnam-un.org/en/vnun.php?id=216&cid=20 (accessed 23 March 2014).

such speeches. ASEAN member states thereby seek to portray themselves, and consequently Southeast Asia, as a region that has developed a "culture of peace" that should be extended to the global level. This peace agenda is, on the one hand, often associated with concepts such as stability and security – both also prerequisites for development – and with values such as tolerance in the face of diversity, reconciliation, interreligious dialogue and a culture of moderation on the other. References to Malaysia's call for the establishment of a Global Movement of Moderates marks one of the few instances where ASEAN member countries approvingly referred to a fellow member in the UNGA. The message, it seems, is that peaceful conflict resolution and the rejection of extremism and radicalism have become inalienable parts of ASEAN's *acquis*. Indonesia, referring to its previous experiences in domestic and regional conflicts, derives from this agenda of peace the image of a successful mediator in international politics. Interestingly, this role is framed by drawing heavily upon the organicist state ideology widely shared among conservative elites in the region and examined in Chapter 3. References of the "human family," "harmony," "harmonious co-existence" and "unity" appear quite frequently in speeches of ASEAN diplomats.

Indonesia and Malaysia often also highlight their Islamic identity in UNGA debates. Both countries are, as mentioned before, leading voices in the OIC. Islamic identity is highlighted by Indonesia's quest to mediate in conflicts in which Islamic countries or Muslims are involved, and, together with Malaysia, it takes a strident anti-Israeli posture in UNGA debates. They particularly target Israel's settlement policies, denouncing them as a "breach of international law," "intransigent" and prone to "human rights violations." Both compete in their support for a two-state solution and in calling for solidarity with Palestinians.[132] Other ASEAN countries like Vietnam and Laos[133] air similar concerns although Vietnam has also urged restraint upon Palestinians,[134] while Singapore takes a more neutral stance.[135]

A final frame to be identified is the Singaporean role concept of a small state. This is underscored by the country's membership in coalitions of small countries such as FOSS, the Global Governance Group (3G) and Small Five (S5) as well as frequent hints in speeches by Singaporean diplomats that Singapore advocates small states' interests. Indonesia, on the other hand, as illustrated by its ambition to become a permanent member in the UN Security Council, often tacitly or openly adopts the positions of an emerging power. A case in point is its rejection of the Arms Trade Treaty that it regards as discriminating against arms importers.[136] Closely associated with arms modernization is the perception in the region that Indonesia, thus far a relatively minor military power despite its size and large population, seeks to acquire attributes of coercive power for which countries with international leadership aspirations strive.[137]

[132] See UNGA, A/RES/67/84, A/RES/66/14 and A/RES/65/13.

[133] See UNGA, A/RES/67/84. [134] See UNGA, A/RES/65/13. [135] See *ibid*.

[136] See UNGA, A/RES/67/234 B.

[137] Statements in this regard abound in the Indonesian domestic foreign and security discourse. For examples, see: security expert Rizal Sukma, *Jakarta Post*, 21 March 2005; *Tempo Interaktif*, 14 March 2005, M. Alfan Alfian M. of Universitas Indonesia, *Kompas*, 24 April 2005, Jaleswari Pramodhawardan (LIPI), *Media Indonesia*, 6 October 2009; Guspiabri

Although the common draft resolution and joint statements have contributed to the perception that ASEAN member countries sometimes frame their positions as a bloc, these frames only reflect broad views and interests and seek to promote a progressive and change-oriented image of the region that, as we have seen above, seeks in reality to preserve conservative Westphalian norms. Indeed, as our content analysis of the speeches of ASEAN diplomats in the UNGA reveals, references to sovereignty norms abound. They are an inevitable rhetorical element in virtually every speech. However, the Third-World developmentalist rhetoric and frames of communication identified in this section are hardly specific to ASEAN and resemble those employed by other actors of the developing world. By contrast, the frames and rhetoric used to elevate the voice and status of ASEAN are much less pronounced than those used to promote the international standing of ASEAN's individual member countries.

5.3 Coalition-building

Like most other members of international forums, ASEAN countries also seek to strengthen their bargaining power through coalition-building. The classic case of successful coalition-building was the mobilization of support for the annual resolutions condemning the Vietnamese occupation

Sumowigeno, "Mempersoalkan Politik Luar Negeri Presiden SBY," 21 August 2010, available at: http://17-08-1945.blogspot.com/2010/08/koran-digital-guspiabri-sumowigeno.html (accessed 3 March 2011) and Christian Donny Putranto (Universitas Atma Jaya Jakarta), *Jakarta Globe*, 27 August 2010.

of Cambodia tabled in the UN General Assembly throughout the 1980s (Narine 2002; Haacke 2003). Over time, ASEAN managed consistently to increase its support between 1980 and 1989. Mobilizing support was a division of labor among ASEAN countries and also often a quid pro quo with partners. Indonesia and Malaysia, for instance, sought to reach out to NAM and OIC members, whereas Singapore, the Philippines and Thailand lobbied ASEAN's Western dialogue partners, offering in exchange support for the West's Afghanistan resolutions after invasion of the country by Soviet forces in 1979 (Snitwongse 1989; Robles Jr. 2004).

However, despite a modicum of unity and quasi-bloc behavior by ASEAN member countries in the UN General Assembly, coalition-building often follows lines that pit ASEAN members against each other. Singapore, for instance, greatly concerned by the excessive vulnerability of small states, launched the Forum of Small States (FOSS) in 1992, which it has headed ever since (Jayakumar 2011: 64). FOSS comprises states with a population of fewer than 10 million and at the time of writing counts 105 members. This number represents formidable voting power that has repeatedly been mobilized when small states run for UN positions. FOSS holds regular meetings where members discuss issues of common interest.[138]

Singapore also played a pivotal role in forming a coalition of the "landlocked" and "shelf-locked" states in the negotiations for a new law of the sea in the 1970s. This caucus, permanently chaired by Singapore and Austria, sought to

[138] *Straits Times*, 3 October 2012.

defend the interests of countries that did not benefit from the extension of maritime boundaries as demanded by large coastal states. The city state was thus adopting a position at variance with fellow ASEAN members such as Indonesia, the Philippines and Malaysia that were in favor of a marked enlargement of maritime boundaries. Yet, in the end, ASEAN maintained a modicum of solidarity: in the vote on a UNGA resolution sponsored by Singapore together with landlocked and shelf-locked states, other ASEAN members abstained despite contradictory national interests (*ibid.* 109).

More recent coalition-building in the UN focused on UN reform. Yet here too it was national interest that primarily guided ASEAN member Indonesia to join an obscure grouping known as the Leaders Network in Support of UN Reform. Indonesian President Susilo Bambang Yudhoyono became one of the fourteen members of this grouping, which was initiated by Sweden's Prime Minister Goran Persson in 2005.[139] Through the membership of this coalition, Indonesia hoped to advance its claims for a permanent Security Council seat. Thailand's Prime Minister Thaksin Shinawatra was the only other ASEAN leader who was a member of the network.[140] This was hardly accidental as Thailand often seeks to

[139] *Merdeka*, 27 October 2005; *Jakarta Post*, 13 October 2006.

[140] Members apart from Indonesia and Thailand include: Sweden, Ukraine, Nigeria, Gabon, Canada, Great Britain, Turkey, South Africa, Mexico, India, Argentina and Egypt. See Thai Press Reports, Meeting of Representatives of Leaders' Network in Support of UN Reform agreed with Thailand's proposal, 26 April 2006: www.accessmylibrary.com/article-1G1-144958330/meeting-representatives-leaders-network.html. No longer available.

match Indonesian ambitions for regional leadership. While at the time of writing the coalition seemed to have become moribund,[141] by contrast, Singapore had been instrumental in building the by now likewise defunct Small-5 (S5) group, which had launched proposals for UN reform envisaged to benefit small countries.[142]

Coalition-building is also practiced in other forums, albeit with limited success and with an ever-declining degree of regional coherence. A good example is ASEAN coalition-building in the WTO. During the Uruguay Round (1986–1994) and the ministerials immediately thereafter, ASEAN was often able to agree on joint positions. At the Singapore ministerial in 1996, for instance, ASEAN submitted a proposal on issues relating to the full implementation of the Uruguay Round agreements and difficulties arising therefrom (Wilkinson 2007: 104). However, this consensus soon began to erode. While in the years following the conclusion of the Uruguay Round Singapore increasingly came to align itself with the positions of developed countries that included the Singapore themes, others, such as Indonesia, Malaysia and the Philippines, upheld their strong opposition to them. However, much to the chagrin of many developing countries, this resistance to the so-called new WTO issues crumbled. Sources present in Green Room meetings prior to the launch of the Doha Round reported that Malaysia gave up its opposition and unexpectedly supported developed country positions on investment rules, giving rise to speculation that it had received side payments from developed countries in exchange for dropping its objections to the new round

[141] Authors' interview, 30 July 2012. [142] See also section 5.2.

(Kwa 2003: 33). While it later resumed its objections to the Singapore themes, the episode shows that national short-term gains have taken precedence over a principled negotiation position and regional cohesion.

During the Doha Round, ASEAN unity further disintegrated. The Asian financial crisis, which had a differential impact on ASEAN countries and diverging economic development perspectives and strategies contributed to the fact that ASEAN countries have increasingly been pursuing national positions. Singapore, for instance, consequently continued its liberalization course, with non-ASEAN partners where necessary, while other ASEAN governments opted for more defensive, and hence protectionist, stances. Member countries' attitudes towards the proliferating cross-regional bilateral free trade areas also varied. While Singapore was a front-runner and ardent proponent, Malaysia and Indonesia responded warily. As Razeen Sally commented years ago, ASEAN cooperation in the WTO "is all but broken down" (Sally 2004: 7) and, one may add, has never been restored to the Uruguay Round level, an increasing number of joint statements notwithstanding. Like in many other areas of ASEAN cooperation, these statements do not transcend very general positions.[143] We join Sally in concluding that "Therefore, ASEAN collectively is not important in the WTO at present" (*ibid.* 14).[144]

[143] See, for instance, the ASEAN Statement on the Occasion of the 8th WTO Ministerial Conference, Geneva 16 December 2011.

[144] A similar response came from a Western diplomat when asked about ASEAN's role in disarmament negotiations. His response: "Is there an ASEAN?" Informal authors' conversation, 11 December 2012.

A watershed for intra-ASEAN cooperation in the WTO was the Seattle ministerial in 1999. Unlike in the period prior to the Uruguay Round, ASEAN countries failed to agree on common terms for a new trade liberalization round (*ibid.* 11). With trade interests increasingly diverging, ASEAN countries subsequently joined different coalitions with non-regional partners. Singapore, for instance, was a member of the Invisibles Group, an informal group of capital-based officials coordinating trade policies with Geneva-based officials. Of its roughly twenty members the majority were developed countries and major emerging economies. Personal accounts of Singaporean officials participating in the meetings of the group suggest that they basically represented national interests rather than joint ASEAN positions (Desker 2009). Singapore was also one of the prime movers of the Friends of a New Round prior to Seattle, later to be joined by Thailand (Sally 2004: 50). Others, like Malaysia and Indonesia, supported developing country positions, demanding implementation of the Uruguay Round agreements before entering a new round.

In some cases the paradoxical situation emerged where countries were formally part of coalitions that worked for quite contradictory goals. Cases in point are Indonesia, Malaysia and the Philippines, which are members of the Cairns Group, a coalition of countries pursuing agricultural liberalization, and at the same time belong to the G33, an Indonesian-led grouping campaigning for the exemption of vital agricultural products from liberalization.[145] Moreover, while most ASEAN members active in the G15 and in the G33

[145] *Jakarta Post*, 25 August 2004 and 23 March 2007.

refuse to negotiate on the so-called Singapore themes (trade facilitation, procurement, investment rules, competition policies),[146] Singapore, as a member of the Colorado Group, was actively promoting a WTO agreement on trade facilitation (*ibid.* 22). Finally, Thailand, Indonesia, Malaysia and the Philippines are members of the G20 Plus,[147] formed prior to the WTO Ministerial of Cancun, whereas, again, Singapore is much closer to developed countries' trade positions.

Even though ASEAN coordination and harmonization of negotiation positions in the G20 appear more coherent than in other forums – on paper at least – the extent to which this interaction preceding G20 meetings enables ASEAN to act as a bloc remains unclear. Doubts prevail in this respect, given that individual ASEAN members belong to broad-based non-regional coalitions that have access to the G20 Chairs (Berensmann et al. 2011). Singapore, for instance, is the leader of the so-called Global Governance Group (3G), a coalition of twenty-eight small and middle-sized countries seeking to increase the influence of non-members on the G20 (Chowdhury 2010).

ASEAN countries have also occasionally tried to use interregional dialogue forums such as ASEM as vehicles for

146 At the Cancun Ministerial, the Malaysian Minister of International Trade and Industry categorically ruled out "to begin negotiation on any of these issues." See World Trade Organization, WT/MIN(03)/ST/30, 11 September 2003, available at: www.wto.org/english/thewto_e/minist_e/min03_e/statements_e/st30.pdf (accessed 6 February 2012).

147 Not to be mixed up with the G20 formed during the Global Financial Crisis in 2008 as a forum to coordinate financial and monetary policies.

coalition-building in global forums. In the late 1990s and early 2000s ASEAN and EU foreign ministers met prior to the UN General Assembly, but as these meetings took place irregularly it is unlikely that they markedly increased the bargaining power of either grouping. One of the topics was UN reform, a theme on which both regional organizations could not even achieve an internal consensus, much less a consensus between them. Also, early attempts to coordinate positions in the WTO under the umbrella of ASEM failed (Yeo 2003; Hänggi et al. 2006). Meanwhile, the New York consultations are no longer conducted "methodologically." If at all, they are conducted on an ad hoc and informal basis at the level of the UN delegations.[148]

5.4 Forum shopping

As elsewhere, forum shopping has also become a widely applied institutional strategy in East Asia (Rüland 2012b). In 1990 Malaysian Prime Minister Mahathir Mohamad proposed the formation of an East Asian Economic Group (EAEG) under Japanese leadership. With the new grouping he sought to balance Western and, in particular, US influence in Pacific Asia (Ravenhill 2001).[149] The proposal overlapped with APEC launched one year earlier by Australia and Japan (*ibid.* 2001), and the older Pacific Economic Cooperation Council (PECC), organizations suspected by Mahathir as strengthening

[148] Email information provided by a European diplomat, 9 August 2012.
[149] The following paragraph draws from Rüland (2012b).

extra-regional, in particular American, influence in East and Southeast Asia (Johnson 2013: 47).

Even though Mahathir's proposal turned out to be a non-starter owing to its limited support from fellow-ASEAN members, and particularly Indonesia (*ibid.*; Rüland 2002), its underlying motivations resurfaced in response to the region's adverse experiences with IFIs and Western governments during the Asian financial crisis. The fact that crisis-stricken ASEAN countries had to kowtow to the IMF for rescue packages with conditionalities that deepened rather than resolved the crisis (Dieter 1998; Rüland 2000) fueled Asian aspirations to dissociate themselves from Western-dominated IFIs. While the Japanese proposal, supported by ASEAN countries, to set up an Asian Monetary Fund (AMF) initially collapsed owing to strong US and (less-vocal) European opposition, the subsequent Miyazawa Initiative paved the way for the Chiang Mai Initiative (CMI) and, in 2008, the Chiang Mai Initiative Multilateralized (CMIM), a regional debt swap arrangement enabling Asian countries to respond to future liquidity crunches without having to resort to IFIs for assistance (Rana 2011; Katada 2011: 274; Grimes 2011: 295; Huotari 2012).[150]

Yet, once more, ASEAN countries did not display unity in their approach towards the new facility. Singapore, for instance, together with South Korea, bypassed the CMI in the wake of the global financial crisis, for whatever reasons, and turned to the US Federal Reserve for a US$30 billion liquidity swap (Rana 2011; Katada 2011: 274; Grimes 2011: 295).

[150] *Jakarta Post*, 4 April 2011.

CMI critics saw this as vindication of their claim that the facility was hardly more than a symbolic exercise.[151]

Other exercises of forum shopping orchestrated by ASEAN members primarily occurred at the regional level, giving rise to a phenomenon that elsewhere has been called "competing regionalism" (Michael 2013: 182). Among the flurry of newly formed and often short-lived fora after the Asian financial crisis are groups such as the Asian Cooperation Dialogue (ACD), the West Pacific Forum, the Bay of Bengal Initiative for Multi-Sectoral Technical and Economic Cooperation (BIMSTEC) and many other initiatives.[152] Some of these fora, such as the ACD in the case of Thailand, were also used for the purpose of mobilizing support in the UN.

An early case of forum shopping in which ASEAN was involved at the global level was the support of the developing countries initiatives in the 1970s intended to make the UN Conference on Trade and Development (UNCTAD) the major forum for the negotiation of trade agreements and to ensure a fairer distribution of economic resources between North and South. Again, however, not all countries supported this agenda, with Singapore, for instance, keeping an aloof attitude. More recently, in the 1990s, ASEAN countries quite uniformly rejected Western attempts to link trade, on the one

[151] Not all, however, agree. Rana, for instance, believes that subsequent measures such as the establishment of the ASEAN+3 Monetary Research Office (AMRO) as a surveillance mechanism in 2011 and the establishment of an Asian bond market "quickened East Asia's journey" towards an AMF, which observers expect to be launched some time between 2016 and 2020 (Rana 2011).

[152] For more examples, see Michael (2013).

hand, and social and environmental issues, on the other. As mentioned earlier, they ultimately succeeded in shifting the labor issue from the WTO to the ILO (Thurman 1996).

Another negotiation strategy must be mentioned in this context, even though – strictly speaking – it is not precisely forum shopping. ASEAN heads of state and governments in particular often hold bilateral talks in the margins of multilateral forums at the global, interregional and the wider East Asian regional levels. The UN General Assembly and the Summits of the G20, ASEM, APEC and EAS have become venues for such bilateral dialogues.[153] Yet, it is quite difficult to establish the extent to which such bilateralism strengthens or weakens ASEAN cohesion. The latter cannot be ruled out if we remember that in many multilateral fora national interests often trump regional interests among ASEAN countries.

Overall, we believe that forum shopping is a strategy that rather tends to weaken regional cohesion as it encourages member countries to "pick and choose" institutions based on short-term tactical advantages (Forman and Segaar 2006: 213). Such strategies also do not bode well for a deeper institutionalization and legalization of the international institutional order, as countries engaged in forum shopping normally show little concern for reconciling new or alternative fora

153 For the Pittsburgh, Toronto and Cannes G20 Summits, see *Jakarta Post*, 29 September 2009; 23 June 2010 and 16 November 2011; for the UN General Assembly, see 11th ASEAN-ECO Joint Ministerial Meeting, New York, 24 September 2011, available at: www.asean.org/news/asean-secretariat-news/item/the-11th-asean-eco-joint-ministerial-meeting (accessed 6 November 2014).

with the existing institutional architecture and are also hardly prepared to invest in the governance costs[154] usually associated with a deepening of institutions. In general, forum shopping seems to contribute to a trend of weakening principled multilateralism that elsewhere has been labeled "diminished multilateralism" (Rüland 2012b).

5.5 Image projection and creation of "soft power"

In Southeast Asia the appreciation of "soft power" as a resource to influence the behavior of others can be traced back to the pre-colonial kingdoms of the region (Nguitragool 2012). More recently, "soft power" has been (re-)discovered as a policy instrument by Indonesian President Yudhoyono in his quest to position his country as a credible regional leader with global ambitions.[155] The Indonesian government tries to derive "soft power" from the country's successful democratic transformation, its reconciliation of democracy, modernity and Islam and its role as a "bridge builder" and "mediator" in regional and global politics. However, it competes in this middleman role with fellow ASEAN member Singapore

[154] On the concept of governance costs, see Lake (1999).

[155] See former Foreign Minister Ali Alatas, *Jakarta Post*, 19 August 2005, current Foreign Minister Marty M. Natalegawa, *Jakarta Post*, 27 January 2010 and Indonesian President Susilo Bambang Yudhoyono in his Opening Statement at the Inaugural Session of the Bali Democracy Forum, Nusa Dua, Bali, 10 December 2008, available at: http://kemlu.go.id/Pages/SpeechTranscriptionDisplay.aspx?Name1=Pidato&Name2=Presiden&IDP=276&l=en (accessed 6 November 2014).

and – outside ASEAN – India and South Korea (Chowdhury 2010: 20; Dobson 2011: 14).

ASEAN member countries have consciously tried to accumulate "soft power" in an attempt to strengthen their influence in international organizations and forums. Part of this strategy is providing services to international organizations. Individual ASEAN countries such as Indonesia, Malaysia and, to a lesser extent, the Philippines have therefore been frequent contributors to UN peace missions. Yet Indonesian proposals to set up an ASEAN peacekeeping force have been rejected by ASEAN members, compelling Indonesia to operate the peacekeeping facility opened in December 2011 in Sentul, Bogor, on a purely national basis.[156]

Another facet of building "soft power" is the hosting of international events. Indonesia and Singapore have especially pursued this strategy. Organizing summits and international meetings is, as the *Jakarta Globe* writes, "a great opportunity for Indonesia to showcase its quality and show the world that it is a nation on the move."[157] The prototype of these conferences is the legendary Bandung Conference of Asian and African countries in 1955, often referred to as the cradle of the Non-Aligned Movement (NAM) (Ricklefs 2001; Acharya 2009). The Bandung Conference, Michael Leifer wrote many years ago, "gave Indonesia a respected place on the map of world politics" (Leifer 1983: 39). Later Jakarta hosted the Jakarta Informal Meetings (JIMs) in the search of a

[156] *Far Eastern Economic Review*, 6 May 2004, p. 19 and *Jakarta Post*, 3 January 2012.

[157] *Jakarta Globe*, 17 November 2011.

solution to the Cambodian conflict in the 1980s, as well as the Non-Alignment Summit in 1992 and the third APEC Summit in Bogor in 1994 (Haacke 2003; Narine 2008; Ba 2009). Other recent events hosted by Indonesia include the 50th anniversary conference commemorating the Bandung Conference,[158] the 2006 D8 Summit in Bali,[159] the Bali Climate Change Conference 2007 (Carrapatoso 2008)[160] and since 2008 the annual Bali Democracy Forum (BDF).[161] In 2013 Indonesia hosted the G20 Summit, the annual APEC Summit and the 9th WTO Ministerial in Bali.[162] Singapore organized the APEC Summit in 1990, the WTO Ministerial in 1996 (Reiterer 1996), the IMF/World Bank annual meeting in 2006 and the APEC Summit in 2009.[163] While Malaysia also held the APEC Summit in 1998 and the NAM Summit in 2003, Thailand hosted the 10th United Nations Conference on Trade and Development (UNCTAD X) in 2000 and APEC Summits in 1992 and 2003. The Philippines and Vietnam also organized the APEC Summits in 1996, 2000 and 2006. Many other, on first sight, minor events also elsewhere in the region could be added.

Whether image-building activities and the display of "soft power" have really strengthened ASEAN countries' negotiation positions in global forums is difficult to establish with certainty. Yet well-organized events convey to the international community aspirations of leadership and the desire to be viewed as active players in the process of global

[158] *Jakarta Post*, 24 April 2005. [159] *Jakarta Post*, 16 May 2006.
[160] *Jakarta Post*, 10 November 2007.
[161] *Jakarta Post*, 12 December 2008 and 12 December 2009.
[162] *Suara Pembaruan*, 22 December 2009; *Jakarta Post*, 21 December 2012.
[163] *Straits Times*, 24 November 2008.

governance. They may indeed generate positive publicity effects, impressing visiting dignitaries and delegates, the foreign media and opinion leaders in the academic community. The ensuing prestige spillover may enhance the region's attractiveness as a cooperation partner and – if it is able to combine the role of a good host with diplomatic skills – it may acquire the reputation of an effective deal-maker, honest broker and entrepreneurial leader (see theoretical chapter). As we have seen, this is partly the case for ASEAN, although the limited success of Indonesia's global activities must be attributed to the fact that the country still has not yet found the undisputed recognition for which it longs. However, such image-building efforts do at least have some impact on ASEAN cohesion owing to the practice of ASEAN member countries to support each other once they have expressed intentions to host major conferences and conventions.[164]

Overall, therefore, ASEAN's strategic behavior in global forums is much closer to a caucus than a bloc or quasi-bloc. This is most evident in the quest for leadership positions that is often highly competitive and where coordination and support are often more lip service than real, even though outright defections of individual countries are rare. Yet countries' behavior in the competition for leadership positions is highly power-conscious and marked by low levels of mutual trust. The same can be said for coalition-building and to a lesser extent forum shopping, where we have seen uncoordinated initiatives in the past. ASEAN's behavior

[164] Authors' interviews, 31 July 2012.

in framing very general messages and cooperation in the generation of "soft power" is closer to quasi-bloc cohesion, even though there is a tendency to reclaim said "soft power" for national purposes rather than for strengthening the regional image.

Chapter 6

Case studies

The previous chapters examined ASEAN's cohesion in international forums, mainly the United Nations (UN) and the World Trade Organization (WTO). We came to the conclusion that in all three major phases of negotiation (Chapter 4) and with regard to five major negotiation strategies, ASEAN's cohesiveness (Chapter 5) is quite in line with what we predicted at the end of Chapter 3 after studying the world views of foreign policy elites, how these cognitive dispositions shaped the grouping's repository of cooperation norms and how the latter reflected on the grouping's organizational structure. ASEAN's collective behavior in international forums is ambiguous and does not reveal stable long-term trends towards greater cohesiveness. It more resembles a caucus than a quasi-bloc, especially in tangible areas of negotiation such as norms and rules of the international order, trade and climate change, and in the application of crucial negotiation strategies such as the quest for leadership positions, coalition-building and, to a lesser extent, forum shopping.

Yet we are aware that these findings rest thus far on a rather broad and eclectic analysis. The subsequent two in-depth case studies have the function of examining the preliminary evidence derived from Chapter 5. We chose, as outlined in the methodology, two cases that are characterized by considerable variation in outcome. In the first case, the material distribution of values is up for negotiation, in the second case, a normative or ideational issue.

6.1 Case 1 ASEAN and GATT/WTO negotiations on agricultural and tropical products

Background: agriculture in the global trade regime

Although it is difficult to determine exactly when agriculture became an agenda for trade negotiation, trade in agricultural products was already part of the discussions at the time of the establishment of the General Agreement on Tariffs and Trade (GATT) in 1947. Despite an increased recognition of the problems related to agricultural products from developing countries in the 1950s, little progress had been made in reforming agricultural trade. The exclusion of agriculture was a legacy of the two world wars in the twentieth century, which enhanced the perception that agriculture was closely linked to national food security and thus deserved special treatment and protection against the vagaries of global market mechanisms. Agricultural protectionism was also a response to the fall in price of agricultural products and the shrinking agricultural sector resulting from the expansion of manufacturing in the post-war period. Trade negotiations during the first thirteen years of GATT thus dealt almost exclusively with industrial products (WTO 2000).

During the Dillon Round of trade negotiation (1960–1961), tariffs on a few agricultural products, including cotton, soya beans, canned fruits and vegetables were discussed as a response to the call of developing countries for increased access to markets in developed countries. Using "development" as a communicative frame, developing countries including ASEAN member governments argued that income from growing trade volume was urgently needed for their development. The developed countries agreed to negotiate market access for agricultural items under the rubric of "tropical products" at subsequent rounds of trade negotiation. During the Uruguay Round of trade negotiation (1986–1994), agriculture for the first time was on the negotiating table as an entire sector (Healy et al. 1998).

ASEAN and agricultural and tropical products negotiations in the Uruguay Round

In the Uruguay Round, the global recession of the early 1980s and, after recovery, the challenges of an accelerating economic globalization from the mid-1980s onward became drivers for closer trade policy coordination. ASEAN countries responded to the global spread of the free-market ideology with increasing liberalization. Indonesia and the Philippines began to abandon their inward-oriented trade strategies, while Malaysia and Thailand intensified their already outward-looking economic policies. Prior to the official launch of the Uruguay Round in Punta del Este in September 1986, ASEAN leaders identified issue areas in trade negotiations that were of particular interest to the region or that entailed opportunities for ASEAN coordination (GATT 1986b). Foremost among them were tropical products, agriculture, dispute settlement, reform of the GATT system, tariffs and non-tariff measures (ASEAN 1988). In an internal division of labor, individual ASEAN members commenced their coordination in different issue areas. While Malaysia and the Philippines worked on the coordination of tropical products, Thailand, Singapore and Indonesia were responsible for agriculture, trade rules and textiles respectively (Meepiarn 2009: 165).

Except for Singapore, whose economy had relied heavily on manufacturing and services (Huff 1994: 38), agriculture was an important economic sector for ASEAN countries, accounting for more than 20 percent of the ASEAN GDP and 55 percent of the region's labor force during the 1980s (GATT 1987a). However, the fact that tropical products were negotiated as a special sector resulted in different levels of engagement of ASEAN countries, although the two sectors were closely related. Despite a lack of definition of "tropical products," the list of tropical commodities adopted before the launch of the Uruguay Round covered many export items of ASEAN countries, including coffee, cocoa, oilseeds, vegetable oils, rice, rubber, tea, tropical fruits and tropical wood (Raghavan 1987).

As a strategy to influence the negotiation, Malaysia took the chairmanship of the tropical products negotiating group in 1987, while Thailand worked assiduously as a representative of ASEAN in the Cairns Group[1] – an issue-based

[1] The Cairns Group was formed at a meeting of agricultural exporters in Cairns, Australia on 27 August 1986. Led by Australia, the group comprised both developed and developing economies, namely Argentina, Australia, Brazil, Canada, Chile, Colombia, Hungary, Indonesia,

alliance whose objective was to push for major reforms in agricultural trade. In 1987 ASEAN tabled a joint proposal, seeking an alignment of tariffs on tropical products and elimination of non-tariff measures on tropical products for developing countries. A similar proposal was also submitted to the WTO negotiating committee on trade and development. ASEAN urged the economically advanced countries to translate into action their political commitment to increase market access for developing countries (GATT 1987b; GATT 1987c).

Within GATT, the idea of "developing countries" was associated with a sense of insecurity amidst an unfolding trade war among major economic powers and fear of economic marginalization, but the simultaneous experiences of successful cooperation in the Cambodia conflict and growing confidence in their economic prowess buoyed by high economic growth rates were the glue that bound ASEAN members together and led them to seek regional solidarity during the negotiations. They were the basis of ASEAN's quasi-bloc cohesion, particularly in tropical products, throughout the Uruguay Round. And with effective intra-regional brokers, diverse national interests notwithstanding, ASEAN member countries were more willing to compromise and speak with one voice so as to increase their bargaining leverage. An examination of the agricultural policies of each individual ASEAN member exemplifies this point.

Malaysia, New Zealand, the Philippines, Thailand and Uruguay. In 2012, Costa Rica, Guatemala and South Africa were also members of the group.

Coordinating diverging positions and coalition-building

Indonesia, although exporting a number of tropical agricultural products (coffee, cocoa, fish, palm oil, spices and tea), was concerned about food security, especially about self-sufficiency in staple products such as rice. This, along with the need to control the price of important food crops, made the freedom to pursue domestic policies and agricultural development issues of paramount concern. In the early 1990s the concept of self-sufficiency was also adopted (Gérard 2010). These factors explained the government's protectionism for the sake of food security.

For Malaysia, the government's attempt to reduce the country's dependence on exports of raw and semi-processed commodities, which accounted for more than 70 percent of foreign exchange earnings (Pura 1988: 41), led to a new focus on manufacturing and services in the early 1980s.[2] This, together with the rapid expansion of large-scale palm oil and cacao plantations, had resulted in a decline in food production. In 1985 Malaysia's imports of food products, including rice, sugar, vegetables and meat rose to slightly over RM3 billion, compared with RM2.3 billion in 1980 (Indrani 2001: 8). In order to restore food security, the Malaysian government subsequently intervened in the production and import of rice through fertilizer subsidies and rice import licensing. At the same time,

[2] In the 1980s, Malaysian Prime Minister Mahathir Mohammad launched a "heavy industries" policy, which he believed would help Malaysia catch up with Western countries in terms of economic development. See Milne and Mauzy (1999: 64–7).

Malaysia's commodity exports faced trade distortion owing to subsidies in the developed countries (e.g., USA and EC) that led to an excessive supply of vegetable oils and fats, such as soya oil, and depressed the world price of palm oil (Salih et al. 1988: 73).

The Philippine position was to some extent similar to that of Indonesia and, to a lesser extent, Malaysia. In the Philippines, a sharp decrease in irrigation investment slowed down domestic rice production in the 1980s. This, together with a drop in the price of rice in the international market, pushed the nominal protection rate (NPR) up from an average of 16 percent during 1985–1989 to 26 percent in 1990–1995 and 67 percent between 1995 and 1999 (Cororaton and Corong 2009: 10). The NPR of corn and beef also increased significantly between 1984 and 1994 (*ibid.*).

The situation was different for Thailand, which, enjoying large surpluses of rice and increasing production of other agricultural products, was less concerned about food security than other ASEAN countries. Therefore, following its entry into GATT in 1982, the Thai government liberalized its agricultural policy. In the mid-1980s it abolished export taxes and the rice premium (Gingrich 1994).[3] Export duties on rubber were significantly reduced and barriers to maize trade were also removed (Thomas and Wang 1995: 39). Other major exported items included cassava, poultry and sugar. Even though Thailand's most exported items were covered by the

[3] Despite exports of many agricultural commodities, Thailand was also an importer of some agricultural products such as soya beans and soya bean meal during the 1980s (Gingrich 1994).

list of tropical products, the country's loss in rice export caused by the adoption of the US Farm Security Act (1985) and the Common Agricultural Policy (CAP) of the EC drove it to take an active part in the negotiations on the liberalization of agriculture (Ajanant et al. 1988: 180).

In brief, although Indonesia, the Philippines and Malaysia exported agricultural products, the issues negotiated in the agricultural negotiation such as subsidies, import barriers and phytosanitary regulations were less urgent to them than they were to Thailand. Their interest rested largely on the negotiation on tropical products such as palm oil, coconut, pineapple, timber and tropical wood products, for which they sought the fastest and fullest liberalization possible (GATT 1987b).[4] And, compared to agriculture, the negotiation on tropical products was in a way less contentious because economically advanced countries were normatively bound to demonstrate their commitment to the economic development of the developing countries. The decision of Thailand, Indonesia, Malaysia and the Philippines to join the Cairns Group therefore largely reflected their desire to demonstrate ASEAN solidarity and to show support to Thailand, rather than the same economic interests in the negotiation (Mangkusuwondo et al. 1988: 50; Meepiarn 2009: 156–157). In return, they also expected Thailand and other members of the Cairns Group, particularly Australia, which possessed greater negotiating capacity, to support them on

[4] Malaysian and Indonesian palm oil, for instance, was subjected to high tariffs in Australia, Canada, South Korea and a number of the EEC countries (Salih et al. 1988: 71).

tropical products (Mangkusuwondo et al. 1988: 50; ASEAN 1989). The support of other ASEAN countries had allowed Thailand to pursue an active role in agricultural negotiation. As the representative of ASEAN in the Cairns Group, Thailand was regarded as an important player and was invited to the Green Room, although not regularly. The existence of the complementary interests in joining the Cairns Group and in coping with the new economic challenges was an important condition for ASEAN to augment its actorness during the negotiation.

It must be noted that although the four ASEAN members joined the Cairns Group, ASEAN also sought recognition as a coherent entity during the Uruguay Round. Aware of the fact that the developed countries, particularly those of the EC and the USA, still dominated the world trading system, ASEAN states saw their participation in GATT as a way to elevate their international standing, reduce their vulnerability and curtail the unilateralism of economically advanced countries.[5] Incidents that enhanced the perception of vulnerability include Washington's removal of Singapore from its Generalized System of Preferences (GSP) schemes, that benefited developing countries in the late 1980s,[6] a trade dispute between ASEAN and the Austrian government in 1992

[5] Authors' interviews, 27 May 2012.

[6] Although Singapore was the only ASEAN country that was removed from the US GSP schemes in 1989, ASEAN joined Singapore in the latter's protest (Kng et al. 1988: 154). The other three newly industrialized economies that were also removed were Hong Kong, South Korea and Taiwan.

over tropical timber[7] and the emergence of new regional and trans-regional economic cooperation schemes such as the European single market, Mercosur (1991), the North American Free Trade Agreement (NAFTA) (1993) and APEC (1989).

Given these new economic challenges, but also given the cooperative successes ASEAN had in the 1980s, academics and the media in the region also supported ASEAN coordination in the negotiations (Ariff and Tan 1988). In a December 1987 report, the *New Straits Times* stated that "The ASEAN members while small individually, command strength collectively. They must make their voice heard in the negotiations that are expected to draw up the rules of international trade for some years to come."[8] Within agricultural and tropical products negotiations, ASEAN succeeded in making its voice heard. Its participation in the Cairns Group contributed to the conclusion of the Agreement on Agriculture that, at least in principle, bound developed countries to reduce their agricultural import tariffs, quotas and export subsidies, thereby providing greater access to the markets of industrialized countries for agricultural products from developing countries.

ASEAN's collective action during the Uruguay Round, however, did not reflect the association's attempt further to develop institutional conditions that could facilitate regional cohesion or collective capacity building at the regional level. In the midst of the Uruguay negotiation, ASEAN also negotiated the ASEAN Free Trade Area (AFTA), the process that, together with GATT negotiation, contributed to the regional

[7] See Montes and Magno (1997).

[8] *New Straits Times*, 10 December 1987, p. 12.

realization of the necessity to pursue deeper cooperation and to strengthen the ASEAN Secretariat. The Singapore Declaration of 1992 laid out important steps to restructure ASEAN, including the expansion of the Secretariat and the endorsement of the Senior Economic Officials Meeting (SEOM), which was tasked with handling every aspect of ASEAN economic cooperation.[9] It also foresees collective efforts to strengthen the negotiations and "enhance ASEAN's competitive posture, and to sustain the expansion of ASEAN agricultural exports in the international markets".[10] However, no concrete measures and strategy to strengthen the negotiations were mentioned. As noted in Chapter 3, the Secretariat had neither the mandate nor the capacity to prepare a common negotiating position of ASEAN in GATT. And even though the gatherings of ASEAN trade officials in negotiation locations such as Geneva took place more often than they do today (Sally 2004) these meetings were not institutionalized as an obligatory process. The Singapore Declaration hence only slightly intensified policy consultation and coordination instead of creating institutional conditions that enhance regional cohesion and bloc-building. As a result, ASEAN members' trade policy developed in different directions, contributing to ASEAN's cohesion deficit in international trade forums in the following two decades.

Agricultural negotiation: from Uruguay to Doha

After the formation of the WTO on 1 January 1995 agriculture remained an important issue for ASEAN. Of the seven ASEAN

[9] Singapore Declaration of 1992, Singapore, 28 January 1992. [10] *Ibid.*

countries that were members of the WTO in 2001, three countries, namely Indonesia, Thailand and the Philippines, still had stakes in agriculture negotiations. Moreover, three of the four countries joining ASEAN in the 1990s, and, subsequently the WTO: Cambodia, Laos and Vietnam, also greatly depended on the agricultural sector.[11]

ASEAN members continued to seek coordination in the WTO, the organization succeeding GATT, at least during the initial stage of the Doha Round (2001 to the present). Policy coordination, however, suffered from several factors. One was the increasing frustration about the influx of agricultural imports in some countries – in particular, Indonesia and the Philippines – as a result of the implementation of the Uruguay commitments, but of perhaps even greater significance was re-emerging mutual distrust, a consequence of the Asian financial crisis (1997–1998), and deepening disagreements over the conclusion of bilateral free trade agreements with non-ASEAN partners, a development particularly spurred by Singapore and Thailand.[12] The confidence in quasi-bloc type cooperation, built up during the Uruguay Round, was used up by the beginning of the 2000s, going hand in hand with a return to the older cognitive dispositions.

Before the Third WTO Ministerial Conference held in November 1999 in Seattle, difficulties in coordinating a

[11] Myanmar was a founding member of the WTO, joining the organization before acceding to ASEAN.

[12] Initially, especially Malaysia and Indonesia articulated their dissatisfaction with the aggressive conclusion of bilateral and mini-lateral free trade agreements, arguing that they undermine AFTA and Southeast Asian regionalism.

common ASEAN position on agriculture became apparent (Sally 2004). The seven ASEAN members in the WTO could not agree over whether they should pursue a common ASEAN position in the new round of negotiation scheduled for the early 2000s and, if so, on what issues and to what extent they should do so. The Indonesian ambassador to the WTO reportedly asked the Indonesian President Abdurrahman Wahid in 1999 to withdraw Indonesia's membership in the Cairns Group – a strategic alliance of ASEAN during the Uruguay negotiations (Hidayat 2002). Calls for the Philippine government to leave the group also emerged in 2000.[13] Despite the increasingly different positions, all ASEAN members shared the general view that ASEAN should at least reiterate the need for a fairer and more stable international trading system as a means of preventing the unpredictable economic shock and crisis they had experienced in 1997–1998. The ASEAN agricultural ministers also expressed their concern over the lack of progress on agricultural policy reforms in the developed countries, particularly in reducing domestic support measures, export subsidies and discriminatory tariffs. They concluded that ASEAN countries should "intensify coordination in strategy and development of positions relative to the agriculture negotiations and the proposed launching of a new round" (ASEAN 2001a).

Before the official launch of the Doha Round, ASEAN submitted a document on "Special and Differential Treatment

[13] *Philippine Star*, 19 April 2000, available at: www.philstar.com/business/100566/solon-urges-govt-withdraw-australia-led-trade-bloc (accessed 18 March 2014).

for Developing Countries" (SDT) to the WTO's Committee on Agriculture (World Trade Organization 2000). For the upcoming negotiations, ASEAN envisaged an elimination of all forms of export subsidies, domestic support measures for developing countries and the removal of protection measures against agricultural products from the developing countries. Like in other international forums, ASEAN framed its interests and negotiation objectives in Third-World developmentalist rhetoric. This entailed persistent references to "fair trade" in order to press for greater market access for agricultural products in the economically advanced countries. In order to increase the salience of the issue, ASEAN employed the principles of non-discrimination and non-reciprocity as enshrined in Paragraph 5 of the "Enabling Clause"[14] as a frame of communication to highlight the fact that the developed and developing countries were competing in "substantially different" playing fields.

The proposal submitted by ASEAN addressed all the major concerns of the individual ASEAN countries in the WTO. It also made direct requests to the developed countries. Conflicts of interest among ASEAN members could thus be temporarily reconciled owing to the existence of the developed Others. In addition to the elimination of all forms of subsidies in the developed countries, ASEAN also stressed the need for policy autonomy in developing countries to address

[14] The "Enabling Clause" is formally known as the 1979 Decision on Differential and More Favorable Treatment, Reciprocity and Fuller Participation of Developing Countries, which provided a legal basis for the Generalized System of Preferences (Keck and Low 2004, 5).

food security. It also included issues such as greater market access for tropical agricultural products through tariff reduction and the elimination of tariff peaks and tariff escalation. Other strategies employed to strengthen its position included campaigning for the candidacy of Thailand's former Minister of Commerce Supachai Panichpakdi, who ran for the WTO Director General position (see Chapter 5), and chairing the negotiating sessions. Thailand chaired the WTO Committee on Agriculture in 2001, a critical time when discussions on the continuation of the agricultural reform process took place (Raghavan 2001). The Philippines also chaired the Committee on Sanitary and Phytosanitary Measures in 2002. Both countries are current ASEAN coordinators in agricultural negotiations.[15]

Cracks and new coalitions

Not long after the Doha Round was launched, however, the coalition of ASEAN members in agricultural negotiation started to disintegrate. Indonesia's unilateral decision not to sign the Cairns Group position statement, which called for considerable tariff reductions in 2002, was an early indication of the crumbling coalition within the Cairns Group. Pressed by concerns over the survival of local farmers and food security following the implementation of the Uruguay commitments, Indonesia demanded exemptions for special products, including rice, maize, sugar and soya from further tariff reduction commitments (Sally 2004). The Philippines also

[15] Authors' interviews, 14 December 2012.

reconsidered its membership of the Cairns Group after the latter abstained from supporting the Philippines and Thailand in a trade dispute with the EU over canned tuna (Asian Political News 2002).[16] Seeing the Cairns Group as still an important player in the agricultural negotiation, Thailand did not complain publicly about the group's lack of support. Frustrated about the situation, however, the Thai Commerce Minister went to the WTO Director General, Supachai Panitchpakdi, to ask for assistance.[17]

Shortly before the WTO ministerial meeting in Cancun in September 2003, Indonesia and the Philippines, together with thirty-one other developing countries, formed the Group of 33 (G33), whose mission was to ensure that food security, rural livelihood and rural development were taken seriously in the agricultural negotiations. The new group promoted "special and differential treatment (SDT)" through "special products (SPs) and special safeguard mechanisms (SSMs) for all developing countries." The G33's proposal was a protective policy that, like ASEAN's proposal on SDT submitted earlier in 2000, sought the much needed flexibility for

[16] Trade dispute between Thailand on the one hand and the EU on the other occurred after the EU signed the Cotonou Agreement in 2000, granting a preferential tariff to canned tuna for the African, Caribbean and Pacific states (ACP countries). The EU's zero-import tariffs for the ACP would impair Thailand's tuna export, which was subject to a tariff of 24 percent. Affected by the preferential tariffs, the Philippines joined Thailand in the dispute.

[17] *The Nation*, 24 September 2002, available at: www.nationmultimedia.com/home/Adisai-seeks-WTO-help-over-tuna-dispute-66280.html, accessed 14 March 2014.

developing countries to pursue their development objectives. The G33's position, however, deviated from ASEAN's proposal significantly. While the latter emphasized the issue of market access through the reduction and elimination of tariffs and non-tariff barriers, the G33 advanced SPs and SSMs as measures to mitigate price fluctuations and import surges that, as the results of increased market access, may threaten food security, livelihood security and rural development (Mably 2007: 8–9). Indonesia and the Philippines also joined a Group of twenty developing countries (G20), which was led by Brazil and India.[18] In order to amend its strategy following the weakening of the Cairns Group, Thailand also joined the G20[19] before the Cancun meeting (Sally 2004: 48).[20]

Despite the effort of the G20 to be a consensus seeker of the Global South,[21] the coalition was in no way a proper alliance within which ASEAN solidarity could be forged. This is because of the low number of ASEAN members within the group. Except Indonesia, the Philippines and

[18] The G20 promotes liberalization and agricultural reforms in the developed countries, with emphases on social justice and development of the developing countries (Ismail 2007: 5). It also takes into account the issues of rural development as well as food and livelihood security concerned by members of the G33.

[19] The G20 formed in the run-up to the Cancun WTO Ministerial is not identical with the G20 enlarging the G8 in the aftermath of the global financial crisis in 2008.

[20] Many developing members of the Cairns Group, including Argentina, Brazil, Indonesia, the Philippines, South Africa, Thailand and Uruguay are now members of the G20.

[21] The G20 has sought to incorporate the concerns of the developing countries and the LDCs in its proposal. See Ismail (2007).

Thailand, no other ASEAN members in the WTO joined the alliance.

ASEAN's collective action was further hampered by Singapore's position, which despite its developing identity has been close to the industrialized countries in general.[22] Indonesia became the most active in the G33 and currently works as the coordinator of the latter. Malaysia has maintained its membership in the Cairns Group, although its interest in agricultural negotiation is restricted to market access for processed tropical products (Sally 2004: 35). Besides which, the growing demand for key export items such as rubber and palm oil in the world market have also made agricultural negotiation less urgent for the country. This had allowed Malaysia to balance its position between the Cairns Group and G33, although the country was much concerned about the G33's proposed SPs (International Centre for Trade and Sustainable Development 2006). This middle ground position was also sought rhetorically to some extent by Thailand, which sometimes sided with the G33 in order to demonstrate its sympathy.[23] The primary task of the Thai negotiators in the WTO agricultural negotiation, however, was to "protect the national interests to the maximum."[24] These

[22] Authors' interviews, 10 October 2013. [23] *Ibid.*

[24] Ministry of Foreign Affairs of the Kingdom of Thailand, 28 June 2012, available at: www.mfa.go.th/main/th/world/7/19901-%E0%B8%AD%E0%B8%87%E0%B8%84%E0%B9%8C%E0%B8%81%E0%B8%B2%E0%B8%A3%E0%B8%81%E0%B8%B2%E0%B8%A3%E0%B8%84%E0%B9%89%E0%B8%B2%E0%B9%82%E0%B8%A5%E0%B8%81-%28World-Trade-Organization:-WTO%29.html (accessed 26 December 2013).

interests include overcoming the tariff and non-tariff barriers mounted against rice import in countries such as Kenya, Indonesia and the Philippines (Department of Foreign Trade 2013).[25]

Like Singapore, Thailand had been subject to other ASEAN members' persuasion to compromise her position.[26] At the 9th Ministerial Conference in December 2013, however, it became clear that Thailand was not ready to make a compromise. Together with the USA and some other members of the Cairns Group, including Pakistan and Uruguay, it rejected India's proposal on food security measures such as farm subsidies.[27] After long discussions a compromise was eventually reached. India and other developing countries, including Indonesia and the Philippines, could maintain and expand their public stockholding for food security until an agreement on a permanent solution for the issue of the public stockholding for food security purposes is concluded (World Trade Organization 2013).

[25] Thailand also joined the USA and the EU in criticizing Indonesia's import-restricting policies and practices, which hindered the importation of horticultural products, fresh fruits and vegetables from Thailand. See meetings of the WTO Council for Trade in Goods on 26 November 2012 and 25 March 2013 WTO, G/C/M/112, 5 March 2012 and G/C/M/113, 2 July 2013.

[26] Authors' interviews, 10 October 2013.

[27] *Guardian*, 6 December 2013, available at: www.theguardian.com/global-development/poverty-matters/2013/dec/06/wto-agreement-bali-helped-developing-countries-india (accessed 24 February 2014).

New ASEAN members and negotiation alliances

Entering the WTO in 2004, Cambodia is a member of the G90 and, like Myanmar and Laos,[28] participates in the group of least developed countries (LDCs). Vietnam has also remained in the group of recently acceded members (RAMs) after it joined the organization in 2007.[29] As agriculture has increasingly been a central pillar of the Vietnamese economy, the country had participated as an observer in the Cairns Group[30] prior to becoming the newest member of the group just before the WTO Ministerial Conference in December 2013.[31]

The only group in agricultural negotiation within which ASEAN has the potential to develop quasi-bloc coherence is the group of thirty Asian Developing Members (ADMs) created in March 2012. To date, the ADMs have played an important role in advancing the accession of Asian developing countries that apply for WTO membership. This is an issue in which ASEAN has been active and has shown quasi-group cohesion in order to accelerate the accession of Laos, the last ASEAN economy to enter the WTO. Outside the ADMs, however, ASEAN only exists as a loose caucus, a network of developing countries, from which other WTO members may seek support.[32] As illustrated in Table 6.1, ASEAN members

[28] In October 2012, the WTO General Council voted for Laos's membership to the organization in early 2013.

[29] RAMs' position is defensive. With less economic capability and experience, the group seeks lesser commitment in the negotiation.

[30] https://dfat.gov.au/geo/vietnam/111213-JTECC-joint-communique.html.

[31] http://cairnsgroup.org/pages/131202-communique.aspx.

[32] Authors' interviews, 14 December 2012.

Table 6.1 *ASEAN countries and their alliances in the agricultural negotiations*

Groups	*Description / Issues*	*Brunei*	*Cambodia*	*Indonesia*	*Laos*	*Malaysia*	*Myanmar*	*Philippines*	*Singapore*	*Thailand*	*Vietnam*
Asian developing members	Asian developing WTO (announced 27 March 2012)	X	X	X	X	X	X	X	X	X	X
G90	African Group + ACP + LDCs	–	X	–	X	–	X	–	–	–	–
Least-developed countries	The world's poorest countries	–	X	–	X	–	X	–	–	–	–
Recently acceded members	Countries that negotiated and joined the WTO after 1995	–	–	–	–	–	–	–	–	–	X
Cairns Group	Countries lobbying for agricultural trade liberalization	–	–	X	–	X	–	X	–	X	X

G20	Developing countries pushing for ambitious reforms of agriculture in developed countries	–	–	X	–	–	–	X	–	X	–
G33	Developing countries pressing for other developing countries to limit market opening in agriculture (known also as "Friends of special products")	–	–	X	–	–	–	X	–	–	–

Source: Authors' compilations, updated from WTO website, WTO (2013).

participate in different groups and coalitions that often compete with one another.

In brief, ASEAN's cohesion in the agricultural negotiations in the WTO has fluctuated throughout the past two decades as a result of the changing constellation of interests and changing levels of trust between ASEAN partners. While ASEAN acted as a quasi-bloc in the tropical products negotiation, a sub-forum of agricultural negotiation during the Uruguay Round, it only existed as a caucus in the agricultural negotiations as a whole in the Doha Development Round. The inclusion of Cambodia, Laos, Myanmar and Vietnam in the 1990s increased a degree of disparity, although it must be noted that the eroded cohesion comes from the disagreement among the founding members. Besides, with a high level of policy autonomy under the existing ASEAN institution (see Chapter 3), ASEAN members could practice the strategy of forum shopping, maneuvering between competing coalitions such as the Cairns Group, the G20 and the G33. As also practiced in the negotiation of trade agreements between ASEAN as a group and a dialogue partner, each individual ASEAN country also negotiates a bilateral protocol with different tariff reductions.[33] The lack of harmonization of trade policy and trade interests, which certainly requires some level of trust, has arguably been an important factor for the lack of ASEAN unity since ASEAN's inception.

ASEAN's loose and fragile cohesion was provided only by the shared "Asian" and "developing" identities, despite the high levels of development of some member

[33] Authors' interviews, 5 April 2012 and 7 April 2012.

countries. These identities were most explicit in the communicative frames they used in ASEAN statements and proposals, and their membership in the Asian Developing Members Group. However, as reflected in the recent disagreement over food security between the India-led G33[34] and net food exporters such as Pakistan and Thailand, these identities tell us little about the actual interests and preferences of the member countries. Hence although ASEAN is recognized as a group in the WTO in general, its high-profile standing in agricultural negotiation has almost ceased to exist.

6.2 Case 2 forced labor in Myanmar and ASEAN's multiple negotiation agenda

Background: Myanmar and the ILO

Established as an agency of the League of Nations in 1919, the International Labor Organization (ILO) has become increasingly popular as an instrument to push for the incorporation of human rights and labor standards in trade agreements and the WTO (Elliott 2000). As one of the most democratic international forums, employer and worker delegates enjoy independent and equal representation apart from governments.

Following the highly publicized detention of the Nobel laureate and opposition leader Aung San Suu Kyi in the early 1990s, Myanmar became a top issue in the ILO when twenty-five workers' delegates from the developed and developing

[34] At the 9th WTO Ministerial in Bali, Indonesia as the host had to play a more mediating role and had to leave leadership in the G33 to India.

countries (including Lebanon, Pakistan, France, Germany, the USA, Japan, India and Malaysia) filed a complaint to the 83rd Session of the International Labor Conference (ILC) in June 1996, accusing Myanmar of gross violation of the 1930 Forced Labor Convention (FLC) (No. 29). In 1997, the Governing Body, comprising fifty-six titular members and sixty-six deputy members,[35] set up a Commission of Inquiry to examine the observance of the FLC by Myanmar. The Commission of Inquiry reported that the violation was indeed "widespread and systematic" and urged the Myanmar government to end forced labor in the country (International Labor Organization 2000a).

Negotiations about the complaint took place as soon as forced labor in Myanmar became an international issue. As a broad political process that aims to change the behavior of ILO norm violators, in this case the military dictators in Myanmar, agenda-setters such as the EU, the USA and their supporters primarily employed "threats" such as sanctions in order to trigger change. Although the charges did not target other Southeast Asian governments, the latter were dragged into the negotiation as direct neighbors of Myanmar as well as members of ASEAN which Myanmar had joined in 1997.

What must be noted is that before Myanmar became a member of the association, ASEAN governments knew that Myanmar had been an object of international scrutiny and

[35] To date, the titular members consist of twenty-eight governments, fourteen employers and fourteen workers. The deputy members comprise twenty-eight governments, nineteen employers and nineteen workers.

pressure. After Myanmar's military junta, the State Law and Order Council, annulled the 1990 elections, which the opposition had won by a landslide, the EU had imposed "smart" sanctions, including an arms embargo, followed by the suspension of defense cooperation, all bilateral aid other than humanitarian assistance and high-level governmental visits to the country. The EU's sanction policy was confirmed by the adoption of the EU common position in October 1996. Two months before Myanmar joined ASEAN in July 1997, the Clinton government issued an Executive Order prohibiting new investments by US citizens and companies in the country (Niksch and Weiss 2008). Australia, Canada, Japan, Switzerland and the UK also imposed lesser restrictions on trade and travel (Friends of the Earth Canada 2005: 7).

In July 1997, despite the devaluation of the Thai Baht, which occurred as the early symptom of fundamental economic problems[36] and subsequently escalated into the Asian financial crisis, ASEAN member countries sensed neither the peril that would further deteriorate their international position nor potential problems associated with the admission of Myanmar into the grouping. As a Thai diplomat stated, ASEAN did not have strict criteria for granting new membership. "The only important criterion is the geographical factor."[37] With abundant natural resources, untapped economic

[36] Thailand began financial market deregulation and liberalization in the early 1990s. However, due to continuous overspending and mismanagement of massive capital inflows, the country ended up in a debt crisis and was vulnerable to speculative attacks that resulted in currency devaluation and the collapse of the Thai stock market.

[37] Authors' interviews, 21 April 2012.

potential and growing concern over China's rapidly expanding influence in Myanmar, ASEAN members welcomed Myanmar's application for full membership in August 1996, although the admission had heightened tension between the association and the EU. At the ASEAN–EU Ministerial Meeting in February 1997 the EU recommended that ASEAN negotiate an agreement with Myanmar to ensure that the latter would improve its political and human rights record prior to admission (Robles Jr. 2004: 161). The lack of compliance with the ILO Convention had also led the 87th ILC in 1999 to impose restrictions on Myanmar, including the suspension of the ILO technical cooperation – except for combating forced labor – and the exclusion from participating in a number of ILO meetings and activities. Since then Myanmar has been an issue that tainted ASEAN's international reputation and damaged relations with Western dialogue partners who sought to use ASEAN as an agent for Myanmar's democratic reform.

Negotiating policy: the ILO and UNSC

At the ILC in 2000, delegates voted to take action against Myanmar and called on its members and all the UN bodies to impose sanctions against the Burmese junta. As members of the ILO and other UN agencies, the Southeast Asian states were in principle bound to follow the ILC resolutions. For many ASEAN leaders, however, sanctions were not a plausible solution to the alleged use of forced labor by the junta of Myanmar. Besides, as members of ASEAN, they felt compelled to take action that could buy time for intra-ASEAN discussion, and to come up with a statement that would help Myanmar as well as prevent potential damage to ASEAN.

The impact of the human rights norms, as well as active participation of non-state activists in the ILO left ASEAN no chance to protect its member. The best that ASEAN states could do was to urge the ILO to postpone sanctions and plead for an adoption of measures other than sanctions.[38] As Myanmar's economy depended largely on investment from the region, individual Southeast Asian governments sought precaution against the potential accusation that they contributed to forced labor in the country. In February 2001 the Thai government issued a letter to the ILO affirming that it had taken measures in compliance with the ILC resolution and that no Thai investment in Myanmar had contributed to forced labor in the country (International Labor Organization 2001a). The governments of Malaysia, the Philippines and Singapore, along with some other ILO members, also stated that "they had no relations with Myanmar that could be taken advantage to perpetuate or extend the practice of forced or compulsory labor" (*ibid.* 6).

In addition to these statements, ASEAN governments made clear their positions towards the ILC resolutions. The Singaporean government reiterated its preference for promotional measures over sanctions, while Malaysia announced that it, along with other ASEAN members, would "urge the Myanmar authorities to implement measures that would bring an end to all practices described as forced labor by the

[38] With the exception of Thailand, all ASEAN governments attended the meeting.

Commission of Inquiry" (*ibid.*). At a special sitting concerning Myanmar's alleged violations of the FLC, a delegate from Malaysia, on behalf of the ASEAN member states of the ILO, sought to defend Myanmar, stating that he recognized the political will of the [Myanmar] Government to resolve the issue and to cooperate with the ILO through the reception of the ILO High-Level Team (HLT), which was scheduled to visit the country to assess the implementation of the measures concerning forced labor and their actual impacts in September 2001. He also noted that the Governing Body should review the measures taken under Article 33 of the ILO Constitution "with a view to removing those measures" (International Labor Organization 2001b). Cooperation should also be sought until the issue was resolved completely (*ibid.* 19, Part 3/6).

Sanctions and restrictions taken against Myanmar adversely impacted ASEAN, including upon ASEAN's credibility, and led to a slowdown of cooperation in many areas. Compelled to intervene in Myanmar's domestic affairs, ASEAN became an unofficial broker for Myanmar's domestic change and Myanmar's negotiation with the ILO. In 2000 the association sought to persuade the government of Myanmar to comply with ILO recommendations by providing technical assistance and experts, and by supporting Myanmar's invitations to the ILO technical team to visit the country (International Labor Organization 2000b; ASEAN 2001b).[39] Signs that the Myanmar government might cooperate with the ILO had resulted in the ILO's adoption of a "wait-and-see"

[39] *New York Times*, 1 August 2000.

approach (Friends of the Earth Canada 2005: 7) and other key actors' temporary suspension of sanctions.

ASEAN became an important mediator between Myanmar and the ILO in 2003. Knowing Myanmar could not actively participate in a number of ILO meetings and activities as a result of the restrictions, ASEAN sought to engage the ILO in regional initiatives. For instance, it invited the ILO to participate in the ASEAN Senior Labor Officials Meeting and Labor Ministers Meeting (ALMM) in Indonesia in May 2003. Although discussion at the meetings centered on the impact of pandemics like SARS and HIV/AIDS and possible cooperation between ASEAN and the ILO, the ILC's resolution on forced labor in Myanmar was included in the Joint Communiqué of the ALMM. Like in previous years, ASEAN ministers called for the removal of ILO measures against Myanmar. The Communiqué stated that:

> The ASEAN Labor Ministers also acknowledged the efforts made by the Myanmar Government in eradicating the practice of forced labor from the country. In particular, the Ministers noted that the Myanmar Government's willingness to cooperate with the ILO by developing a Plan of Action and continue discussions with the ILO Liaison Officer in the efforts to eliminate forced labor. The ASEAN Labor Ministers reaffirmed their support for the Government of Myanmar in their quest to comply with the ILO Core Convention 29 on Forced Labor and called upon the ILO to consider removing the measures taken against Myanmar by the ILO (International Labor Organization 2003: 6).

In addition to the ILC resolutions, the United Nations General Assembly Resolution No. 54/186 adopted in 1999 on the Situation of Human Rights in Myanmar gave the UN Secretary General a mandate to continue discussions with the Myanmar government. Then UN Secretary General Kofi Annan appointed the Malaysian diplomat Razali Ismail to the position of Special Envoy for Myanmar. Razali's efforts contributed to progress in a number of areas, including the release of Aung San Suu Kyi from detention in May 2002. The use of diplomacy, however, faced a severe setback when Aung San Suu Kyi was again detained on 30 May 2003 and Myanmar's Prime Minister Khin Nyunt and the Foreign Minister Win Aung were dismissed in 2004 by the ruling military junta now known as the State Peace and Development Council (SPDC). Razali was also barred from entering the country.[40] The failure of the UN mechanisms to bring about changes allowed ASEAN to play a greater role.

Intra-regional negotiation and international lobbying

Myanmar became a regional agenda requiring intensive regional negotiation when Thailand's then-Foreign Minister Surakiart Sathirathai proposed the idea of a roadmap to reconciliation and democracy in 2003. Instead of using ASEAN as a vehicle for rallying international support, the Thai government went its own way to lobby participants at the foreign ministers meeting of the Asia–Europe Meeting (ASEM)

[40] *Taipei Times*, 4 December 2005.

that year. The initiative was clearly intended to strengthen Thailand's international status and leadership in the region. Because of a long history of hostile relations, however, the Myanmar government did not regard Thailand to be an honest broker.[41] In August 2003 it announced its own roadmap comprising seven steps to democratic reform, including the drafting of a new constitution and the holding of free and fair elections.[42] Civil society activists criticized the roadmap for its lack of temporal precision and for omitting the release of political prisoners and dialogue for national reconciliation.[43]

Competing with Thailand for a leading position in the negotiation with Myanmar, Indonesia appointed Ali Alatas as Special Envoy for Myanmar. The military junta, however, refused to recognize Alatas as a representative of ASEAN (Wallensteen et al. 2004). Frustrated with the lack of progress, other ASEAN member governments formed a common position and made it clear that they could assist Myanmar only if the latter coordinated with ASEAN and signaled its willingness to reform, which included releasing Aung San Suu Kyi and cooperating with the ILO. Despite several promises to release the Nobel laureate and a pledge to continue its cooperation with the ILO (ASEAN 2004),[44] the lack of concrete steps towards reform led the ILO to threaten

[41] *The Nation*, 28 March 2009. [42] *Asia Times*, 4 December 2007.

[43] See statements of regional human rights NGOs and from 2005 onward the ASEAN Inter-parliamentary Myanmar Caucus (AIPMC).

[44] In March 2007, the ASEAN Secretariat and the ILO signed a cooperation agreement, which provided another mechanism to influence Myanmar in addition to the joint Action Plan signed by the Myanmar government and the ILO.

the imposition of harsher measures to end forced labor in the country. Seeking to exert more pressure, the USA also brought the political situation in Myanmar to the discussion at the UN Security Council. Washington framed the issue as "refugee flows" and "drug trade" that constituted threats to international peace and security.[45] The USA also brought up the issue at the 2006 APEC Summit in Hanoi, where President George W. Bush once more urged ASEAN leaders to persuade the junta to initiate democratic and human rights reforms.[46]

Although ASEAN members agreed in principle that they should have a common position on the issue of Myanmar, they faced practical difficulties. One problem was the diverging policy preferences among member states that resulted in the reliance on a bilateral, rather than a regional, approach. Influenced by its close ties with the USA, the Philippines explicitly stated that it would support Washington's proposed UN resolution, while other members such as Indonesia and Thailand preferred to continue with "constructive engagement," an approach pursued by ASEAN countries since Myanmar's accession to the grouping in contrast to the confrontation and sanction policy of the West. Such differences contributed to ASEAN's inability to argue

[45] United Nations Security Council, Updated Report No. 4, Myanmar, 15 December 2005, available at: www.securitycouncilreport.org/site/c.glKWLeMTIsG/b.1304015/k.247A/UPDATE_REPORT_NO_4brMYANMARBR15_DECEMBER_2005.htm (accessed 23 July 2012).

[46] United Nations Security Council, Update No. 3, Myanmar, 22 November 2006, available at: www.securitycouncilreport.org/site/c.glKWLeMTIsG/b.2263725/k.9F86/Update_No_3_br_Myanmar_br_22_November_2006.htm (accessed 23 July 2012).

convincingly with one voice in many UN debates, including that of the United Nations General Assembly in July 2006 (Jones 2008: 283).

In July 2006 Malaysian legislators organized an ASEAN Inter-parliamentary Myanmar Caucus (AIPMC), a network of parliamentarians that came into existence in November 2004 in Kuala Lumpur to push for discussion and debate on Myanmar in the Security Council.[47] At the same time, the governments of Thailand, Singapore, Malaysia and Indonesia continued to try to persuade the Myanmar junta bilaterally while avoiding policies that would jeopardize their bilateral relations. As one Indonesian diplomat stated: "One argument Indonesia used in persuading the junta was that the world has changed, and that it was necessary to adopt a certain level of democracy or risk being expelled from the international community." The military need not necessarily be a victim of democratization: "If they can adjust themselves, and become an element of democracy, they can also play a significant role."[48] Indonesia's policy of engaging Myanmar also led the country to abstain from the UN Security Council voting on a resolution against Myanmar in January 2007.[49] Together with Congo and Qatar, it engaged in forum shopping, arguing that the UN Human Rights Council was a more appropriate venue for addressing Myanmar's human rights

[47] Reuters, "South East Asian Lawmakers Call for UN Debate on Myanmar," *Epoch Times*, 22 July 2006, available at: www.theepochtimes.com/news/6-7-22/44155.html (accessed 24 July 2012).

[48] Authors' interviews, 24 April 2012.

[49] See www.un.org/News/Press/docs/2007/sc8939.doc.htm (accessed 22 March 2014).

problems than the Security Council.[50] South Africa, Russia and, in particular, China, Myanmar's most influential ally, voted against the US resolution, contending that "the situation in this country does not pose any threat to international or regional peace," and that such a view was shared by many states, including Myanmar's neighbors.[51] The division within the Security Council has thus been a factor in why the UN has not adopted a strong policy towards Myanmar.

Constructive engagement: facilitating ASEAN's policy brokerage

Compared with the Security Council, the ILO is a forum where ASEAN could play a more significant role. This can be seen from the frequent reference to "constructive engagement," a policy initiated by the former Thai Prime Minister Anand Panyarachun in 1991 to deal with the human rights problems in Myanmar through regional cooperation, and to eventually integrate Myanmar into ASEAN (Bunyanunda 2002). This idea goes against the use of legal mechanisms and punishments such as sanctions, and can thus be conceived to deflect the American and European pressures (*ibid.*). Knowing that the Myanmar government was suspicious about every action taken by other actors, including their own, ASEAN uses "constructive engagement" and other communicative frames to deal with Myanmar's distrust and suspicion.

[50] *Washington Post*, 13 January 2007. [51] *Ibid.*

As maintained by Alatas in the typical organicist language ASEAN officials often use (see also Chapter 3), Myanmar is part of the "ASEAN family," and every member of the ASEAN family has an obligation to interact with and help one another (Chalermpalanupap 2009: 8–9). Malaysian Foreign Minister Abdullah Badawi referred to ASEAN in a similar vein. According to him, ASEAN is "a community bounded in cooperation" (*ibid.*). As rhetoric and ideology, the "family" and "community" metaphors[52] serve to overcome the misgiving among ASEAN leaders. Within these frames, dialogue, cooperation and peaceful resolution were the appropriate ways to end political problems in Myanmar. If successfully promoted at the international level, constructive engagement could help to prevent the adverse impact of the imposition of punishments (such as trade sanctions) on an ASEAN country with a dismal human rights record, which would taint the international image of the association as a whole. While pushing for constructive engagement, ASEAN governments also encouraged Myanmar to keep them fully informed about the implementation of its roadmap (*ibid.* 9–18).

While some constituents such as the Italian workers' delegate criticized the approach and agreed that the issue of forced labor in Myanmar should be taken to the International Court of Justice in The Hague, most ASEAN members saw engagement through dialogue and cooperation as a more appropriate approach. Speaking on behalf of ASEAN, the Indonesian delegate urged the Myanmar government and the ILO to continue their dialogue. ASEAN's stance was

[52] For the strategic use of these metaphors, see also Rüland (2012a).

supported by a number of countries, including Belarus, China and Cuba as well as the ILO workers' delegates (International Labor Organization 2005).

The acknowledgement of ASEAN's policy of engagement is owed partly to the success of ASEAN in persuading Myanmar to become more open to cooperation with the ILO. In early 2005 Myanmar's Minister of Labor informed the ILO that his country's authorities were willing to seek a "constructive dialogue" with the ILO's High-Level Team, and that Myanmar was ready for "constructive cooperation" with the ILO based on mutual trust and interest (*ibid.* 20). More importantly, in 2006 ASEAN managed to persuade Myanmar voluntarily to give up the ASEAN chairmanship. The relinquishment, according to the Malaysian Foreign Minister Syed Hamid Albar, was an indication of Myanmar's "greatest interest on ASEAN unity," which was increasingly difficult to achieve owing to the unwillingness of Cambodia, Laos and Vietnam to intervene in Myanmar's domestic affairs.[53] Myanmar's action persuaded ILO members of ASEAN's contribution to political development in the country. The former US Secretary of State Condoleezza Rice, who was mobilizing support in Southeast Asia in 2006 in order to exert pressure on Myanmar, stated that ASEAN's policy on Myanmar had evolved significantly into one that was "more clear about the challenge that the international system faces with Burma."[54] The representative of the German government noted at the

[53] Agence France-Presse, 27 July 2005, available at: www.freerepublic.com/focus/f-news/1451258/posts (accessed 18 March 2014).

[54] *Daily Times*, 29 July 2006.

ILO special sitting that examined the compliance of Myanmar with the 1930 Forced Labor Convention in 2007 that he hoped ASEAN would support the Myanmar authorities in implementing the Supplementary Understanding agreed earlier in February 2006 after three years of negotiation (International Labor Organization 2007).[55]

Yet, despite the Understanding, the government of Myanmar's policy was far from predictable. In that year, the humanitarian situation in the country deteriorated. Small protests organized by the "88 Generation Students" in Yangon escalated into the Saffron Revolution – a clash between the Buddhist monk demonstrators and the junta's security forces in September 2007. ASEAN responded to the ruling junta's use of force by issuing a statement expressing "revulsion."[56] The military government also expelled the UN diplomat Charles Petri from the country[57] and in April 2008 arrested eight labor activists, who were also members of the oppositionist National League for Democracy (NLD).[58]

The erratic and unpredictable behavior of the Myanmar junta heightened the degree of frustration among the five ASEAN founding members. Singapore, which acted

[55] The agreement sets out a complaints mechanism within which the residents of Myanmar can submit complaints about forced labor to the ILO Liaison Officer.

[56] Reuters, 27 September 2007, available at: www.reuters.com/article/2007/09/27/idUSN27379289 (accessed 3 January 2013).

[57] *New York Times*, 2 November 2007.

[58] Agence France-Presse, 4 April 2008, available at: www.aucampaignforburma.org/announcements/myanmar-arrests-8-labour-activists (accessed 14 March 2014).

as the ASEAN chair, invited UN Special Envoy for Myanmar Ibrahim Gambari to brief at the East Asia Summit in 2007 so as to put more pressure on the Myanmar leaders. Prior to the arrival of Gambari, the Singaporean government organized what George Yeo called a "family dinner where each member is invited to speak his mind."[59] According to the *Straits Times*, "heated" discussion took place over the dinner. Myanmar's President Thein Sein, supported by Cambodia, Laos and Vietnam, firmly objected the envoy's briefing. The divide between the ASEAN Six and the CLMV marked "the end of the consensus."[60]

The disagreement prevented ASEAN from achieving a common statement. Singapore, in its capacity as the ASEAN Chairman, launched a statement on Myanmar in November 2007, announcing that the group "would respect Myanmar's wishes and make way for Myanmar to deal directly with the UN and the international community on its own."[61] ASEAN, however, was ready to play a role if Myanmar wish it to do so.[62] Regional observers interpreted the Chairman's statement, along with Singapore's and Malaysia's attempts to engage China, India, the UN and the USA, as an undeclared policy of "disengagement" between ASEAN and Myanmar (Jones 2008; Roberts 2010b).

In February 2008 the junta took a major step towards implementing its roadmap to democracy by promising to

59 *Straits Times*, 21 November 2007. 60 *Ibid.*

61 ASEAN Chairman Statement, 18–22 November, 2007, Singapore, available at: www.asean.org/news/item/asean-chairman-statement-on-myanmar (accessed 3 January 2014).

62 *Ibid.*

hold a referendum on a new Constitution and an election in 2010. Cyclone Nargis, which hit the country in May 2008, gave ASEAN and the UN another opportunity to exert more influence on the junta. Although the government initially blocked the delivery of the international aid to Myanmar, ASEAN managed to depoliticize the delivery and convince the junta to cooperate with the association and the international community. ASEAN was thus a critical mediator between the UN agencies and Myanmar (Roberts 2010a: 5). ASEAN's success owed a great deal to the cyclone disaster as well as the role of ASEAN Secretary General Surin Pitsuwan who assiduously sought contact with Myanmar's leaders, as well as with other ASEAN member governments. Singapore, the Chair of ASEAN at that time, also called for a meeting of the ASEAN Foreign Ministers to discuss the disaster in mid-May (ASEAN 2010a; ASEAN 2010b). More importantly, it was ASEAN's continuous efforts to engage Myanmar through a less confrontational policy that had made the junta less suspicious of ASEAN's assistance and eventually accept the ASEAN-led aid coordinating mechanism. The Myanmar government also agreed to participate in a Tripartite Core Group, comprising ASEAN, the government of Myanmar and the UN, for long-term recovery of the cyclone-affected areas. Other significant positive response of the junta was the inclusion of the ban on forced labor in the 2008 Constitution (Article 359) and a reiterated promise to hold a national election in 2010, the first election in twenty years, as an implementation of the roadmap.[63]

[63] *New York Times*, 27 March 2008.

ASEAN and recent negotiations

At this juncture, it became apparent that from the mid-2000s onward, and despite internal disagreements, ASEAN's function as an organization working for the interests of the Southeast Asian countries had extended to that of a member of the international community and multilateral forums such as the UN. This new role coincided with the writing of the ASEAN Charter, a document that signifies some, albeit varying, regional acceptance of previously rejected seemingly liberal principles such as democracy, protection of human rights and fundamental freedoms. The adoption of the Charter and the newly adopted liberal norms largely reflect ASEAN leaders' pragmatism in rhetorically adapting to both domestic and international ideational pressures. ASEAN member states thereby sought to protect ASEAN's international reputation and to retain their stature as relevant international players, but to what extent it complies with internationally accepted norms is context-based.

Clearly, the ASEAN states share the interests of solving credibility and cooperation problems caused by the junta's inaction and pressures from ASEAN's dialogue partners, namely the EU and the USA. That the ASEAN founding members sought to intervene in the human rights situation in Myanmar thus does not necessarily mean that ASEAN worked against the interests of one of its members. Rather, what constitutes "interest" is a matter of perception, which may change as a result of interaction and social learning. Unlike hard pressures such as public shaming and sanction, the measures other ASEAN members imposed on the Myanmar junta included attempts to alter the latter's view towards the outside world. It aimed to make the junta realize its interests such as lucrative business deals that would follow the restoration of economic and political relations between Myanmar and other countries. As an Indonesian diplomat argued, if the junta followed the path to democracy like some Indonesian generals, "they can become respectable political leaders. This would allow them to play, but with a different hat."[64] Indonesia's economic growth and leading position in Southeast Asia provided a convincing example of how changes could occur, a model Myanmar could emulate.

After Cyclone Nargis, international and regional pressures continued, particularly on the release of political prisoners. In March 2010, the Myanmar government announced a new law that barred individuals with criminal convictions, including Aung San Suu Kyi, from becoming members of a political party. Consequently, the opposition National League for Democracy (NLD) did not take part in the election, allowing the pro-junta Union Solidarity and Development Party (USDP) to gain more than 76 percent of the contested seats.[65] The UN Secretary General Ban Ki-moon warned that ASEAN's reputation could suffer if no tougher measure was taken (Witcher 2010). The Vietnamese government issued an ASEAN Chair statement emphasizing the need for the Myanmar government "to work with ASEAN and the United

[64] Authors' interviews, 24 April 2012.

[65] *Democratic Voice of Burma*, Final Election Results Announced, available at: www.dvb.no/elections/final-election-results-announced/12942 (accessed 25 July 2012).

Nations in the road to democracy."[66] The release of Aung San Suu Kyi shortly after the election signaled the junta's willingness to comply with these demands.

The EU sought to pressure Myanmar further, demanding that the junta release thousands of political prisoners. Together with other members, it tabled in the UN General Assembly the draft Resolution No. A/C.3/65/L.48/Rev.1 on the Situation of Human Rights in Myanmar, which sought a greater role for the UN Secretary General, including providing assistance to the Special Advisor and Rapporteur, and reporting to the UNGA and Human Rights Council regarding the implementation of the resolution. At the 47th meeting of the UNGA Third Committee in November 2010 Brunei, Cambodia, Laos, Malaysia, Myanmar and Vietnam voted against the resolution, while Indonesia, the Philippines, Singapore and Thailand abstained. Through majority voting, the resolution was adopted by ninety-six votes to twenty-eight, with sixty abstentions (UNGA 2011: 11).

Although ASEAN members did not have a common vote on the resolution in the UNGA, they continued coordination and negotiation elsewhere. One result of the intra-regional coordination was ASEAN's call on the international community to lift economic sanctions against Myanmar. This came in January 2011, only two months after the controversial elections. The call was the result of the negotiation between the nine ASEAN members and Myanmar, with the latter's

66 "ASEAN Chair Issues Statement on Myanmar Elections," 11 November 2010, available at: http://web.archive.org/web/20120519073000/http://www.aseansec.org/25580.htm (accessed 6 November 2014).

promise to "cease to be a problem of ASEAN in its engagement with the international community" in exchange for the ASEAN Chairmanship in 2014.[67]

At least three factors contributed to the softening of Myanmar's position. First was the friendly bilateral relation between Indonesia and Myanmar. Roberts maintained that the two countries had traditionally enjoyed some level of camaraderie. Myanmar's military forces were modeled after the Indonesian structures of *dwi-fungsi* and territoriality developed during the Suharto era. Hence, while Senior General Than Shwe refused to meet with other ASEAN leaders, he agreed to see the Indonesian President Susilo Bambang Yudhoyono (Roberts 2010b: 146). Second was the decision to transform the socialist state of Myanmar "into a modern market-oriented nation" (Chachavalpongpun 2012). This can be seen from the eagerness of the Myanmar leaders in boosting business relations with neighboring countries. In 2010 it signed an agreement with the Italian–Thai Development Public Company Limited (ITD) to develop the Dawei port project worth at least US$58 billion. Third, according to former ASEAN Secretary General Surin Pitsuwan, there existed a changing perception towards Myanmar's relations with China. "The Myanmar government no longer wants to stay under the Chinese influence. [...] Besides, Myanmar would like to catch up with ASEAN and be fully integrated in the ASEAN community" (Pitsuwan 2012: 78).

[67] "ASEAN to Push Myanmar on Democracy, Wants Sanctions Lifted," available at: www.reuters.com/article/2011/01/16/us-asean-idUSTRE70F0D320110116 (accessed 25 July 2012).

The three factors above point to the importance of a modicum of trust (such as that between Myanmar and Indonesia), power of persuasion through the use of "carrots" and closed-door diplomacy, as well as the ongoing implementation of the plans to build an ASEAN Community – all of which have contributed to the reconsideration of Myanmar's position in ASEAN as well as its relations with China. However, improved ASEAN–Myanmar relations and positive political developments over the past few years may remain fragile owing to domestic power struggles and historical antagonism. Particularly with Thailand, a long history of conflict as well as enemy and inferiority images are still prevalent.[68] As a Myanmar observer noted, his country is "a traditional enemy of Thailand's ancient Lanna and Siamese Kingdoms."[69] Besides, ethnic friction and domestic rebels have hindered the junta from nurturing economic relations with the Thais. The suspension of the construction of a power plant financed by ITD in Dawei Special Industrial Zone in early 2012 is a case in point. It may be a result of public protests over social and environmental impacts, in combination with the government's concern over the potential attack on the plant by the Karen National Liberation Army (KNLA).[70]

[68] *Irrawaddy*, June 2001, available at: www2.irrawaddy.org/article.php?art_id=2276 (accessed 24 December 2013). See also Chachavalpongpun (2005).

[69] *Irrawaddy*, 24 July 2012, available at: www.irrawaddy.org/commentary/love-thy-neighbor-thai-burmese-relations.html (accessed 24 December 2013).

[70] *Asian Correspondent*, 10 January 2012, available at: http://asiancorrespondent.com/73450/power-plants-dams-and-mind-games-in-burma/ (accessed 24 December 2013).

The need to ensure domestic security made ASEAN's cooperation norms that prioritize national autonomy and non-intervention an indispensable element in ASEAN's intramural negotiation. As President Thein Sein maintained, Myanmar still needs all the necessary measures to defend its "national interests and sovereignty," despite reforms.[71] Thein Sein's concerns were well understood by other ASEAN governments. After various rounds of high-level discussions, ASEAN agreed in November 2011 that Myanmar would be the Chair of the group in 2014.[72] Affirming the ASEAN Way, Indonesian Foreign Minister Marty M. Natalegawa noted that ASEAN's decision was "not a vote of confidence" but a way to engage with Myanmar and encourage it to live up to international expectations.[73] Assured that its desire to chair ASEAN would be honored, the Myanmar government announced in December 2011 that the by-elections for forty-eight seats (forty in the Lower House, six in the Upper House and two in the regional/state assemblies) had been scheduled for 1 April 2012 (Kuppuswamy 2012). After the by-elections, in which the NLD won a landslide victory and Aung San Suu Kyi a seat, ASEAN immediately sought talks with the EU, the USA and ILO to lift sanctions and harsh measures against the former rogue state.[74]

[71] Reuters, "Myanmar President Thein Sein Supports Changing Constitution, Making Suu Kyi Eligible to Lead," 3 January 2014, available at: www.abc.net.au/news/2014-01-02/an-myanmar-constitution/5182916 (accessed 25 February 2014).

[72] *Jakarta Post*, 18 November 2011. [73] *Asia Times*, 18 May 2012.

[74] *Al Jazeera*, 4 April 2012.

Because of Myanmar's "remarkable transformation that is under way," the EU, which was concurrently negotiating bilateral FTAs with ASEAN states, announced on 23 April 2012 that it would suspend a range of trade, economic and individual sanctions on the country for one year.[75] A year later the sanctions were lifted, although the arms embargo remained effective.[76] In May 2012 the Obama administration followed the EU, allowing US investment in Myanmar.[77] ASEAN officials, mostly at the expert level, work assiduously to canvas support for Myanmar from ILO members.[78] At the 101st ILC in June 2012 the representative of Vietnam, on behalf of ASEAN, urged Western countries to lift trade restrictions and other sanctions on Myanmar. Expressing appreciation for Myanmar's cooperation with the ILO, he noted that ASEAN, as well as the UN Secretary General, recognized positive developments in the country, which included the President of Myanmar's commitment to eliminate all forms of forced labor. ASEAN thus "called upon the ILO to reciprocate Myanmar's genuine efforts, tangible achievements and continued political will in eliminating forced labor by reviewing the resolution adopted [. . .] in 1999 and 2000" (International Labor Organization 2012a: 7–8). Referring to the ASEAN statement, the Myanmar Ambassador stressed that his government had complied sufficiently with the recommendations

[75] "Myanmar: ASEAN-EU Meeting Marks New Chapter," available at: www.siiaonline.org/?q=programmes/insights/myanmar-asean-eu-meeting-marks-new-chapter (accessed 25 July 2012).

[76] Reuters, 22 April 2013, available at: www.reuters.com/article/2013/04/22/us-myanmar-eu-idUSBRE93L11G20130422 (accessed 14 March 2014).

[77] *ABC News*, 19 May 2012. [78] Authors' interviews, 14 December 2012.

of the ILO Commission of Inquiry (International Labor Organization 2012b). He also added that his government aimed completely to eradicate forced labor by 2015 (Ministry of Labour 2012). The ILC eventually decided to suspend many restrictions imposed in 1999 and 2000, allowing Myanmar to restore its relations with many international organizations and trading activities. In November 2013 the Myanmar government signed an agreement with the ILO to conduct the first comprehensive national labor force survey (LFS) since 1990.[79] In the following month, it ratified the ILO Worst Forms of Child Labor Convention.[80]

In sum, over the past two decades ASEAN members were compelled to find a common solution to the organization's eroding credibility and international pressures caused by Myanmar's human rights violations. ASEAN has faced a number of difficulties in establishing cohesion in dealing with the Myanmar issue. These difficulties arose mostly from the diverging positions towards human rights violations between the old and the new members. Despite disagreements as reflected in the Gambari briefing and attempts by Singapore and Malaysia to engage other actors, ASEAN acted more as a quasi-bloc than a caucus after Cyclone Nargis, mediating between Myanmar on the one hand and the international

79 "ILO, Myanmar Sign Agreement on National Labour Force Survey," 14 November 2013, available at: www.ilo.org/global/about-the-ilo/activities/all/WCMS_229675/lang–en/index.htm (accessed 25 February 2014).

80 "Myanmar Ratifies the Worst Forms of Child Labour Convention," 19 December 2013, available at: www.ilo.org/global/standards/information-resources-and-publications/news/WCMS_233060/lang–en/index.htm (accessed 25 February 2014).

community on the other. Important conditions for the increased cohesion included the Myanmar leaders' changing perception of the region and attempts to reposition the country in the international world. These were possible partly because of the cordial relations between Myanmar and Indonesia as well as the genuine attempt to integrate Myanmar into ASEAN for economic reasons.

Cultivation of "trust" and cooperation between Myanmar and the other nine member states was the issue of common interest that underpinned ASEAN's position at the international level. ASEAN has sought trust by promoting the sense of belonging through rhetoric such as the "ASEAN family" and "ASEAN community." Although the idea of community and the associated economic opportunities might have contributed to the Myanmar government's reconsideration of its engagement in the ASEAN region, domestic conflicts and history of inter-state wars have impeded full-fledged cooperation with the neighboring countries. Moreover, as also the case in the previous two chapters, ASEAN did not have a policy of bowling together, but left a large degree of flexibility to its members when it came to voting in the UNGA. Despite the different preferences demonstrated in the voting record for the 2010 resolution on the situation of human rights in Myanmar, the association was most consistent and cohesive in rhetorically promoting the policy of constructive engagement in international forums, while occasionally practicing undeclared disengagement.

Chapter 7

Conclusions and future options

Examining ASEAN's behavior in international forums from different angles leads us to the question of what we can conclude in general terms for regional organizations of the Global South and in more specific terms for ASEAN? At a theoretical level we have added a new explanatory approach to the literature on international negotiations, which has thus far been strongly dominated by neo-functionalist and rational choice approaches. In a constructivist reinterpretation of the neo-functionalist externalization thesis, we argued that more than material institutional factors such as functional specificity, heterogeneity and centralization, it is cognitive factors such as the world views – shaped by historical experiences – of decision-makers that have a major bearing on the cohesiveness of regional organizations. The more these cognitive factors are entrenched in the collective memory of a region's elites the more they tend to impact on the normative underpinnings of a regional organization and the latter's organizational structure. The more new experiences reproduce these historical experiences the more they strengthen ideational path dependencies, thereby externalizing the regional organization's intra-regional ideational dispositions regarding interactions with third states and in international organizations.

Even though we have to be careful in drawing far-reaching generalizations from a single case study, our examination of ASEAN's behavior and cohesion in international organizations has brought to the fore more considerable evidence for our theoretical argument. These insights are mainly based on diachronic in-case comparisons. We can, most importantly, marshal abundant evidence that the world views determining the behavior of foreign policy elites in ASEAN member countries have not changed much over time. They may have temporarily fluctuated somewhat depending on contextual conditions, but overall they have remained the same. Power sensitivity, lingering distrust of partners and fear of Great Powers inside and outside the wider East Asian perimeter continue to fuel a proclivity for sovereignty-based cooperation norms. As a result, the national interest still dominates the behavior of member states towards each other as well as towards third parties. Such skeptical world views inevitably have a negative impact on regional cohesion; they have indeed – despite the enactment of the ASEAN Charter – thus far prevented a substantive deepening of regional integration in Southeast Asia. The deeply internalized historical legacies of conquest, threats, violence and power politics have been persistently reproduced even after the formation of ASEAN and during much of the period under investigation in this study. Analysts often highlight the fact that ASEAN member countries have never been at war with each other after accession to the grouping (Kivimäki 2008), that the association has become a major regional security manager (Haacke 2006: 130) and that welfare levels in the region have risen tremendously over the preceding decades. These are certainly valid observations and stand for the successes of ASEAN. Yet they have been overshadowed by less felicitous experiences. The exigencies of the Cold War, deep global socioeconomic inequalities, power asymmetries in international organizations in the region itself, the Indochina wars, the Asian financial crisis, armed border disputes before and after accession to ASEAN such as between Thailand and Laos (1984 and 1987) and Thailand and Myanmar throughout much of the 1980s and 1990s, the military clashes between Thailand and Cambodia over territory surrounding the Preah Vihear temple and the war between Vietnam and China in 1979, the genocide under the Khmer Rouge in Cambodia, disputes over resource-rich maritime territories between Malaysia and Indonesia and the conflict over EEZs in the South China Sea, the unresolved Philippine claim on Sabah and the tense relations between Malaysia and Singapore have all kept highly skeptical pre-existing perceptions of the external world very much alive. Governments thus saw the best way of coping with such seemingly adverse circumstances as fostering national resilience and relying on a highly pragmatic and flexible foreign policy in which defection from regional solidarity is a frequent occurrence where it serves vital short- and long-term national interests.

Also reproducing mutual distrust and thereby undermining regional cohesion are the increasing leadership ambitions of individual countries based on a surge of neo-nationalist populism in domestic politics (Desker 2009; Rüland 2009). With its democratization and successful economic recovery after the disastrous Asian financial crisis, Indonesia in particular has formulated leadership claims with increasing assertiveness since the mid-2000s.[1] It has

[1] On the relationship between democratization and nationalist populism, see Snyder (2000).

repeatedly demanded a permanent seat in the UN Security Council and it expresses its self-styled regional and even global leadership role through its membership of the G20. Indonesian leadership claims are not new to the region but what makes them even less palatable than before for many fellow members is the fact that they no longer merely rest on physical attributes such as population and size, but increasingly on a normative rationale. By emphasizing democracy and human rights as key values underpinning its foreign policy, Indonesia has elevated itself to a moral high ground and by portraying itself as a model for the region, it tacitly promotes a self-image based on exceptionalism (Rüland 2014). Most other ASEAN members resent these hegemonic aspirations, even though the Indonesian leadership seeks to project the image of a benign regional leader.[2] Yet these aspirations revitalize existing distrust and provoke resistance against such seemingly dominant behavior. The lowest common denominator of the ASEAN Charter – on the one hand, retaining the sovereignty-based core values of the ASEAN Way and, on the other, complementing it in an uneasy coexistence with the democracy and human rights norms Indonesia in particular championed – is a reflection of these tensions and a recipe for non-cohesive collective behavior. Seeming lack of deference by fellow ASEAN members and the ignoring of its leadership ambitions in turn deepen Indonesian sentiments of frustrated entitlement[3] and also facilitate a strongly national

[2] For different types of regional hegemons, see Prys (2010).

[3] An attitude already observed decades ago by Leifer in his study on Indonesian foreign policy elites (Leifer 1983: 365).

interest-driven foreign policy, as demanded by Rizal Sukma in his plea for a post-ASEAN foreign policy.[4] Conflicting leadership claims, often pursued in search of international recognition, but possibly at the expense of fellow ASEAN members, have repeatedly jeopardized ASEAN unity: cases in point are Indonesian and Malaysian rivalries for leadership in the OIC and NAM, between Thailand and Indonesia in the Cambodian conflict in the 1980s or between Indonesia and Singapore for the intellectual leadership in ASEAN.

Neo-functionalist theories and other variants of rationalist scholarship have tended to regard heterogeneity as an obstacle for regional cohesion. Enlargements such as that of ASEAN in the 1990s may then be a process of increasing regional heterogeneity. Yet the study seems to confirm our earlier argument that enlargement per se may not necessarily contribute to greater heterogeneity of a regional organization. It only becomes an obstacle for regional cohesion if prior relationships with the accession countries are burdened with negative historical legacies and reminiscences of past hostilities. In contrast to the assumption of neo-functionalist and rational choice approaches, heterogeneity of a regional organization is not merely an issue of the number of its members. What counts much more are the perceptions and cognitive dispositions of members that may or may not add new cleavages to the organization.

Empirical evidence that heterogeneity is not necessarily a numerical question is provided by our in-depth case study on agricultural negotiations in the WTO. At first sight

[4] See Rizal Sukma, *Jakarta Post*, 30 June 2009.

it seems to support neofunctional and rationalist arguments, as ASEAN did indeed act quite cohesively as ASEAN-5[5] during the GATT's Uruguay Round in the 1980s and the first half of the 1990s. Cohesion then increasingly declined and eventually collapsed after ASEAN's enlargement in the second half of the 1990s and throughout the 2000s. However, our case study suggests that this decline in cohesion has little to do with enlargement and growing heterogeneity as the new ASEAN members (except Myanmar) were not WTO members at the time of their accession. And even after joining the WTO, our analysis shows that disagreements deepened between the ASEAN-5, not between the ASEAN-5 and the new members. It was the lack of harmonization of trade interests of ASEAN's core members which, in the wake of new distrust sown by the Asian financial crisis and the aggressive policy of setting up bilateral and minilateral free trade agreements with partners outside the region, that eroded regional cohesion in the WTO, driving the core members to join very different coalitions in the negotiation process.

Additionally, the second case study examining the negotiations on forced labor in the ILO does not lend support to neo-functionalist and rationalist explanations of regional cohesion in international forums. In this case ASEAN maintained a modicum of unity despite the fact that after the issue was brought up in the ILO the association was in the process of expansion from six to ten members, and hence seemingly increasing in terms of heterogeneity. The new members were less democratic than the ASEAN-5, some still adhered to a

[5] Brunei Darussalam became a member of the WTO in 1995.

socialist economic system and they also differed markedly from the older ASEAN members in terms of development. But the issue confirmed another lesson that tallies well with ASEAN's engagement in the Cambodian crisis of the 1980s: ASEAN develops unity precisely when key concerns and the image of the region as a whole are at stake. Myanmar's pariah status threatened to deeply embarrass all ASEAN members in the same way and, hence, also to markedly weaken their political leverages in international forums.

In the UN there is also no decline of unity after ASEAN enlargement. Overall, ASEAN-10 even displayed a slightly more cohesive voting behavior than ASEAN-6 (Burmester and Jankowski 2013: 9). ASEAN was also not less cohesive in campaigns for leadership positions. It succeeded in capturing the UNGA presidency as ASEAN-5 in 1971 and repeated this success as ASEAN-7 in 1998. Shortly thereafter it also successfully supported the campaign of the ASEAN candidate for the post of WTO Director General. ASEAN's record was less impressive thereafter, but it did also succeed in placing Supachai Panichpakdi at the head of the UNCTAD in the mid-2000s. In cases where ASEAN was less successful, such as, for instance, in Surakiart Sathirathai's bid for the post of UN Secretary General, there was no open competition within ASEAN, but tensions, disagreements and mutual distrust resulted in (at best) lackluster support of the campaign from fellow members and a persistent fear on the part of the candidate of being double-crossed by partners through the nomination of a candidate of their own.

As regards functional specificity, the picture we encountered in our empirical analysis was rather ambiguous.

ASEAN member countries' interests did indeed differ across functional domains, but over time they also differed markedly within them (such as in the WTO or in climate change negotiations) to such a degree that cohesion in international organizations remained rather low. Moreover, we also found that, despite increasing functional breadth, voting behavior in the UN became slightly more cohesive over time, even though it differed across policy fields.

ASEAN's level of centralization increased only slightly over the years: with the envisaged creation of a single market and an ASEAN Economic Community by 2015 perhaps most strongly in the sphere of economic cooperation. Yet, as we have seen, this development did not have a unifying impact on the grouping in WTO negotiations. According to our interviews, the number of joint statements in the WTO (and also in the UN) has increased markedly in recent years; but many of these statements were of a declaratory nature and of little consequence for the commitment of ASEAN's member states. They did not substantively change ASEAN members' behavior in decision-making and coalition-building.

Pending more in-depth case studies of specific negotiation processes, our empirical analysis also suggests that ASEAN acts more as a caucus than as a bloc or quasi-bloc in international forums. As we have shown in our theoretical section, these types of cohesion are also strongly guided by the world views of the member countries' foreign policy elites. Caucus-type behavior predominates in crucial negotiation stages, such as in processes of agenda-setting, norm entrepreneurship and decision-making, as well as in significant global issues such as UN reform, trade liberalization and climate change, whereas we found quasi-bloc behavior mainly in less significant issues. Caucus-type behavior also prevails in the application of key negotiation strategies such as occupying leadership positions in international forums, coalition-building and, to a lesser extent, forum shopping. Only in negotiation strategies such as the framing of positions and image and "soft power" building activities does ASEAN approach the form of a quasi-bloc.

7.1 Strengthening cohesiveness, but how?

Even though we have not been able to provide empirical evidence for other regional organizations of the Global South, we believe that they behave similarly in international organizations. Many other world regions look back on a similarly turbulent history and a continuity of power asymmetries, neocolonial domination by Great Powers, external interferences into their region, violence, regular economic crises; in short frequently repeating experiences of vulnerability and victimization. This gives rise to a similarly skeptical world view, including a lingering distrust towards fellow members and a penchant for heavily prioritizing the national interest over common regional interests, as we have found among foreign policy stakeholders in ASEAN. Yet such propositions must be tested through empirical studies. Still, the question remains what must happen for regional organizations of the Global South to become more cohesive actors in international forums.

If our theoretical assumptions in this study are correct, then the strengthening of regional cohesion is basically a factor of changing perceptions of the external world and of the way international politics is seen to be operating. Such behavioral change can be the product of severe external shocks and critical junctures such as the Second World War in Europe. The latter facilitated a far-reaching change of mind among foreign policymakers who realized the devastating effects of extreme forms of nationalism and hence promoted the idea that deep regional integration promotes peace and markedly strengthens individual members of the EU. Only if such cognitive changes have taken place can we expect a new assessment of opportunity structures associated with regional cooperation. But such cognitive changes may also occur incrementally as a result of an increasing number of positive experiences in regional and global politics. Under such circumstances it is perceptible that foreign policy elites regard the regional and global environment more than hitherto as a factor enabling cooperation. Our in-depth case study on agricultural negotiations in the WTO, which in a conducive political and economic environment exhibited temporary cohesion, corroborates such a proposition.

Temporary changes in the region's external political environment are pivotal. While economic globalization of the 1980s and 1990s seemed to have created new threats and challenges, they did not markedly enhance ASEAN sentiments of insecurity and vulnerability. In fact, ASEAN countries were quite well prepared to meet them. At the time, ASEAN member countries had experienced unprecedented, sometimes double-digit, economic growth rates and had become preferred destinations for foreign investments. Economically, they increasingly appeared to be winners of globalization,[6] giving rise to highly optimistic outlooks such as the rise of a Pacific Century with gravitational shifts in global economic and political power. Moreover, with the end of the Cold War, major security threats such as the communist expansion had subsided. The optimism that after the end of the Cold War a global peace dividend with a strengthening of multilateral institutions would be imminent was also shared by many in Southeast Asia.[7] The reduced uncertainties thus seemed to increase the trust of ASEAN states in the external world. Such notions also seemed to reflect the positive experiences in security cooperation that crystallized in the search for a solution to the Cambodia problem in the 1980s. Thus, overall, there was less reason than before to refer to established power-sensitive patterns of behavior vis-à-vis the external world that had previously led to non-cohesive negotiation behavior.

To have long-term effects on ASEAN's cohesion in international organizations, such experiences must repeat themselves over a long time in order to overshadow the more skeptical world views persistently reproduced through the overwhelming impact of negative experiences in the past. This, however, did not happen in ASEAN's case. Ten years later, in the second half of the 1990s, these enabling conditions for closer regional cooperation no longer existed. With the conceptually ill-prepared enlargement of ASEAN from the

[6] Also, Southeast Asians regarded themselves initially as beneficiaries of globalization, at least until the Asian financial crisis of 1997/1998. See press commentary, *Jakarta Post*, 15 November 1999.

[7] See, for instance, Alatas (2001: 583).

mid-1990s onward, ASEAN also imported additional historical legacies of enmity and distrust, making it more cumbersome and more costly to coordinate ASEAN positions at the regional level as well as in the global arena. Perhaps even more importantly, by then post-Cold War hopes for a peace dividend had waned. The expectations of a greater institutionalization, legalization, contractualization and constitutionalization of international politics were increasingly suspected in the non-Western world of being a normative offensive by the West, and the USA in particular, with the objective of preserving its dominance in global forums against challenges associated with the rise of new power centers in the non-Western world.

A watershed for ASEAN cohesion was the Asian financial crisis, which painfully reminded the region that, irrespective of their breath-taking economic growth in preceding decades, ASEAN countries were still highly dependent on international organizations dominated by the West. Rather than uniting in order to negotiate more favorable rescue packages with the IMF, crisis-stricken countries such as Thailand and Indonesia negotiated bail out schemes individually. The traumatic experience of the Asian financial crisis corroborated and reproduced the skepticism of ASEAN foreign policy elites towards a seemingly hostile external world and re-emphasized the region's vulnerability. Conspiracy theories of an economic war launched by the Western industrialized countries against unwelcome competitors pervaded the public discourse in the region (Ba 2009: 204). For some years, at least, revitalized sentiments of insecurity, vulnerability and victimization have prompted beggar-thy-neighbor policies and facilitated the resurfacing of enmities deeply inculcated in collective memories (Rüland 2000). These suspicions were only superficially glossed over by strategies of damage control and the launching of new cooperative projects inside and outside the region. These moves climaxed with the Bali Concord II of 2003 and the enactment of the ASEAN Charter in 2008. However, below the surface of the ASEAN Charter quite substantial disagreements over cooperation norms and notions of sovereignty among member countries continue to linger.

7.2 Reforming ASEAN

We do not believe that substantial changes in ASEAN's cohesion in international organizations can be brought about quickly and easily without major changes in the world view of foreign policy stakeholders. The future generation of foreign policy elites, however, is perhaps a source for qualified optimism. Even though the majority of international relations students surveyed by Nguitragool in Indonesia adhere to world views guided by political realism, there was also a substantial percentage of students (31 percent) that favored a liberal theoretical outlook on international relations (Nguitragool 2013: 10). Yet, we should not overestimate such perceptions as they may be thrown overboard when these students come of age, becoming decision-makers themselves, and when they are confronted with similarly adverse experiences and circumstances to those of their predecessors. Moreover, the survey results only cover Indonesia, where, under the impact of democratization, a more open foreign policy discourse is taking place that also exposes foreign policy stakeholders to novel ideas from outside the country. Such conditions do not prevail in the majority of ASEAN member countries. Authoritarian governments especially perceive themselves confronted with a highly insecure external environment, but, in addition, their hallmark is a deep fear of domestic challenges. Hence, for them, the uncompromising pursuit of the national interest in the international arena is a major element of legitimization. Very often domestic opposition rallies around international issues such as trade – if it is perceived to be jeopardizing the welfare of major segments of society – or territorial issues that seem to question the country's sovereignty and dignity. The underlying cognitive dispositions are deep-seated and this is the main reason why we believe that ASEAN's cohesion in international fora cannot be fostered through merely technical and organizational reforms. Without cognitive changes, we doubt that in the short run a better and more effective coordination of ASEAN's global interests can be achieved within the respective regional bodies.

Thus, it is inevitable that also the following proposals to upgrade ASEAN's knowledge base as a major prerequisite for successful international negotiations are contingent on cognitive changes. Nevertheless, in the subsequent sections we discuss three proposals that we believe have some potential to strengthen ASEAN's cohesion in international negotiations: (1) upgrading the process of knowledge generation; (2) better coordination between the regional level and negotiators in global fora; and (3) further professionalizing and strengthening the ASEAN Secretariat.

7.3 Upgrading the process of knowledge generation

One key problem the majority of ASEAN countries encounter is their deficit in expert knowledge in global forums. As policy matters become increasingly technical, complex and complicated, cutting edge know-how is increasingly a key requisite for success in negotiations. Most economically advanced countries demonstrate this with an extensive academic staff that assists their negotiation teams. The USA and the EU, for instance, usually have delegations in excess of 800 people during WTO Ministerials, whereas developing countries including the majority of ASEAN members have a few dozen personnel at best (Wilkinson 2007: 126). Given the advanced state of research in developed countries, much better networking among ASEAN institutions of knowledge is pivotal in order to match this structural disadvantage in international negotiations. It is no longer sufficient to rely on the ASEAN–ISIS network and – as in Singapore – a few additional specialized think tanks. Despite an intensifying regional discourse on non-traditional security issues, we have seen in Chapter 3 that with a few exceptions ASEAN think tanks have thus far developed only limited and variable research capacity to deal at a cutting edge level with highly sophisticated legal and technical special issues in areas such as trade, climate change, food and energy security and disarmament. Enhancing the existing specialized knowledge available to negotiators would necessitate a dramatic increase of investment in the region's research capacities. However, it will not suffice for investments to be channeled into individual institutes; any agenda to produce more tangible know-how for negotiators must involve the creation of regional knowledge networks that would systematically include the region's top universities. The creation of links between regional networks and global networks should also be stepped up. The new, less-developed ASEAN members in particular must be more effectively incorporated into such networks, even if this results in substantial costs in the form of aid programs to be shouldered by the economically advanced ASEAN countries. Enhanced knowledge generation in these countries also reduces political elites' sentiments of insecurity and fears that may easily translate into obstructive behavior when it comes to developing common ASEAN positions, the consequences of which they cannot properly assess.

7.4 Better coordination of multi-level governance

The second proposal concerns the need for an improved coordination process between the regional policy level and member countries' negotiators in global fora. Our interviews suggest that negotiators in Geneva or New York often have considerable leeway in deciding how to act in the respective forum. In other cases, however, they have to report back to the capital before they can formulate a negotiation position and strategy. Yet it is questionable how far the positions in the capitals have been the result of careful coordination with the governments of fellow members.

The singularity and the inaction of ASEAN's G20 Contact Group are telling in this respect. Such groups should be established and activated at the regional level if positioning and strategies in UN bodies, the WTO and climate change negotiations are to be better coordinated. Even though there is a proliferation of ASEAN meetings, preparatory meetings must be organized immediately prior to major international conferences. At these meetings it is essential that ASEAN makes greater efforts, supported by better and broader-based professional know-how, to transcend the ubiquitous joint statements and declarations, which are often hardly more than declaratory politics and symbolism, into more substantive frameworks that allow negotiators in Geneva and New York to develop a more concerted ASEAN position. To this end, the ASEAN presidency must also be strengthened as, perhaps with the exception of Vietnam, the new members in particular hardly have the bureaucratic capacities competently to deal with the wide range of international negotiation themes.

7.5 Reforming the ASEAN Secretariat

As the means of the smaller countries to build up a stronger bureaucratic apparatus for preparing common ASEAN positions in international negotiations are particularly limited, the focus of reforms must inevitably lie on the ASEAN Secretariat. The Secretariat is the only ASEAN entity that has developed a strong regional identity and is therefore particularly suited to strengthening ASEAN's negotiation capacity. However, while opting for a strengthening of the ASEAN Secretariat, we do not propose a supranational role for it. This means that we do not suggest that the ASEAN Secretariat adopt negotiating functions on behalf of ASEAN. This is absolute anathema for ASEAN member governments and would be a non-starter. Yet the Secretariat must cease to act "as a simple agent awaiting tasks from the principals," that is, ASEAN member governments (Conceição-Heldt 2006: 162).

What we propose, therefore, is a marked expansion of the Secretariat's expert staff with the capacity to manage knowledge. This expert staff could help in preparing negotiations in global forums by providing access to the respective legal and disciplinary know-how. Moreover, it could devise and analyze the pros and cons of policy options for negotiations and suggest choices for issue linkages and package solutions (*ibid.* 162). Furthermore, it could facilitate the coordination process at the regional level and help to broker frameworks for common negotiation strategies and positions. These staff resources should be built up step by step by prioritizing key issue areas such as trade, international finance, climate change and disarmament. Expert staff should not, as currently, only be hired from the open market of the region, but should be sought on a global scale. The Secretariat should be enabled, as ASEAN Deputy Secretary General Bagas Hapsoro demanded, to make work in the Secretariat attractive for highly specialized professionals with working experience in international organizations such as the United Nations, the World Trade Organization, the World Bank or the European Union.[8] This would facilitate the expansion of the Secretariat's functions and help it to become a nodal point in the association's organization.

[8] See *Jakarta Post*, 12 August 2011. Similar points have also been raised by Rizal Sukma, Djisman Simantunjak and former ASEAN Secretary General Surin Pitsuwan: see *Jakarta Post*, 2 November 2011.

Inevitably, a multiplication of expert staff would entail a substantial increase of the Secretariat's funding needs, even though – as mentioned in Chapter 3 – the ASEAN Secretariat has been successful in attracting third-party funds.[9] However, the realization of an adequate budget to enable the Secretariat to perform these new functions of knowledge management would necessitate ASEAN member countries ending their symbolic elevation of the Secretariat to an embodiment of member equality. It would also require the region's economically advanced countries to shoulder the lion's share of the Secretariat's budget. However, Indonesian proposals to link contributions to the Secretariat with member countries' GDP have been rejected by other countries, including Singapore, which due to its high level of economic development would have to shoulder a much higher share of the Secretariat's costs (Jayakumar 2011: 98). Nonetheless, the controversy is puzzling as even ASEAN's poorer member countries could markedly increase their budgetary share of the Secretariat as the current contributions hardly exceed a symbolic level and are an expression of member governments' lack of political will to strengthen the Secretariat's capacities.

A better-staffed and more professional ASEAN Secretariat could adopt the functions of a catalyst in knowledge generation. It could establish close networks with the region's centers of knowledge and with extra-regional academic institutions, which may provide advanced know-how on the issues under negotiation in global forums. This would

[9] Another point addressed by Bagas, see *Jakarta Post*, 12 August 2011.

also include a more effective tapping of know-how available in civil society organizations and various types of interest groups. A side-effect of connecting the Secretariat more systematically with non-government stakeholders would be the transformation of ASEAN into a more people-oriented organization, as envisaged in the ASEAN Charter.

Acting as a catalyst of knowledge would also necessitate the establishment of more channels of communication between the Secretariat and the ASEAN Committees in Geneva and New York. Such channels currently hardly exist and it seems that ASEAN negotiators and governments have little interest in establishing them. Yet such feedback channels would provide the Secretariat with insights into the dynamics of the negotiation process and make the proposed policy options and know-how generation more attuned to the requirements of negotiators.

While such a transformation of the Secretariat from merely auxiliary functions to a catalyst for expertise can be expected to help ASEAN strengthen its negotiation capacities, there are certainly risks that may give rise to objections from member countries. One is the classic principal–agent problem: drawing from more recent studies on international organizations one cannot rule out that a strengthened Secretariat may seek increasing autonomy from its principals, that is, ASEAN governments (Barnett and Finnemore 2004). Such autonomy, which is increasingly difficult to control by member governments, includes a possible mission creep, that is, the performance of additional functions that have not been mandated to the Secretariat, setting its own agenda and the interpretation of information (*ibid.* 7) that reflects the Secretariat's organizational interests but not necessarily that of ASEAN governments. An empowered Secretariat may even shape and change the policy preferences of member states (*ibid.* 11).

ASEAN governments may also fear the bureaucratic pathologies that large organizations often tend to contract, including the emergence of routines, the ossification of the organization and a declining ability to change (*ibid.* 8–9). Bureaucratic culture and social environment may increasingly deviate and become causes for internal bureaucratic conflict, especially when it becomes apparent that organizational behavior deviates from the stated mission and publicly proclaimed goals (*ibid.* 36). Member states may also fear a politicization of the Secretariat that is inevitable if, for instance, the larger countries or those bearing a major share of the budget try to manipulate the Secretariat for their political objectives or for promoting their normative preferences.

We may therefore expect that ASEAN governments with their normative underpinnings and penchant for national sovereignty would strongly resent a development in which the Secretariat would become increasingly autonomous. We thus doubt that ASEAN member governments would agree to such wide-ranging reforms as proposed above with their centralizing effects for the grouping and the emergence of the Secretariat as a powerful organizational entity. Additionally, we therefore believe that without critical junctures such as major crises and external shocks ASEAN member states will not substantially change the role of the Secretariat. While triggering change in ASEAN, even the Asian financial crisis was not such a critical juncture (Jetschke and Rüland 2009).

Consequently, we assume that member governments will proceed with incremental, albeit largely symbolic, reforms of the Secretariat. The latter will hardly go to the point of transforming the Secretariat into a catalyst for and manager of knowledge in the association. Member governments will remain responsible for the management of know-how relevant for international negotiations. Moreover, a weak and small ASEAN Secretariat would tally well with the normative disposition of member governments. With their predilection for pragmatism and flexibility, most of them would perceive uniform bloc-type cohesion as imposing an undesirable rigidity on their policy options in negotiation processes. They will argue that the caucus-type cohesion suits their needs best, because they could easily shift to a more cohesive quasi-bloc behavior if major common regional interests are at stake, or if issues are insignificant and quasi-bloc behavior does not entail costs for member countries. Furthermore, speaking individually in global fora would give them an even more effective voice, because in the process ASEAN arguments can be presented not only once but several times. This, at least, is a lesson that has been learned in the EU (Smith 2006).

7.6 Future research directions

What ASEAN's behavior means and how it relates to other regional organizations is difficult to assess at this point. More fieldwork-based studies on the negotiation behavior of regional organizations and their members, their negotiation strategies at different stages of the negotiation processes and in a broad cross-section of issue areas including linkages between negotiation arenas are direly needed. This implies taking into account that regional organizations and their members act in a broad array of policy fields and hence a great number of international fora. Assuming that they act homogeneously across these fora is certainly not tenable. More in-depth research is also needed with respect to world views, education, professional background, expectations of negotiators and the preparatory processes preceding international negotiations. All these important issues could be touched upon in this study only in a preliminary way. Also, greater methodological sophistication is needed. That is, better and more measurable operationalization of what regional cohesion means for negotiations in global forums. Studies focusing only on the voting behavior of the members of regional organizations (Ferdinand 2013) are insufficient for gaining a better understanding of regional organizations as collective negotiators and actors in major international forums. Only looking at the frequency of joint voting fails to provide any information about the significance of the issues on which members voted jointly. It may well be that members of a regional association act collectively when little is at stake, but fail to develop joint positions when issues of great significance are being voted upon as has often happened in the UNGA.

Through more nuanced and longitudinal studies will it be possible to capture the peculiarities in different arenas of international negotiation. The political environment may change and hence impact on the world view of negotiators, new generations of negotiators may emerge and opportunities for negotiators may differ across issue areas. Drawing from the methodology of the more recently developed concept of

Comparative Area Studies (CAS) (Basedau and Köllner 2007; Ahram 2010; Huotari and Rüland 2014), these studies should have a comparative and, in particular, cross-regional dimension. Yet, unlike what is practiced in the field of comparative regionalism (de Lombaerde et al. 2010), these studies should not elevate the EU to the position of a model to be emulated by other regional organizations. Critics of the current state of affairs in comparative regionalism studies are right to emphasize that the EU should not be treated as the gold standard for non-European regional organizations. Comparison should therefore mainly focus on the regional organizations to which the literature often refers as "new regionalism," that is, groupings mainly established in the Global South in the 1990s. This study is a first step in this direction. But much work is still to be done.

EXECUTIVE SUMMARY

This book addresses a topic that in the proliferating literature on the Association of Southeast Asian Nations (ASEAN) has so far been almost entirely neglected. While ASEAN's practices in intra-regional cooperation are well covered and some information exists about ASEAN's agency in international forums of the East Asian and Asia-Pacific region, hardly anything is known about ASEAN as an actor and negotiator in global forums such as the United Nations, the World Trade Organization (WTO), the International Monetary Fund (IMF) or the climate change and non-proliferation regimes. Available information is unsystematic, scattered and often anecdotal.

In this study, we argue that in global forums regional cohesion has to contend with four major constraints: first, the ASEAN Way as the grouping's repository of shared cooperation norms and, second, as a direct outflow of the former, ASEAN's organizational structure. Neither ASEAN's value system nor its internal structure is conducive to collective action in the global political arena. Both are legacies of a "cognitive prior" shaped by centuries of conflict, threats, instability and political uncertainties that have deeply engrained distrust, suspicion and ill-feelings towards the external world in the minds of decision-makers and major parts of the public. These legacies are reflected in the strong emphasis of the ASEAN Way on sovereignty norms. The seemingly cosmopolitan liberal norms ASEAN adopted with the Bali Concord II of 2003 and elevated to quasi-constitutional status in the ASEAN Charter enacted in 2008 may have eased external normative pressures on ASEAN, but have done little to overcome ASEAN's cohesiveness dilemma. On the contrary, they have, and this is our third major point, exacerbated the association's collective action problems by creating a value base that is contradictory below the surface of rhetorical unity. Fourth and finally, we argue that Southern regional organizations such as ASEAN also grapple with an uneven institutional playing field. While it is true that the legitimacy of the established international institutional order including its representativeness, decision-making procedures and normative underpinnings is coming under siege, the institutional power of the mainly Western creators of this order is only gradually eroding and thus markedly curtailing the scope for effective collective action of Southern regional actors.

The study proceeds in six major steps. Following the introductory chapter that lays out the research questions, we develop in Chapter 2 an analytical framework. After identifying shortcomings of neo-functionalist and rational choice-based neo-institutional approaches applied in the analysis of the negotiating behavior of the EU in international forums, we propose a constructivist reinterpretation of the neo-functionalist externalization hypothesis. It makes the argument that ASEAN externalizes its weakly developed internal cohesion that is the result of a cognitive prior that has deeply inculcated in the region's collective memory notions of a hostile external world. Repeated experiences of insecurity and vulnerability and a long history of victimization by

Great Powers have on the one hand given rise to attempts to overcome these adverse legacies through regional cooperation but on the other have also preserved lingering sentiments of distrust and suspicion towards neighbors. The result was a continued concern for self-help, national resilience, the protection of national sovereignty and shallow regional integration that has been reproduced whenever political events seemed to have affirmed the experiences of the past. This led ASEAN member states to pursue a pragmatic, flexible and context-sensitive foreign policy that responds seismically to global and regional power shifts. The norms and institutions guiding regional cooperation fit this state of mind quite well and impede the deepening of regional cohesion. It is thus hardly surprising that ASEAN member states also practice collective action in global forums only in issues of minor relevance or when there is a high degree of congruence of their interests. ASEAN's repository of cooperation norms and its institutional set-up may foster a certain level of mutual consultation and coordination, but rarely full-fledged collective action. We try to measure ASEAN's cohesion in global forums by developing a four-dimensional typology of cohesion (bloc, quasi-bloc, caucus, non-cooperation). Based on negotiation theory, we lay the ground for the empirical analysis by conceptualizing international negotiations as a multi-staged process in which actors employ a range of strategies including leadership, framing, coalition-building, forum shopping as well as image-building and the generation of "soft power."

The empirical part (Chapters 3–6) is the result of comprehensive data collection and data mining. Much of the information comes in the form of newly collected primary data such as content analysis of official documents and speeches, intensive newspaper analysis, statistics and interviews with diplomats from ASEAN member countries, former and current officials of the ASEAN Secretariat as well as think tank and university scholars.

Chapter 3 seeks to capture the cognitive prior, that is, the historically grown ideational context in which ASEAN operates. The chapter portrays Southeast Asia as a region that in pre-colonial times have localized Hindu–Brahmanic and Sinic power-sensitive state craft, the essence of which has been persistently reproduced through wars, colonial conquest, Great Power interventions and a highly asymmetric global distribution of power. These ideational and historical legacies have translated into a normative and institutional structure that limits the depth of cooperation and impedes the development of collective negotiation capacities that would match those of the economically advanced nations.

Chapter 4 explores ASEAN behavior during three stages of international negotiation. Evidence for cohesive cooperation is ambiguous. ASEAN's role as an initiator, innovator and agenda-setter in international negotiations is largely confined to minor or special issues: in key issues of the global order such as UN reform, trade liberalization and climate change it has rather been a reactive force. ASEAN can also hardly be considered an innovative norm entrepreneur in international relations. By and large, it stands for rather conservative and conventional Westphalian sovereignty norms. Although framing its negotiation position in Third Worldist and developmentalist language, ASEAN has rarely been a radical challenger of the existing international institutional architecture. Even where the association as a whole or individual member states saw their interests jeopardized in international negotiations, it has usually abstained from pursuing obstructive and intransigent negotiation strategies. Yet, ASEAN members' pragmatic behavior that has made them amenable to package deals, side payments and second-best solutions also prevented a stronger bloc-type attitude at the end of the negotiation process when decisions are prepared and eventually made. In the decision-making process, we found on closer scrutiny a comparatively high degree of ASEAN unity at least in the UN General Assembly. Yet, we observed quasi-bloc behavior primarily in votes on rather insignificant issues. Compliance, too, was rather mixed. It was higher in the international trade regime than in human rights and environmental issues.

As regards ASEAN's negotiation strategies we found no clear pattern, either. Our evidence suggests that in the application of negotiation strategies ASEAN cohesion fluctuates between quasi-bloc and caucus. Our evidence suggests that ASEAN's degree of unity is greatest in the attempt at generating and projecting "soft power" and in framing its goals in negotiations, resulting in quasi-bloc behavior. Much less cohesive, and, hence, much more caucus-type behavior prevails in the pursuit of leadership and executive positions as well as in coalition-building and, to a lesser extent, forum shopping. These three strategies are more often and more strongly dominated by national interests than the two negotiation strategies mentioned before. Hence the tendency for bowling alone and acting in an uncoordinated way.

The empirical part of the study (Chapter 6) ends with two case studies: one exploring ASEAN's behavior as negotiator on an issue where material values were at stake (WTO agricultural negotiations) and another one on an issue where ideational values mattered (human rights issues in the UN and the ILO). Although ASEAN's behavior at first glance might appear puzzling in the two cases, on closer scrutiny it fitted very well with our main argument in which ASEAN was strongly guided by its cognitive prior.

This final chapter (Chapter 7) concludes the study, summarizes major findings, relates them to our initial set of theoretical assumptions and outlines recommendations on how ASEAN's cohesion in global forums may be strengthened. It focuses on improvements in the process of knowledge generation for international negotiation, better multi-level processes of coordination and reforms of the ASEAN Secretariat. We propose to upgrade the Secretariat to a catalyst of knowledge and specialized know-how that member states may tap in order to act more cohesively and competently in international negotiations. This entails a marked expansion of the Secretariat's expert personnel, a massive increase of funding and the acceptance on the part of member states that the Secretariat becomes a nodal point in the organization including a certain degree of centralization, albeit without supranational competences. We also discuss the drawbacks of such a strategy that ASEAN countries may fear. They include a mission creep of the Secretariat and a tendency to seek autonomy from its principals, the member governments. We believe that these fears, given ASEAN's normative disposition, weigh strongly and explain why the grouping may at best strengthen its Secretariat incrementally. Despite the ASEAN Charter that also pursues the objective of making ASEAN a more assertive and more cohesive player in global fora, its impact will remain limited in the foreseeable future.

REFERENCES

Acharya, A. (2001) *Constructing a Security Community in Southeast Asia: ASEAN and the Problem of Regional Order*, London and New York: Routledge.

(2004) "How Ideas Spread: Whose Norms Matter? Norm Localization and Institutional Change in Asian Regionalism," *International Organization* 58: 239–275.

(2009) *Whose Ideas Matter: Agency and Power in Asian Regionalism*, Ithaca, NY and London: Cornell University Press.

(2012) "Comparative Regionalism: A Field Whose Time has Come?," *International Spectator* 47(1): 3–15.

Ahram, A. (2010) "The Theory and Method of Comparative Area Studies," *Qualitative Research* 11(1): 69–90.

Ajanant, J., Chirathivat, S. and Iamkamala, C. (1988) "Trade Policy Options for Thailand." In M. Ariff and L.-H. Tan (eds.), *Asean Trade Policy Options: The Uruguay Round*, Singapore: Institute of Southeast Asian Studies.

Alatas, A. (2001) *A Voice for a Just Peace. A Collection of Speeches*, Jakarta and Singapore: PT Gramedia Pustaka Utama in cooperation with Institute of Southeast Asian Studies.

Alburo, F., Medalla, E. and Pante Jr., F. (1988) "Trade Policy Option for the Philippines." In M. Ariff and L.-H. Tan (eds.), *Asean Trade Policy Options: The Uruguay Round*, Singapore: Institute of Southeast Asian Studies.

Allen, D. and Smith, M. (1991) "Western Europe's Presence in the Contemporary International Arena." In M. Holland (ed.), *The*

Future of European Political Cooperation, New York: St. Martin's Press.

(1998) "The European Union's Presence in the New European Security Order: Barrier, Facilitator or Manager?" In C. Rhodes (ed.), *The European Union in the Global Community*, Boulder, CO: Lynne Rienner, pp. 213–230.

Alter, K. J. and Meunier, S. (2006) "Nested and Overlapping Regimes in the Transatlantic Banana Trade Dispute," *Journal of European Public Policy* 13(3): 362–382.

Anderson, B. R. O'G. (1972) "The Idea of Power in Javanese Culture." In C. Holt (ed.), *Culture and Politics in Indonesia*, Ithaca, NY and London: Cornell University Press, pp. 1–70.

Anggoro, K. (2005) "Geopolitik, Pengedalian Ruang Laga dan Strategi Pertahanan Indonesia." In B. Bandoro (ed.), *Perspektif Baru Keamanan Nasional*, Jakarta: Center for Strategic and International Studies, pp. 61–79.

Anwar, D. F. (1992) *Indonesia and the Security of Southeast Asia*, Jakarta: Center for Strategic and International Studies.

(1994) *Indonesia in ASEAN: Foreign Policy and Regionalism*, Singapore: Institute of Southeast Asian Studies.

Asian Political News (2002) "Philippines Threatened to Pull Out of Cairns Group," 11 February 2002, available at: http://business.highbeam.com/435555/article-1G1-84268849/philippines-threatens-pull-out-cairns-group (accessed 13 November 2012).

Ariff, M. and Tan L.-H. (eds.) (1988) *Asean Trade Policy Options: The Uruguay Round*, Singapore: Institute of Southeast Asian Studies.

ASEAN (1988) "The 20th ASEAN Economic Ministers Meeting, Thailand, 17–19 October 1988," available at: http://web.archive.org/web/20081202001004/http://www.aseansec.org/7136.htm (accessed 4 November 2014).

(1989) "Joint Communiqué of the 22nd ASEAN Ministerial Meeting Banda Seri Begawan, 3–4 July 1989," available at: www.asean.org/communities/asean-political-security-community/item/joint-communique-of-the-22nd-asean-ministerial-meeting-bandar-seri-begawan-3-4-july-1989 (accessed 8 November 2012).

(1999) "Listen to Southeast Asia in Seattle by Rodolfo C. Severino Secretary General of ASEAN, for International Herald Tribune," 25 November 1999, available at: http://web.archive.org/web/20120514165122/http://www.aseansec.org/2824.htm (accessed 4 November 2014).

(2001a) Joint Press Statement, The Twenty-Third Meeting of the ASEAN Ministers on Agriculture and Forestry (23rd AMAF), 5 October 2001, Medan, North Sumatera, Indonesia, available at: http://web.archive.org/web/20080907064543/http://www.aseansec.org/1071.htm (accessed 4 November 2014).

(2001b) Joint Communiqué, The Fifteenth ASEAN Labour Ministers Meeting, 10–11 May 2001, Kuala Lumpur, Malaysia, available at: www.asean.org/communities/asean-socio-cultural-community/item/joint-communique-the-fifteenth-asean-labour-ministers-meeting-10-11-may-2001-kuala-lumpur-malaysia (accessed 8 January 2013).

(2004) Joint Communiqué, The Eighteenth ASEAN Labour Ministers Meeting, 13–14 May 2004, Bandar Seri Begawan, Brunei Darussalam, available at: www.asean.org/communities/asean-socio-cultural-community/item/joint-communique-the-eighteenth-asean-labour-ministers-meeting (accessed 23 July 2012).

(2010a) *A Humanitarian Call: The ASEAN Response to Cyclone Nargis*, Jakarta: ASEAN Secretariat.

(2010b) *The Story of the ASEAN-Led Coordination in Myanmar: Compassion in Action*, Jakarta: ASEAN Secretariat.

Assmann, Jan (2002) *Kollektives Gedächtnis. Schrift, Erinnerung und politische Identität in frühen Hochkulturen*, Munich: Beck'sche Reihe.

Ba, A. (2009) *(Re)Negotiating East and Southeast Asia: Region, Regionalism and the Association of Southeast Asian Nations*, Stanford, CA: Stanford University Press.

Barnett, M. and Duvall, R. (2005) "Power in International Politics," *International Organization* 59(1): 39–77.

Barnett, M. and Finnemore, M. (2004) *Rules for the World: International Organizations in Global Politics*, Ithaca, NY and London: Cornell University Press.

Basedau, M. and Köllner, P. (2007) "Area Studies, Comparative Area Studies, and the Study of Politics: Context, Substance, and Methodological Challenges," *Zeitschrift für Vergleichende Politikwissenschaft* 1(1): 105–124.

Beck, U. (1997) *Was ist Globalisierung?*, Frankfurt am Main: Suhrkamp.

Beeson, M. and Stone, D. (2013) "The European Union Model's Influence in Asia after the Global Financial Crisis," *European Journal of East Asian Studies* 12(2): 167–191.

Berensmann, K., Fues, T. and Volz, U. (2011) *Die G20: Rolle und Herausforderungen*, Bonn: Deutsches Institut für Entwicklungspolitik.

Bellamy, A. J. and Beeson, M. (2010) "The Responsibility to Protect in Southeast Asia: Can ASEAN Reconcile Humanitarianism and Sovereignty?," *Asian Security* 6(3): 262–279.

Benford, R. D. and Snow, D. A. (2000) "Framing Processes and Social Movements: An Overview and Assessment," *Annual Review of Sociology* 26: 611–639.

Boesch, E. E. (1970) *Zwiespältige Eliten. Eine sozialpsychologische Untersuchung über administrative Eliten in Thailand*, Berne: Huber.

Boesche, R. (2002) *The First Great Political Realist: Kautilya and his Arthasastra*, Lanham, MD: Lexington Books.

Börzel, T. A. and Risse, T. (2009) "The Transformative Power of Europe: The European Union and the Diffusion of Ideas," Kolleg-Forschergruppe (KFG) Working Paper 1, Freie Universität Berlin.

Bourchier, D. (1999) "Positivism and Romanticism in Indonesian Legal Thought." In T. Lindsey (ed.), *Indonesia: Law and Society*, Sydney: The Federation Press, pp. 186–196.

Bretherton, C. and Vogler, J. (1999) *The European Union As a Global Actor*, London: Routledge.

Bunyanunda, M. (2002) "Burma, ASEAN, and Human Rights: The Decade of Constructive Engagement, 1991–2001," *Stanford Journal of East Asian Affairs* 2(1): 118–135.

Burmester, N. and Jankowski, M. (2013) "The Unsolved Puzzle: Pacific Asia's Voting Cohesion in the United Nations General Assembly – A Response to Peter Ferdinand," *British Journal of Politics and International Relations*, http://onlinelibrary.wiley.com/doi/10.1111/1467-856X.12028/abstract.

Buruma, I. and Margalit, A. (2005) *Okzidentalismus. Der Westen in den Augen seiner Feinde*, Vienna: Hanser.

Caballero-Anthony, M. (2004) "Non-State Regional Governance Mechanism for Economic Security: The Case of the ASEAN People's Assembly," *Pacific Review* 17(4): 567–585.

Capie, D. (2012) "The Responsibility to Protect Norm in Southeast Asia: Framing, Resistance and the Localization Myth," *Pacific Review* 25(1): 75–93.

Carrapatoso, A. (2008) "Ein Klima der Veränderung? Ergebnisse des Weltklimagipfels in Bali 2007," *GIGA Focus*, 3 (2008), Hamburg: German Institute of Global and Area Studies.

Chachavalpongpun, P. (2005) *A Plastic Nation: The Curse of Thainess in Thai–Burmese Relations*, Lanham, MD: University Press of America.

(2010) *Reinventing Thailand: Thaksin and His Foreign Policy*, Singapore: Institute of Southeast Asian Studies.
(2012) "Thailand Set to Profit from Burma's New Dawei Port Project," *East Asia Forum*, 24 February 2012, available at: www.eastasiaforum.org/2012/02/24/thailand-set-to-profit-from-burma-s-new-dawei-port-project/ (accessed 24 December 2013).
Chalermpalanupap, T. (2009) "ASEAN and Myanmar: From Flexible Engagement to Enhanced Interactions, Shared Commitment and Collective Responsibility Building," presented at the workshop "Myanmar/Burma: Outside Interests and Inside Challenges," Washington, DC, 28–30 October 2009.
Chandra, A. C. (2005) "Indonesia and Bilateral Trade Agreements (BTAs)," *Pacific Review* 18(4): 541–565.
Chowdhury, I. A. (2010) "The Global Governance Group (3G) and Singaporean Leadership: Can Small Be Significant?," Working Paper 108, Institute of South Studies, National University of Singapore.
Coleman, W. D. and Tangerman, S. (1999) "The 1992 CAP Reform, the Uruguay Round and the Commission: Conceptualizing Linked Policy Games," *Journal of Common Market Studies* 37(3): 385–405.
Collins, A. (2008) "A People-Oriented ASEAN: A Door Ajar or Closed for Civil Society Organizations?," *Contemporary Southeast Asia* 30(2): 313–331.
Collinson, S. (1999) "'Issue-Systems,' 'Multi-Level Games' and the EU's External Commercial and Associated Policies: A Research Agenda," *Journal of European Public Policy* 6(2): 206–224.
Conceição-Heldt, E. (2006) "Integrative and Distributive Bargaining Situations in the European Union: What Difference Does it Make?" *Negotiation Journal* 22(2): 145–165.
Cororaton, C. B. and Corong, E. L. (2009) "Philippine Agricultural and Food Policies: Implication for Poverty and Income Distribution,"

Research Report 161, International Food Policy Research Institute (IFPRI), available at: www.ifpri.org/publication/philippine-agricultural-and-food-policies (accessed 5 November 2012).

Czempiel, E.-O. (1994) *Die Reform der UNO. Möglichkeiten und Missverständnisse*, Munich: Beck'sche Reihe.

Davidson, P. J. (1994) "ASEAN: The Legal Framework for Its Trade Relations," *International Journal* 49(3): 588–612.

de Lombaerde, P., Baert, F. and Felício, T. (eds.) (2012) *The United Nations and the Regions: Third World Report on Regional Integration*, Dordrecht: Springer.

de Lombaerde, P., Söderbaum, F., van Langenhove, L. and Baert, F. (2010) "The Problem of Comparison in Comparative Regionalism," *Review of International Studies* 36: 731–753.

Dent, C. M. (2004) "The Asia–Europe Meeting (ASEM) and Inter-Regionalism: Towards a Theory of Multilateral Utility," *Asian Survey* 44(2): 213–236.

Department of Foreign Trade (2013) "สถานการณ์ ข้าว โลก เดือน พฤษภาคม 2556" [world rice production and marketing, May 2013], Ministry of Commerce, Government of Thailand, available at: http://pcoc.moc.go.th/wappPCOC/62/upload/File_IPD_FILE62228625.doc (accessed 25 February 2014).

Desierto, D. A. (2010–2011) "ASEAN's Constitutionalization of International Law: Challenges to Evolution under the New ASEAN Charter," *Columbia Journal of Transnational Law* 268: 267–320.

Desker, B. (2001) "Asian Developing Countries and the Next Round of WTO Negotiations," Singapore: Institute of Defence and Strategic Studies.

(2009) "Informal Caucuses within the WTO: Singapore in the 'Invisibles Group'," Working Paper 188, S. Rajaratnam School of International Studies (RSIS), Nanyang Technological University, Singapore.

(2011) "Asian Developing Countries and the Next Round of WTO Negotiations," Singapore: Institute of Defence and Strategic Studies.

Desker, B. and Ng, J. (2011) "Responsibility to Protect: Tensions between Sovereignty and Security," RSIS Commentaries 142/2011, S. Rajaratnam School of International Studies, Nanyang Technological University, Singapore.

Devies, P. (2001) "Spies as Informants: Triangulation and the Interpretation of Elite Interview Data in the Study of the Intelligence and Security Services," *Politics* 21: 73–80.

Dieter, H. (1998) *Die Asienkrise. Ursachen, Konsequenzen und die Rolle des Internationalen Währungsfonds*, Marburg: Metropolis Verlag.

Dobson, H. (2011) "The G20: Engine of Asian Regionalism?," Working Paper 179, German Institute of Global and Area Studies (GIGA), Hamburg.

Doidge, M. (2011) *The European Union and Interregionalism: Patterns of Engagement*, Burlington, VT: Ashgate.

Dörflinger, J.-S. (2009) "Die Reform des Sicherheitsrates der Vereinten Nationen," Master's thesis, University of Freiburg.

Dosch, J. (1997) *Die ASEAN. Bilanz eines Erfolges. Akteure, Interessenlagen, Kooperationsbeziehungen*, Hamburg: Abera Network.

(2003) "The Post Cold War Development of Regionalism in East Asia." In F.-K. Liu and P. Regnier (eds.), *Regionalism in East Asia: Paradigm Shifting*, London and New York: Routledge, pp. 30–51.

Druckman, J. N. (2011) "What's it all about? Framing in Political Science." In G. Keren (ed.), *Perspectives on Framing*, New York: Psychology Press, pp. 279–302.

Elliott, K. A. (2000) "The ILO and Enforcement of Core Labor Standard," International Economics Policy Briefs 00–6, available at: www.iie.com/publications/pb/pb00-6.pdf (accessed 20 July 2012).

Fawcett, L. and Hurrell, A. (eds.) (1995) *Regionalism in World Politics*, New York and Oxford: Oxford University Press.

Ferdinand, P. (2013) "Foreign Policy Convergence in Pacific Asia: The Evidence from Voting in the UN General Assembly," *British Journal of Politics and International Relations* 16(4): 662–679, available at: http://onlinelibrary.wiley.com/doi/10.1111/1467-856X.12019/abstract.

Forman, S. and Segaar, D. (2006) "New Coalition for Global Governance: The Changing Dynamics of Multilateralism," *Global Governance* 12: 205–225.

Freistein, K. (2008) "Beyond the Taboos?: The Opportunities and Limitations of Asian-European Track-two Dialogue." In J. Rüland et al. (eds.), *Asian-European Relations: Building Blocks for Global Governance*, London: Routledge, pp. 348–381.

Friends of the Earth Canada (2005) "A Civil Society Handbook: International Labour Organization," www.foecanada.org.

General Agreement on Tariffs and Trade (GATT) (1986a) "WTO/GATT Ministerial Declaration on the Uruguay Round (Declaration of 20 September 1986)", available at: www.jus.uio.no/lm/wto.gatt.ministerial.declaration.uruguay.round.1986/d.html (accessed 7 November 2012).

(1986b) "ASEAN: Statement at the Meeting of the GATT Contracting Parties at Ministerial Level, 15–19 September 1986, Punta del Este, Uruguay," MIN(86)/ST/4, 15 September 1986, available at: www.wto.org/gatt_docs/English/SULPDF/91240016.pdf (accessed 7 November 2012).

(1987a) "Negotiating Group on Agriculture, 26–27 October 1987: Statement by the ASEAN Countries on Cairns Proposal," MTN.GNG/NG5/W/25, 5 November 1987, available at: www.wto.org/gatt_docs/English/SULPDF/92030077.pdf (accessed 29 October 2012).

(1987b) "Tropical Products: Submission by ASEAN Countries," MIN.GNG/NG6/W/9, 14 July 1987, available at: www.wto.org/gatt_docs/English/SULPDF/92020219.pdf (accessed 7 November 2012).

(1987c) "Negotiating Group on Tropical Products, Meeting of 26 February 1987: Note by the Secretariat, MTN.GNG/NG6/1, 10 March 1987, available at: www.wto.org/gatt_docs/English/SULPDF/92020043.pdf (accessed 7 November 2012).

George, A. L. and Bennett, A. (2005) *Case Studies and Theory Development in the Social Sciences*, Cambridge, MA: Belfer Center for Science and International Affairs, Harvard University.

Gérard, F. (2010) "Indonesian Experience in Rice Price Stabilization," Groupe de recherche et d'échanges sur la régulation des marchés agricoles (GREMA), available at: www.inter-reseaux.org/IMG/pdf/Indonesian_experience_in_rice_price_stabilization.pdf (accessed 19 March 2014).

Gerard, K. (2013) "From the ASEAN People's Assembly to the ASEAN Civil Society Conference: The Boundaries of Civil Society Advocacy," *Contemporary Politics* 19(4): 411–426, www.tandfonline.com/doi/abs/10.1080/13569775.2013.835113?journalCode=ccpo20.

Gerring, J. (2008) *Case Study Research: Principles and Practices*, Cambridge: Cambridge University Press.

Gill, B., Green, M., Tsuji, K. and Watts, W. (2009) *Strategic Views on Asian Regionalism: Survey Results and Analysis*, Washington, DC: Center for International and Strategic Studies.

Gingrich, C. D. (1994) "GATT and the Thai Agricultural Economy," GATT Research Paper 94-GATT 16, April 1994, available at: www.card.iastate.edu/publications/dbs/pdffiles/94gatt16.pdf (accessed 5 November 2012).

Goldstein, J. and Keohane, R. O. (1993) "Ideas and Foreign Policy: An Analytical Framework." In J. Goldstein and R. O. Keohane (eds.), *Ideas and Foreign Policy: Beliefs, Institutions and Political Change*, Ithaca, NY and London: Cornell University Press, pp. 3–30.

Gordon, B. K. (1966) *The Dimensions of Conflict in Southeast Asia*, Englewood Cliffs, NJ: Prentice-Hall.

Grieco, J. M. (1996) "State Interests and Institutional Rule Trajectories: A Neorealist Reinterpretation of the Maastricht Treaty and European Economic and Monetary Union." In B. Frankel (ed.), *Realism: Restatements and Renewal*, London: Frank Cass, pp. 262–305.

Grimes, W. W. (2011) "The Future of Regional Liquidity Arrangements in East Asia: Lessons from the Global Financial Crisis," *Pacific Review* 24(3): 291–310.

Guggenheim, S. (2012) "Indonesia's Quiet Springtime: Knowledge, Policy and Reform." In A. Reid (ed.), *Indonesia Rising: The Repositioning of Asia's Third Giant*, Singapore: Institute of Southeast Asian Studies, pp. 141–169.

Haacke, J. (2003) *ASEAN's Diplomatic and Security Culture: Origins, Development and Prospects*, London and New York: RoutledgeCurzon.

(2006) "Regional Security Institutions: ASEAN, ARF, SCO and KEDO." In S. Hoadley and J. Rüland (eds.), *Asian Security Reassessed*, Singapore: Institute of Southeast Asian Studies, pp. 128–170.

Haas, E. B. and Rowe, E. T. (1973) "Regional Organizations in the United Nations: Is There Externalization?," *International Studies Quarterly* 17(1): 3–54.

Haas, M. (1997) "ASEAN's Pivotal Role in Asian-Pacific Regional Cooperation," *Global Governance* 3: 329–348.

Halbwachs, M. (1985) *Das Gedächtnis und seine sozialen Bedingungen*, Frankfurt am Main: Suhrkamp.

Hänggi, H. (1992) *Neutralität in Südostasien. Das Projekt einer Zone des Friedens, der Freiheit und der Neutralität*, Berne: Haupt.

Hänggi, H., Roloff, R. and Rüland J. (eds.) (2006) *Interregionalism and International Relations*, London: Routledge.

He, K. and Feng, H. (2008) "If Not Soft Balancing, Then What? Reconsidering Soft Balancing and US Policy Toward China," *Security Studies* 17(2): 363–395.

Healy, S., Pearce, R. and Stockbridge, M. (1998) "The Implications of the Uruguay Round Agreement on Agriculture for Developing Countries," Rome: Food and Agriculture Organization of the United Nations, available at: www.fao.org/docrep/004/w7814e/w7814e00.htm (accessed 31 October 2012).

Hernandez, C. G. (2007) "The Coming of Age of Participatory Enlargement: Bringing the People to the ASEAN Table." In H. Soesastro and C. Joewono (eds.), *The Inclusive Regionalist: A Festschrift Dedicated to Jusuf Wanandi*, Jakarta: Centre for Strategic Studies, pp. 281–289.

Hicks, J. (2012) "A False Start? Indonesian Business Associations as Democratic Actors in the Immediate Post-Soeharto Era," Indonesian Studies Working Paper 15, University of Sydney.

Hidayat, N. (2002) "WTO, Indonesian Agriculture, and Food Security," paper prepared for AFTINET seminar on alternatives to the WTO, Sydney, 8 November, available at: www.aftinet.org.au/papers/hidayat1.html (accessed 18 March 2014).

Hook, G., Gilson, J., Hughes, C. and Dobson, H. (2005) *Japan's International Relations: Politics, Economy and Security*, London: Routledge.

Hopf, T. (1998) "The Promise of Constructivism in International Relations Theory," *International Security* 23(1): 171–200.

Huff, W. G. (1994) *Economic Growth of Singapore: Trade and Development in the Twentieth Century*, Cambridge: Cambridge University Press.

Huotari, M. (2012) "Practices of Financial Regionalism and the Negotiation of Community in East Asia," Occasional Paper Series 8, Southeast Asian Studies, University of Freiburg.

Huotari, M. and Rüland, J. (2014) "Context, Concepts and Comparison in Southeast Asian Studies," Introduction to special issue, *Pacific Affairs* 87(3): 415–439.

Hurrell, A. (2006) "Hegemony, Liberalism and Global Order: What Space for Would-Be Great Powers?," *International Affairs* 82(1): 1–19.

Igarashi, S. (2011) "The New Regional Order and Transnational Civil Society in Southeast Asia: Focusing on Alternative Regionalism from Below in the Process of Building the ASEAN Community," *World Political Science Review* 7(1): 1–31.

Indrani, T. (2001) "Agriculture and Food Security: Developments in Malaysia," in *Situation of Agriculture in Malaysia – A Cause for Concern*, Education and Research Association for Consumers (ERA Consumer), Malaysia.

International Centre for Trade and Sustainable Development (ICTSD) (2006) "Malaysian Informal Paper on Special Products Draws Objections from G-33," *Bridges Weekly Trade News Digest* 10(12), available at: http://ictsd.org/i/news/bridgesweekly/6289/ (accessed 17 March 2014).

International Labor Organization (ILO) (2000a) "International Labour Conference Adopts Resolution Targeting Forced Labour in Myanmar (Burma)," press release, 14 June, available at: www.ilo.org/global/about-the-ilo/newsroom/news/WCMS_007899/lang–en/index.htm (accessed 20 July 2012).

(2000b) "Effect Given by the Government of Myanmar to the Recommendations of the Commission of Inquiry Established to Examine the Observance of the Forced Labour Convention, 1930 (No. 29)," GB 279/6/1, 279th Session, Geneva, November,

available at: www.ilo.org/public/english/standards/relm/gb/docs/gb279/pdf/gb-6-1.pdf (accessed 20 July 2012).
(2001a) "Developments Concerning the Question of the Observance by the Government of Myanmar of the Forced Labour Convention, 1930 (No. 29)," GB 280/6, 280th Session, Geneva (March), available at: www.ilo.org/public/english/standards/relm/gb/docs/gb280/pdf/gb-6.pdf (accessed 20 July 2012).
(2001b) Provisional Record, Eighty-ninth Session, Geneva, 19, Part Three, Special Sitting Concerning the Application by Myanmar of the Forced Labour Convention, 1930 (No. 29), in Application of the Resolution Adopted by the International Labour Conference at its 88th (2000) Session, available at: www.ilo.org/public/english/standards/relm/ilc/ilc89/pdf/pr-19-3.pdf (accessed 20 July 2012).
(2003) ASEAN Senior Labour Officials Meeting and Labour Ministers Meeting, Mataram, Indonesia, 5–9 May, Mission Report, available at: www.ilo.org/public/english/region/asro/mdtbangkok/download/almmay.pdf (accessed 20 July 2012).
(2005) Provisional Record, Ninety-third Session, Geneva, 22, Part Three, Special Sitting to Examine Developments concerning the Question of the Observance by the Government of Myanmar of the Forced Labour Convention, 1930 (No. 29), available at: www.ilo.org/public/english/standards/relm/ilc/ilc93/pdf/pr-22-3.pdf (accessed 24 July 2012).
(2007) Provisional Record, Ninety-sixth Session, Geneva, 22, Part Three, Observations and Information concerning Particular Countries, Special Sitting to Examine Developments concerning the Question of the Observance by the Government of Myanmar of the Forced Labour Convention, 1930 (No. 29), available at: www.ilo.org/public/english/standards/relm/ilc/ilc96/pdf/pr-22-part3.pdf (accessed 24 July 2012).

(2012a) Third Item on the Agenda: Information and Reports on the Application of Conventions and Recommendations, Provisional Record, 101st Session, Geneva, May–June, 19, Part Three, Observations and Information concerning Particular Countries, Special Sitting to Examine Developments concerning the Question of the Observance by the Government of Myanmar of the Forced Labour Convention, 1930 (No. 29), available at: www.ilo.org/wcmsp5/groups/public/—ed_norm/—relconf/documents/meetingdocument/wcms_183283.pdf (accessed 26 July 2012).

(2012b) Reports of the Selection Committee, Provisional Record, 2–4, 101st Session, Geneva, May–June, available at: www.ilo.org/wcmsp5/groups/public/—ed_norm/—relconf/documents/meetingdocument/wcms_182971.pdf (accessed 25 July 2012).

Ismail, F. (2007) "The G20 and NAMA11: The Role of Developing Countries in the WTO Doha Round," lecture presented as part of Global Economic Governance's seminar series, Making Globalization Work for Developing Countries, 23 November, Oxford.

Jagan, L. (2000) "Burma Sanctions Imminent," BBC News, 16 November 2000, available at: http://news.bbc.co.uk/1/hi/world/asia-pacific/1027114.stm (accessed 19 July 2012).

Jayakumar, S. (2011) *Diplomacy: A Singaporean Experience*, Singapore: Straits Times Press.

Jetschke, A. (2009) "Institutionalizing ASEAN: Celebrating Europe through Network Governance," *Cambridge Review of International Relations* 22(3): 407–426.

Jetschke, A. and Rüland, J. (2009) "Decoupling Rhetoric and Practice: The Cultural Limits of ASEAN Cooperation," *Pacific Review* 22(1): 179–203.

Jetschke, A. and Portela, C. (2012) "ASEAN-EU Beziehungen: Von regionaler Integrationsförderung zur Sicherheitsrelevanz,"

GIGA Focus, 12 (2012), Hamburg: German Institute for Global and Area Studies.

Johnson, C. (2013) "Mainland China's Place in the New World Regional Groupings." In B. J. Lin and J. T. Myers (eds.), *Forces for Change in Contemporary China*, Columbia: University of South Carolina Press.

Johnston, A. I. (1996) "Cultural Realism and Strategy in Maoist China." In P. J. Katzenstein (ed.), *The Culture of National Security: Norms and Identity in World Politics*, New York: Columbia University Press, pp. 216–270.

Jones, D. M. and Smith, M. L. R. (2007) "Making Process, Not Progress: ASEAN and the Evolving East Asian Regional Order," *International Security* 32(1): 148–184.

Jones, L. (2008) "ASEAN's Albatross: ASEAN's Burma Policy, from Constructive Engagement to Critical Disengagement," *Asian Security* 4(3): 271–293.

(2012) *ASEAN, Sovereignty and Intervention in Southeast Asia*, Basingstoke: Palgrave Macmillan.

Jorgensen-Dahl, A. (1977) "The Emerging External Policies of the Association of Southeast Asian Nations (ASEAN)," *Australian Journal of Politics and History* 24(1): 36–51.

Kasetsiri, C. (1976) *The Rise of Ayudhya: A History of Siam in the Fourteenth and Fifteenth Century*, Kuala Lumpur: Oxford University Press.

Katada, S. N. (2011) "Seeking a Place for East Asian Regionalism: Challenges and Opportunities under the Global Financial Crises," *Pacific Review* 24(3): 273–290.

Katsumata, H. (2009) "ASEAN and Human Rights: Resisting Western Pressure or Emulating the West?" *Pacific Review* 22(5): 619–637.

Katzenstein, P. and Sil, R. (2008) "Eclectic Theorizing in the Study and Practice of International Relations." In C. Reus-Smit and

D. Snidal (eds.), *The Oxford Handbook of International Relations*, Oxford: Oxford University Press, pp. 109–130.

Kausikan, B. (2005) "Some Fundamentals of Singapore's Foreign Policy." In T. Koh and L. L. Chang (eds.), *The Little Red Dot: Reflections by Singapore's Diplomats*, Singapore: World Scientific and Institute of Policy Studies, pp. 103–110.

Keck, A. and Low, P. (2004) "Special and Differential Treatment in the WTO: Why, When and How?," Staff Working Paper ERSD-2004-03, World Trade Organization, Geneva; reprinted in S. Evenett and B. Hoekman (eds.), *Economic Development and Multilateral Trade Co-operation*, Washington, DC: Palgrave Macmillan and World Bank, 2005, pp. 147–188.

Khong, T. B. (2014) "Vietnam in International Institutions," Ph.D. thesis, Victoria University of Wellington.

Kinder, D. R. and Sanders, L. M. (1996) *Divided by Color: Racial Politics and Democratic Ideals*, Chicago: University of Chicago Press.

Kivimäki, Timo (2008) "Power, Interest or Culture: Is there a Paradigm that Explains ASEAN's Political Role Best?" *Pacific Review* 21(4): 431–450.

Kng, C. M., Low, L. and Toh, M. H. (1988) "Trade Policy Option for Singapore." In M. Ariff and L.-H. Tan (eds.) *Asean Trade Policy Options: The Uruguay Round*, Singapore: Institute of Southeast Asian Studies, pp. 132–168.

Koh, T. and Chang L. L. (eds.) (2005) *The Little Red Dot: Reflections by Singapore's Diplomats*, Singapore: World Scientific and Institute of Policy Studies.

Kraft, H. J. S. (2000) "The Autonomy Dilemma of Track Two Diplomacy in Southeast Asia," *Security Dialogue* 31(3): 343–356.

Kuppuswamy, C. S. (2012) "Myanmar: By-Elections and the National League for Democracy (NLD)," South Asia Analysis Group, No. 4860 (13 January 2012), available at: http://web.arc

hive.org/web/20120312133721/http://www.southasiaanalysis.org/papers49/paper4860.html (accessed 4 November 2014).

Kwa, A. (2003) *Power Politics in the WTO*, 2nd edn., Bangkok: Focus on the Global South.

Laatikainen, K. V. and Smith, K. E. (eds.) (2006) *The European Union at the United Nations: Intersecting Multilateralisms*, Basingstoke: Palgrave Macmillan.

Lake, D. A. (1999) "Global Governance: A Relational Contracting Approach." In A. Prakash and J. A. Hart (eds.), *Globalization and Governance*, London and New York: Routledge, pp. 31–53.

Laksmana, E. (2008) "Strategic Theory, Clausewitz, and the Indonesian Military," *Indonesian Quarterly* 36(1): 86–106.

Legro, J. W. (2000) "The Transformation of Policy Ideas," *American Journal of Political Science* 44(3): 419–432.

Leifer, M. (1983) *Indonesia's Foreign Policy*, London: Allen & Unwin.

(2000) *Singapore's Foreign Policy. Coping with Vulnerability*, London: Routledge.

Liang, M. (2005) "Evolution of the WTO Decision-Making Process," *2005 Singapore Year Book of International Law and Contributors* 22(1): 125–132.

Lowenfeld, A. F. (1996) "The USA, The EEC, and The GATT: The Road Not Taken," *University of Pennsylvania Journal of International Economic Law* 17(2): 533–538.

Mably, P. (2007) "The Role of Research on Trade Policy Changes Affecting the Developing World: Group of 33 Influence at the World Trade Organization," Latin American Trade Network, FLACSO Working Paper 77, available at: www.redlatn.org/wp-content/uploads/2013/03/wp-77.pdf (accessed 16 March 2014).

McCloud, D. G. (1976) "Indonesia in Southeast Asia: An Events Data Assessment of Indonesia's Primary Foreign Policy Environment," *Asian Forum* 9: 61–83.

(1995) *Southeast Asia: Tradition and Modernity in the Contemporary World*, Boulder, CO: Westview.

MacIntyre, A. (1994) "Organising Interests: Corporatism in Indonesian Politics," Working Paper 43, Asia Research Centre, Murdoch University.

Madriaga-Quinsaat, S. (2013) "The Philippines Waltzes with the Big Boys: Coalition-building Strategy in the WTO," *Asian Survey* 52(5): 570–594.

Mahbubani, K. (1993) "The Dangers of Decadence," *Foreign Affairs* 72(4): 11–14.

(1995) "The Pacific Way," *Foreign Affairs* 74(1): 100–111.

(1998) *Can Asians Think? Understanding the Divide between East and West*, Singapore: Marshall Cavendish Editions.

(2005) "Singapore in the United Nations Security Council." In T. Koh and L. L. Chang (eds.), *The Little Red Dot: Reflections by Singapore's Diplomats*, Singapore: World Scientific and Institute of Policy Studies, pp. 91–96.

(2008) *The New Asian Hemisphere: The Irresistible Shift of Power to the East*, New York: Public Affairs.

Mahoney, J. and Thelen, K. (2010) *Explaining Institutional Change: Ambiguity, Agency and Power*, Cambridge: Cambridge University Press.

Mangkusuwondo, S., Simandjuntak, D. and Surono, S. (1988) "Trade Policy Option for Indonesia." In M. Ariff and L.-H. Tan (eds.), *Asean Trade Policy Option: The Uruguay Round*, Singapore: Institute of Southeast Asian Studies, pp. 38–64.

Manners, I. (2002) "Normative Power Europe: A Contradiction in Terms?," *Journal of Common Market Studies* 40(2): 235–258.

Manz, T. (2007) "Allianzen und Gruppen im Global Governance-System – Multilateralismus zwischen partikularen Interessen und universellen Anforderungen," *Internationale Politik und Gesellschaft* 2: 25–44.

Martin, L. G. (1987) *The ASEAN Success Story: Social, Economic and Political Dimensions*, Honolulu: East-West Center.

Meepiarn, W. (2009) "Bargaining Strategies for Developing Countries at the WTO: The Case of Thailand and the Agreement on Agriculture in the Uruguay Round of Multilateral Trade Negotiations," Ph.D. thesis, Department of Politics and International Studies, University of Warwick.

Meunier, S. (2005) *Trading Voices: The European Union in International Commercial Negotiation*, Princeton, NJ: Princeton University Press.

Michael, A. (2013) *India's Foreign Policy and Regional Multilateralism*, Basingstoke: Palgrave Macmillan.

Milne, R. S. and Mauzy, D. K. (1999) *Malaysian Politics under Mahathir*, London and New York: Routledge.

Ministry of Labour, Republic of the Union of Myanmar (2012) "Myanmar Delegation Requests to 101st ILC to Fully Lift Sanctions Imposed on Myanmar," available at: www.mol.gov.mm/en/ilc-myanmar-delegation/ (accessed 25 July 2012).

Montes, M. F. and Magno, F. A. (1997) "Trade and Environmental Diplomacy: Strategic Options for ASEAN," *Pacific Affairs* 70(3): 351–371.

Moravcsik, A. (1998) *The Choice for Europe: Social Purpose and State Power from Rome to Maastricht*, Ithaca, NY and London: Cornell University Press.

Morrison, C. E. (2006) "Track 1/Track 2 Symbiosis in Asia-Pacific Regionalism." In H. E. S. Nesadurai (ed.), *Globalization and Economic Security in East Asia: Governance and Institutions*, London and New York: Routledge, pp. 200–217.

Muhibat, S. F. (2006) "D-8 Summit, Regional Issues and Indonesia's International Diplomacy," *Indonesian Quarterly* 34(2): 132–142.

Nabbs-Keller, G. (2013) "Reforming Indonesia's Foreign Ministry: Ideas, Organizations and Leadership," *Contemporary Southeast Asia* 35(1): 56–82.

Nair, D. (2010) "Do Stated Goals Matter? Regional Institutions in East Asia and the Dynamic of Unstated Goals," Working Paper 199, S. Rajaratnam School of International Studies, Nanyang Technological University, Singapore.

Narine, S. (2002) *Explaining ASEAN*, Boulder, CO: Lynne Rienner.

(2008) "Forty Years of ASEAN: A Historical Review," *Pacific Review* 21(4): 411–429.

Narlikar, A. (2003) *International Trade and Developing Countries: Bargaining Coalitions in the GATT and WTO*, London and New York: Routledge.

(2006) "Peculiar Chauvinism or Strategic Calculation?: Explaining the Negotiating Strategy of a Rising India," *International Affairs* 82(1): 59–76.

Narlikar, A. and Tussie, D. (2004) "The G20 at the Cancun Ministerial: Developing Countries and their Evolving Coalitions in the WTO," *World Economy* 27(7): 947–966.

Nguitragool, P. (2011a) *Environmental Cooperation in Southeast Asia: ASEAN's Regime for Transboundary Haze Pollution*, London and New York: Routledge.

(2011b) "Negotiating the Haze Treaty: Rationality and Institutions in the Negotiations for the ASEAN Agreement on Transboundary Haze Pollution (2002)," *Asian Survey* 51(2): 356–378.

(2012) "God-King and Indonesia: Renegotiating the Boundaries between Western and Non-Western Perspectives on Foreign Policy," *Pacific Affairs* 85(4): 723–743.

(2013) "Indonesia, the West and International Politics: A Survey of Indonesian Student Perceptions of Self and Others in International Relations," Occasional Paper Series 16, Southeast Asian Studies, University of Freiburg.

Niksch, L. A. and Weiss, M. A. (2008) "Burma: Economic Sanctions," CRS Report for Congress, Order Code RS22737 (updated 30 January 2008), available at: http://fpc.state.gov/documents/organization/101738.pdf (accessed 12 July 2012).

Novotny, D. (2010) *Torn Between America and China: Elite Perceptions and Indonesian Foreign Policy*, Singapore: Institute of Southeast Asian Studies.

Nye, J. S. (1967) "Central American Regional Integration," *International Conciliation* 562 (March): 5–66.

(1971) "Comparing Common Markets: A Revised Neo-Functionalist Model." In L. N. Lindberg and S. A. Scheingold (eds.), *Regional Integration: Theory and Research*, Cambridge, MA: Harvard University Press, pp. 191–231.

(1988) "Soft Power," *Foreign Policy* 80: 153–171.

Odell, J. S. (2002) "Creating Data on International Negotiation Strategies, Alternatives and Outcomes," *International Negotiation* 7: 39–52.

(2005) "Chairing a WTO Negotiation," *Journal of International Economic Law* 8(2): 425–448.

(2010) "Three Islands of Knowledge about Negotiation in International Organizations," *Journal of European Public Policy* 17(5): 619–632.

Palmer, N. D. (1991) *The New Regionalism in Asia and the Pacific*, Lexington, MA: Lexington Books.

Pangestu, M., Soesastro, H. and Ahmad, M. (1992) "A New Look at Intra-ASEAN Economic Co-operation," *ASEAN Economic Bulletin* 8(3): 333–352.

Panke, D. (2013a) *Unequal Actors in Equalizing Institutions: Negotiations in the United Nations General Assembly*, Basingstoke: Palgrave Macmillan.

(2013b) "Regional Power Revisited: How to Explain Difference in Coherency and Success of Regional Organizations in the

United Nations General Assembly," *International Negotiation* 18: 265–291.

Perwita, A. A. B. (2007) *Indonesia and the Muslim World: Islam and Secularism in the Foreign Policy of Soeharto and Beyond*, Copenhagen: NIAS Press.

Pitsuwan, S. (2012) อาเซียน รู้ไว้ได้เปรียบแน่ [Competitive Advantage in Knowing ASEAN]. Bangkok: Amarin Printing and Publishing.

Prys, M. (2010) "Hegemony, Domination Detachment: Differences in Regional Powerhood," *International Studies Review* 12(4): 479–504.

Pura, R. (1988) "Doubts Over Heavy Industrialization Strategy." In K. S. Jomo (ed.), *Mahathir's Economic Policies*, Kuala Lumpur: Institute of Social Analysis, pp. 38–43.

Putnam, R. D. (1988) "Diplomacy and Domestic Politics: The Logic of Two-Level Games," *International Organization* 42(3): 427–460.

Raghavan, C. (1987) "The World Asked to Liberalise in Tropical Products," 4 March 1987, docsonline.wto.org (no longer available).

(2001) "Agri-Talks Mark Time, for End of Peace Clause not New Round?," Third World Network, available at: www.twnside.org.sg/title/agri.htm (accessed 8 January 2013).

Rana, P. B. (2011) "Asian Monetary Fund: Getting Nearer," RSIS Commentaries 79/2011, S. Rajaratnam School of International Studies, Nanyang Technological University, Singapore.

Ravenhill, J. (2001) *APEC and the Construction of Pacific Rim Regionalism*, Cambridge: Cambridge University Press.

(2008) "Fighting Irrelevance: An Economic Community with ASEAN Characteristics," *Pacific Review* 21(4): 469–488.

Reeve, D. (1985) *Golkar of Indonesia: An Alternative to the Party System*, Singapore: Oxford University Press.

Reid, A. (1998) "Political 'Tradition' in Indonesia: The One and the Many," *Asian Studies Review* 22(1): 23–38.
Reinhard, D. (2013) "Brasiliens Rolle in Südamerika: Detached Power or Regional Dominator?," term paper, Department of Political Science, University of Freiburg.
Reiterer, M. (1996) "The First Ministerial Conference of the WTO: The Road to Singapore," *Aussenwirtschaft* 3: 383–416.
Rhinard, M. and Kaeding, M. (2006) "The International Bargaining Power of the European Union in 'Mixed' Competence Negotiations: The Case of the 2000 Cartagena Protocol on Biosafety," *Journal of Common Market Studies* 44(5): 1023–1050.
Ricklefs, M. C. (2001) *A History of Modern Indonesia since* c.*1300*, Basingstoke: Macmillan.
Risse, T. (2000) "'Let's Argue!' Communicative Action in World Politics," *International Organization* 54(1): 1–39.
Roberts, C. (2007) "Affinity and Trust in Southeast Asia: A Regional Survey," paper presented at the ASEAN 40th Anniversary Conference, *Ideas and Institutions: Building an ASEAN Community?*, jointly organized by the Friedrich-Ebert-Stiftung (FES) and the S. Rajaratnam School of International Studies, Nanyang Technological University, Singapore, 31 July–1 August, available at: http://library.fes.de/pdf-files/bueros/singapur/04601/2007-3/chris.pdf (accessed 14 August 2010).
Roberts, C. (2010a) "Is Myanmar Changing or Has Myanmar Changed Us?," paper presented at the 24th Asia-Pacific Roundtable, 7–9 June, Kuala Lumpur, available at: http://ebookbrowse.com/christopher-roberts-pdf-d57699775 (accessed 25 July 2012).
(2010b) *ASEAN's Myanmar Crisis: Challenges to the Pursuit of a Security Community*, Singapore: Institute of Southeast Asian Studies.
Robles Jr., A. C. (2004) *Political Economy of Interregional Relations: ASEAN and the EU*, Aldershot: Ashgate.

Roloff, R. (2001) *Europa, Amerika und Asien zwischen Globalisierung und Regionalisierung. Das interregionale Konzert und die ökonomische Dimension internationaler Politik*, Paderborn: Schöningh.

Rosenau, J. N. (1992) "Governance, Order, and Change in World Politics." In J. N. Rosenau and E.-O. Czempiel (eds.), *Governance without Government: Order and Change in World Politics*, Cambridge: Cambridge University Press, pp. 1–30.

Rüland, J. (2000) "ASEAN and the Asian Crisis: Theoretical and Practical Consequences for Southeast Asian Regionalism," *Pacific Review* 13(3): 421–451.

(2002) "APEC, ASEAN and EAEC: A Tale of Two Cultures of Cooperation." In J. Rüland, E. Manske and W. Draguhn (eds.), *Asia-Pacific Economic Cooperation (APEC): The First Decade*, London: RoutledgeCurzon, pp. 40–71.

(2009) "Deepening ASEAN Cooperation through Democratization? The Indonesian Legislature and Foreign Policymaking," *International Relations of the Asia-Pacific* 9(3): 373–402.

(2010) "Balancers, Multilateral Utilities or Identity Builders? International Relations and the Study of Interregionalism," *Journal of European Public Policy* 17(8): 1268–1280.

(2011) "Southeast Asian Regionalism and Global Governance: 'Multilateral Utility' or 'Hedging Utility?'," *Contemporary Southeast Asia* 33(1): 83–112.

(2012a) "The Limits of Democratizing Interest Representation: ASEAN's Regional Corporatism and Normative Challenges," *European Journal of International Relations*, DOI 10.1177/1354066112455289, published online 16 July.

(2012b) "The Rise of 'Diminished Multilateralism': East Asian and European Forum Shopping in Global Governance," *Asia-Europe Journal* 10(1): 255–270.

(2014) "Constructing Regionalism Domestically: Local Actors and Foreign Policymaking in Newly Democratized Indonesia," *Foreign Policy Analysis* 10(2): 181–201.

Salih, K., Piej, M. H. and Sahathavan, M. (1988) "Trade Policy Option for Malaysia." In M. Ariff and L.-H. Tan (eds.), *ASEAN Trade Policy Options: The Uruguay Round*, Singapore: Institute of Southeast Asian Studies, pp. 65–103.

Sally, R. (2004) *Southeast Asia in the WTO*, Singapore: Institute of Southeast Asian Studies.

Sally, R. and Sen, R. (2005) "Trade Policies in Southeast Asia in the Wider Asian Perspective," *World Economy* 34(4): 568–601.

Schimmelfennig, F. (2006) "*Prozessanalyse*." In J. Behnke, T. Gschwend, D. Schindler and K.-U. Schnapp (eds.), *Methoden der Politikwissenschaft: Neuere qualitative und quantitative Analyseverfahren*, Baden-Baden: Nomos, pp. 273–285.

Schirm, S. A. (1997) "Transnationale Globalisierung und regionale Kooperation. Ein politikökonomischer Ansatz zur Erklärung internationaler Zusammenarbeit in Europa und den Amerikas," *Zeitschrift für Internationale Beziehungen* 4(1): 69–106.

Schmidt, M. G. (1995) *Wörterbuch zur Politik*, Stuttgart: Kröner Verlag.

Schmidt, V. A. (2010) "Taking Ideas and Discourse Seriously: Explaining Change through Discursive Institutionalism as the Fourth 'New Institutionalism'," *European Political Science Review* 2: 1–26.

Schmitter, P. C. (1969) "Three Neo-Functional Hypotheses about International Integration," *International Organization* 23: 161–166.

(1971) "A Revised Theory of Regional Integration." In L. N. Lindberg and S. A. Scheingold (eds.), *Regional Integration: Theory and Research*, Cambridge, MA: Harvard University Press, pp. 232–264.

Schwarz, A. (1994) *A Nation in Waiting: Indonesia in the 1990s*, Sydney: Allen & Unwin.

Severino, R. C. (2006) *Southeast Asia in Search of an ASEAN Community: Insights from the Former ASEAN Secretary General*, Singapore: Institute of Southeast Asian Studies.

Simon, S. W. (2002) "Evaluating Track II Approaches to Security Diplomacy in the Asia-Pacific: The CSCAP Experience," *Pacific Review* 15(2): 167–200.

Sjöstedt, G. (1977) *The External Role of the European Community*, Westmead: Gower Press.

Smith, A. L. (2000) "Indonesia's Foreign Policy under Abdurrahman Wahid: Radical or Status Quo State?," *Contemporary Southeast Asia* 22(3): 498–526.

Smith, K. E. (2006) "Speaking with One Voice? European Union Co-ordination on Human Rights Issues at the United Nations," *Journal of Common Market Studies* 44(1): 113–137.

Snitwongse, K. (1989) "Interaction and Collaboration of the EC and ASEAN in the UN System and International Conferences." In G. Schiavone (ed.), *Western Europe and South-East Asia. Co-operation or Competition?*, Basingstoke: Macmillan, pp. 229–258.

Snyder, J. (2000) *From Voting to Violence: Democratization and Nationalist Conflict*, New York and London: W. W. Norton & Company.

Sohn, I. (2007) *East Asia's Counterweight Strategy: Asian Financial Cooperation and Evolving International Monetary Order*, New York and Geneva: United Nations Conference of Trade and Development.

Solidum, E. (1974) *Towards a Southeast Asian Community*, Quezon City: University of the Philippines Press.

Spiller, R. (2008) *Das Management multilateraler internationaler Verhandlungen. Eine Untersuchung von UN-Konferenzen zur*

Verabschiedung internationaler Konventionen, Baden-Baden: Nomos.

Strezhnev, A. and Voeten, E. (2013) "United Nations General Assembly Voting Data," UNF:5:NpHV5DXWPNWMWOrLGTj-QYA==Erik Voeten [Distributor] V5 [Version], http://hdl.handle.net/1902.1/12379 (accessed 13 January 2014).

Stone, D. (2000) "Non-Governmental Policy Transfer: The Strategies of Independent Policy Institutes," *Governance* 13(1): 45–70.

Stubbs, R. (2008) "The ASEAN Alternative? Ideas, Institutions and the Challenge to 'Global' Governance," *Pacific Review* 21(4): 451–468.

Sukma, R. (2000) "Indonesia and Non-Intervention: Debate in Southeast Asia." In D. Dickens and G. Wilson-Roberts (eds.), *Non-Intervention and State Sovereignty in the Asia-Pacific*, Wellington: Centre for Strategic Studies, pp. 86–96.

(2012) "The ASEAN Political and Security Community (APSC): Opportunities and Constraints for R2P in Southeast Asia," *Pacific Review* 25(1): 135–152.

Sunardi, R. M. (2004) *Pembinaan Ketahanan Bangsa: Dalam Rangka Memperkokoh Keutuhan Negara Kesatuan Republik Indonesia*, Jakarta: Kuaternita Adidarma.

Tallberg, J. (2008) *Leadership and Negotiation in the European Union*, Cambridge: Cambridge University Press.

Tan, S. S. (2012) "ASEAN, the United Nations and the Security of Southeast Asia: Problems, Prospects and Paradox." In P. de Lombaerde, F. Baert and T. Felício (eds.), *The United Nations and the Regions: Third World Report on Regional Integration*, Dordrecht: Springer, pp. 157–166.

Tay, S. (2013) "Growing an ASEAN Voice?: A Common Platform in Global and Regional Governance," ERIA Discussion Paper 2013–16: Economic Research Institute of ASEAN and East Asia, Jakarta.

Taylor, R. H. (1987) *The State in Burma*, London: C. Hurst.

Thambipillai, P. and Saravanamuttu, J. (1985) *ASEAN Negotiations: Two Insights*, Singapore: Institute of Southeast Asian Studies.

Than, M. and Gates, C. L. (2001) *ASEAN Enlargement: Impacts and Implications*, Singapore: Institute of Southeast Asian Affairs.

Thomas, M. and Orden, D. (2004) "Agricultural Policies in Indonesia: Producer Support Estimates 1985–2003," MTID Discussion Paper No. 78, Markets, Trade and Institutions Division of the International Food Policy Research Institute, available at: www.ifpri.org/sites/default/files/publications/mtidp78.pdf (accessed 2 November 2012).

Thomas, V. and Wang, Y. (1995) "Structural Adjustment: Gradualism or Big Approach?" In D. Umali-Deininger and C. Maguire (eds.), *Agriculture in Liberalizing Economies: Changing Roles for Governments*, Washington, DC: World Bank, pp. 25–58.

Thompson, E. C. (2012) "Anthropology in Southeast Asia: National Tradition and Transnational Practices," *Asian Journal of Social Science* 40: 664–689.

Thongthep, Mechai (1993) *Ramakien: The Thai Ramayana*, Bangkok: Naga Books.

Thurman, J. E. (1996) "Employment, Labor Standards, and the Social Clause." In C. S. Yue and J. L.-H. Tan (eds.), *ASEAN in the WTO: Challenges and Responses*, Singapore: Institute of Southeast Asian Studies, pp. 58–50.

Tongthep, M. (1993) *Ramakien: The Thai Ramayama*, Bangkok: Naga Books.

Tsebelis, G. (1990) *Nested Games: Rational Choice in Comparative Politics*, Berkeley: University of California Press.

United Nations General Assembly (UNGA) (2009) "Implementing the Responsibility to Protect," Report of the Secretary General: www.un.org/en/ga/search/view_doc.asp?symbol=A/63/677 (accessed 16 July 2014).

(2011) Third Committee, "Summary Record of the 47th Meeting Held at Headquarters, New York, on Thursday, 18 November 2010."

University of Helsinki (2006) *An Evaluation of ASEM in its First Decade and an Exploration of its Future Possibilities*, Helsinki: University of Helsinki, Network for European Studies.

von Lübke, C. (2012) "Striking the Right Balance: Economic Concentration and Local Government Performance in Indonesia and the Philippines," *European Journal of East Asian Studies* 11(1): 17–44.

Wallensteen, P., Staibano, C. and Eriksson, M. (2004) "Routes to Democracy in Burma/Myanmar: The Uppsala Pilot Study on Dialogue and International Strategies," available at: http://pcr.uu.se/digitalAssets/112/112143_burmareport_april_8.pdf (accessed 24 July 2012).

Walton, R. E. and McKersie, R. B. (1965) *A Behavioral Theory of Labor Negotiations: An Analysis of Social Interaction Systems*, New York: McGraw-Hill.

Warr, P. and Kohpaiboon, A. (2007) "Distortions to Agricultural Incentives in Thailand," Agricultural Distortions Working Paper 25, available at: http://siteresources.worldbank.org/INTTRADERESEARCH/Resources/544824-1146153362267/Thailand_0308rev.pdf (accessed 5 November 2012).

Weinstein, F. B. (1976) Indonesian Foreign Policy and the Dilemma of Dependence: From Sukarno to Suharto, Ithaca, NY and London: Cornell University Press.

Weintraub, A. N. (2004) *Power Plays: Wayang Golek Puppet Theater of West Java*, Singapore: Institute of Southeast Asian Studies.

Wesley, M. (1999) "The Asian Crisis and the Adequacy of Regional Institutions," *Contemporary Southeast Asia* 21(1): 54–73.

Whalley, J. (1996) "Developing Countries and System Strengthening in the Uruguay Round." In M. Will and L. A. Winteres (eds.), *The*

Uruguay Round and the Developing Countries, Cambridge: Cambridge University Press.

Widjajanto, A. (2008) "Transforming Indonesia's Armed Forces," available at: http://lesperssi.org/id/conference/workshop-mainmenu-6/5-security-sector-in-democratic-oversight/43-transforming-indonesias-armed-forces (accessed 4 November 2014).

Wilkinson, R. (2007) *The WTO: Crisis and the Governance of Global Trade*, London and New York: Routledge.

Wisma Putra (Ministry of Foreign Affairs of Malaysia) (2009) "Strategic Plan, 2009–2015," Putrajaya: Wisma Putra, available at: www.kln.gov.my/c/document_library/get_file?uuid=bf7282c4-3cad-49cd-a525-15a3e67702a0&groupId=10136 (accessed 17 March 2014).

Witcher, T. (2010) "UN Chief Urges Asia Nations to Pressure Myanmar," 26 September, available at: http://taungzalatnews.blogspot.co.uk/2010/09/un-chief-urges-asia-nations-to-pressure.html (accessed 6 November 2014).

World Bank (2009) "Cambodia Trade Brief," World Trade Indicators 2009/10: Country Trade Briefs, Washington, DC: World Bank, available at: http://info.worldbank.org/etools/wti/docs/Cambodia_brief.pdf (accessed 13 November 2012).

Wouters, J. and Burnay, M. (2011) "The EU and Asia in the United Nations Security Council," Working Paper 78, Centre for Global Governance Studies, Leuven.

World Trade Organization (2000) "Special and Differential Treatment for Developing Countries in World Agricultural Trade," G/AG/NG/W/55, 10 November, available at: http://docsonline.wto.org/imrd/directdoc.asp?DDFDocuments/t/G/AG/NGW55.doc (accessed 13 November 2012).

(2013) "Public Stockholding for Food Security Purposes" (Draft Ministerial Decision), WT/MIN(13)/W/10, 6 December, available at: https://mc9.wto.org/system/files/documents/w10_1.pdf (accessed 13 March 2014).

Wunderlich, J. U. (2012) "The EU as Actor Sui Generis? A Comparison of EU and ASEAN Actorness," *Journal of Common Market Studies* 50(4): 653–669.

Wyatt, D. K. (1984) *Thailand: A Short History*, London and Bangkok: Yale University Press/Thai Wattana Panich Co. Ltd.

Wyatt-Walter, A. (1995) "Regionalism, Globalization and the World Economic Order." In L. Fawcett and A. Hurrell (eds.), *Regionalism in World Politics*, New York and Oxford: Oxford University Press, pp. 74–120.

Yeo, L. H. (2003) *Asia and Europe: The Development and Different Dimensions of ASEM*, London: Routledge.

Yoshimatsu H. (2007) Regional Integration and Business Interests: A Comparative Study of Europe and Southeast Asia, *European Journal of East Asian Studies* 6(2): 217–243.

Young, O. (1991) "Political Leadership and Regime Formation: On the Development of Institutions in International Society," *International Organization* 45(3): 281–308.

Zangl, B. and Zürn, M. (2004) "Make Law, Not War: Internationale und transnationale Verrechtlichung als Baustein für Global Governance." In B. Zangl and M. Zürn (eds.), *Verrechtlichung: Baustein für Global Governance?*, Bonn: Verlag J. H. W. Dietz Nachfolger, pp. 12–46.

Zimmer, H. (1976) *Philosophien und Religionen Indiens*, Frankfurt am Main: Suhrkamp.

Zürn, M. (1992) *Interessen und Institutionen in der internationalen Politik. Grundlegung und Anwendung des situationsstrukturellen Ansatzes*, Opladen: Westdeutscher Verlag.

INDEX

INDEX

Lightning Source UK Ltd.
Milton Keynes UK
UKOW07f0323270415

250365UK00002B/5/P

9 781107 503885